Becoming Activists in Global China

Becoming Activists in Global China is the first purely sociological study
of the religious movement Falun Gong and its resistance to the Chinese
state. The literature on Chinese protest has intensively studied the 1989
democracy movement while largely ignoring opposition by the Falun
Gong, even though the latter has been more enduring. This comparative
study explains why the Falun Gong protest took off in diaspora and the
democracy movement did not. Using multiple methods, *Becoming
Activists in Global China* explains how Falun Gong's roots in
proselytizing and its ethic of volunteerism provided the launch pad for
its political mobilization. Simultaneously, diaspora democracy activists
adopted practices that effectively discouraged grassroots participation.
The study also shows how the policy goal of eliminating Falun Gong
helped shape today's security-focused Chinese state. Explaining the
Falun Gong's two decades of protest illuminates a suppressed piece of
Chinese contemporary history and advances our knowledge of how
religious and political movements intersect.

Andrew Junker is Adjunct Assistant Professor in Sociology at the
Chinese University of Hong Kong. He earned a PhD from Yale
University, where his research was awarded Yale's annual Sussman
Award for best sociology dissertation. He is also a recipient of
a National Science Foundation grant and a University of Chicago
Harper Fellowship.

Becoming Activists in Global China

Social Movements in the Chinese Diaspora

ANDREW JUNKER

Chinese University of Hong Kong

CAMBRIDGE
UNIVERSITY PRESS

CAMBRIDGE
UNIVERSITY PRESS

University Printing House, Cambridge CB2 8BS, United Kingdom

One Liberty Plaza, 20th Floor, New York, NY 10006, USA

477 Williamstown Road, Port Melbourne, VIC 3207, Australia

314-321, 3rd Floor, Plot 3, Splendor Forum, Jasola District Centre, New Delhi - 110025, India

103 Penang Road, #05-06/07, Visioncrest Commercial, Singapore 238467

Cambridge University Press is part of the University of Cambridge.

It furthers the University's mission by disseminating knowledge in the pursuit of education, learning and research at the highest international levels of excellence.

www.cambridge.org
Information on this title: www.cambridge.org/9781108716017
DOI: 10.1017/9781108685382

First published 2019
First paperback edition 2022

A catalogue record for this publication is available from the British Library

Library of Congress Cataloging in Publication data
NAMES: Junker, Andrew, author.
TITLE: Making activists in global China : transnational mobilization in the Falun Gong and the Chinese democracy movement / Andrew Junker.
OTHER TITLES: Sacred and secular protest in the Chinese diaspora
DESCRIPTION: Cambridge, United Kingdom ; New York, NY : Cambridge University Press, 2019. | Revision of author's thesis (doctoral) – Yale University, 2012, titled Sacred and secular protest in the Chinese diaspora : Falun Gong and the Chinese democracy movement. | Includes bibliographical references and index.
IDENTIFIERS: LCCN 2018051974 | ISBN 9781108482998 (alk. paper)
SUBJECTS: LCSH: Social movements – China. | Protest movements – China. | Democratization – China. | Transnationalism – Political aspects – China. | Chinese – Political activity – Foreign countries. | China – Politics and government – 1976–2002. | China – Politics and government – 2002– | Falun Gong (Organization) | China – History – Tiananmen Square Incident, 1989.
CLASSIFICATION: LCC HN733.5 .J85 2019 | DDC 303.48/40951–dc23
LC record available at https://lccn.loc.gov/2018051974

ISBN 978-1-108-48299-8 Hardback
ISBN 978-1-108-71601-7 Paperback

Contents

Figures

Tables

Acknowledgments

This volume certainly would never have made it to publication without several key people. First on that list is my Yale advisor and friend, Julia Adams, who not only provided intellectual guidance, but also insisted over and over again that I press on until the book is published. I would like also to thank Yale sociology faculty Deborah Davis, Philip Gorski, and Jeffrey Alexander. A special thank you is due to Roberto Franzosi at Emory University for his tireless help in adapting PC-ACE to use with my materials. The book was primarily researched and written while I was at Yale as a graduate student and at the University of Chicago when I was a member of the Society of Fellows in the Liberal Arts. I am grateful to many colleagues, professors, and mentors at Yale and the University of Chicago who read and provided feedback on earlier drafts of this work. While at Yale, I received generous support from the Council on East Asian Studies MacMillan Center, a John F. Enders Fellowship from the Graduate School of Arts and Sciences, and a Camp Grant from the Department of Sociology. In addition, I am grateful to the National Science Foundation for a Doctoral Dissertation Research Improvement Grant (#0961624) from the Methodology, Measurement, and Statistics (MMS) Program in 2010. While at Chicago, I also received two grants for research in Hong Kong from the University of Chicago Center in Hong Kong. Several research assistants both at Yale and at the University of Chicago helped at various stages of this project, to each of whom I am grateful. Dan put in an enormous number of hours coding. Thanks also to Jack for sending me the ten yuan "truth currency" reproduced in Chapter 5. Finally, I wish to express my gratitude to my parents, whose support and encouragement were, and remain, invaluable.

Introduction

The student-led democracy movement of 1989 and Falun Gong are famous cases of popular opposition movements in reform-era China, but scholars do not typically see them as belonging to a common class of social phenomenon. The 1989 student movement, which was part of a broader Chinese democratic movement known as *Zhongguo minzhu yundong* or just "Minyun," is seen as a progressive social movement and a pivotal turning point in modern Chinese history. Before and after June 4, 1989, domestic Chinese politics were starkly different. For better or worse, the significance of Minyun for contemporary Chinese history is widely recognized. The Falun Gong case, by contrast, more often than not goes unseen. When it is beheld, it is usually noted as a reactionary, semireligious aberration in Chinese politics-as-usual. Falun Gong[1] had spectacular, but ephemeral, importance in 1999 and shortly thereafter, but today remains a topic left mostly to the rare subfield specialist. This book takes the unconventional stance that these two movements ought to be apprised together. The stance is unconventional, but not unprecedented. In June 1999, Chinese President Jiang Zemin famously also adopted this stance, declaring that Falun Gong was the "most serious political incident" to threaten the Chinese Communist Party (CCP) since the democracy protests of 1989 (Tong 2009: 6; Zong 2002: 66). Seeing Falun Gong and the democracy protests of 1989 as similar threats had enduring and influential consequences for Chinese politics and policy. For example, in February 2001, Jiang Zemin convened over 2,000 CCP

---

[1] In keeping with the scholarly literature, I use the term "Falun Gong". Today, the Falun Gong community generally refers to itself as Falun Dafa.

leaders for "an extraordinary, closed-door meeting" to shore up party unity. According to *The New York Times* (Eckholm and Rosenthal 2001), "Mr. Jiang wanted to make sure that the ruling party remained firmly unified on two divisive issues: the campaign to crush the Falun Gong spiritual movement and the correctness of the party's decision to use troops against the 1989 pro-democracy protesters in Tiananmen Square." All seven members of the politburo Standing Committee – the seven most powerful men in China at the time – "stood up one by one to endorse the anti-Falun Gong campaign as an urgent necessity and to justify the 1989 crackdown." The meeting illustrates that seeing Falun Gong and the Chinese democracy movement as a common object for consideration is not unprecedented nor out of keeping with historical context.

Why Western scholarship has generally not seen the democracy movement and Falun Gong together is due in part to Falun Gong's peculiar status within China studies and social science generally. Two factors in particular have distorted our apprehension of the new religious movement that was banned in China in 1999: first, Chinese state propaganda and severe repression have turned Falun Gong into a pariah community within the Chinese popular imagination and, indirectly, within academia. Even a neutral scholarly analysis that avoids rights advocacy, as found in this book, risks severe professional sanction for simply being out of keeping with CCP policy and propaganda. Falun Gong and the democracy movement are two of the most taboo subjects in China – in conducting serious research on them, both Chinese and non-Chinese researchers accept many risks, including lost job opportunities and access to China (see also He 2014: 29–31). Second, secularist biases within modernist social science incline scholars to see Falun Gong only as a curious sideshow to the real forces of history. The combined result of these two factors is a kind of blindness. As we try to stand outside the historical episode of Falun Gong and peer in, it is as if one of our eyes has been poked out by the Chinese state, whereas we cover the other eye with our own hand.[2]

The reason we disable our own vision is related to the unstable theoretical position of religion in social science theory. Even though secularization theory has been debunked, many still take its premise as the paradigmatic frame for understanding history. As Susanne Rudolph put it, "Modernist social scientists cannot imagine religion as a positive force, as practice and worldview that contributes to order, provides meaning,

---

[2] Thanks to Dan Slater for this vivid metaphor.

and promotes justice" (1997: 6). Following a similar line of critique, Craig Calhoun argued that "the secularism of academics particularly and post-Enlightenment intellectuals generally may have made collective action based on religious and other more spiritual orientations appear somehow of a different order from the 'real' social movement of trade union–based socialism or from liberal democracy" (Calhoun 2012: 254). In misunderstanding "the relationship of tradition and resistance to social change" (2012: 8), Calhoun argued that social theorists have failed to see that "the most effective challenges to the established social order often come in the name of tradition." As Calhoun also pointed out, a tradition-inspired, ideologically reactionary movement may not "always shape a better future, but it can" (2012: 8, 21). Actual outcomes are contingent, but there is no *a priori* justification for excluding tradition-inspired radicalism from the stream of social movement analysis. Even if the ideological project of the group is envisioned as recovering values and institutions under assault by the disenchanting and immoral forces of modernity, the form that collective action takes and its actual consequences might be a source of progressive social change. Progressive and reactionary potentialities are simultaneously present. In the case of Falun Gong, contemporary Chinese state propaganda and entrenched social science habits of interpreting the world have converged to make it harder to see Falun Gong's effects and potentialities with theoretical and empirical clarity.

If social science is disinclined to see Falun Gong as a politically significant social movement, then which Chinese protest movements are regularly examined? Much Western scholarship and journalism have focused on movements that are more appealing to scholars than Falun Gong. The Tiananmen protests of 1989 have been, and continue to be, intensely scrutinized.[3] Another major focus has been on "the weak and disadvantaged left behind by China's economic boom" (O'Brien 2008: 21). Such research includes studies of aggrieved and laid-off workers; rural protesters using "righteous resistance" (O'Brien and Li 2006); *wei-quan* "rights defense" lawyers (Al Saud 2012; Pils 2006, 2015); and *xinfang* petitioners who appropriate official complaint channels for "trouble making" tactics (Chen 2008, 2012; Hurst et al. 2014). Still other common topics are the expansion of civil society and critical public debate through grassroots nongovernmental organizations (NGOs)

---

[3] Publications on the 1989 Tiananmen protests include: (Black and Munro 1993; Brook 1998; Calhoun 1995; Han and Zhang 1990; He 2014; Lim 2014; Nathan and Link 2001; Saich 1990; Wasserstrom and Perry 1994; Zhao 2001).

(Spires, Tao, and Chan 2014; Spires 2011, 2012), environmentalism and environmental NGOs (Sun and Zhao 2008; Yang 2005), and online activism by "netizens" (Yang 2009). Similarly, elite dissidents, like Liu Xiaobo, Xu Zhiyong, or Ai Weiwei, have commonly attracted international media attention.

These more or less familiar cases all share a common feature lacked by Falun Gong: they are all movements that can be represented to the Western community in a valorizing light. They reinforce a tacit teleology common in the modernist imagination, depicting a world historic progression from tyranny to freedom and from tradition, with its fusion of religion and politics, to modernity. Modernity, in this view, includes public politics fully differentiated from private religion and scientific knowledge fully differentiated from private belief. All the movements previously described are easy to represent in harmony with core liberal political ideals. Perhaps because of this political and aesthetic compatibility, such Chinese movements have been widely studied in academia and reported on in the press. They harmonize with the taken-for-granted association between social movements and progressive social change.

The Falun Gong case runs entirely against this grain. Like the "rooted radicalism" described by Craig Calhoun, Falun Gong "radically challenged both the existing social order and liberal agendas for 'progressive' change" (2012: 4). Its inability to be reduced to the progressive narrative left it stuck in a kind of blind spot in the prevailing Western political imagination. "Blind spot" may, in fact, be an understatement. In researching Falun Gong in the field, at times it has felt to me like the movement is in a black hole – all light cast in its direction gets sucked in rather than bounced back, rendering the community invisible to those outside of itself.

Many features of the Falun Gong case lead to its exclusion: it is a new religious movement, founded only in 1992, and, therefore, does not enjoy the acceptability that might accompany true affiliation with any world religion. It is led by a living man, Mr. Li Hongzhi, whose authority is based not on tradition or formal statute, but on the belief by his followers that what he declares is true. According to Max Weber, this kind of authority is "charismatic," meaning that it is ultimately based upon the "extraordinary and personal *gift of grace*" that followers attribute to the leader (Weber 1958 [1946]: 79). Many Falun Gong practitioners regard their leader as fully enlightened, set apart from others, and, thus, divine. Although many of his teachings emphasize being honest, acting with integrity, and cultivating one's spirituality, scholars, journalists, and critics have often emphasized his more exotic claims, such as about miracle healing, supernatural powers, aliens, and an ancient nuclear reactor in Africa.[4] Moreover, as the movement evolved after repression began in 1999, it increasingly relied upon charismatic leadership and a totalizing and transcendent ideology to extract extraordinarily high levels of commitment from its members. Janja Lalich cites that particular combination of qualities as characteristic of a "cult" (2004: 5) – a label that is arguably apt, but politically troubling. The Chinese government has systematically used the term "cult" to justify severe repression, widely said to have included detention without due process, brutal and frequent torture to "de-convert" practitioners, and several thousand deaths.

Another reason for Falun Gong's invisibility is that it has cultural roots in a centuries-old form of Chinese religiosity that is not widely understood, even among scholars of China. Although Falun Gong is certainly a product of modernity, globalization, and China's socialist era, it also has deep historical precedents in China's marginal traditions of salvationist movements and apocalyptic sects (Goossaert and Palmer 2011; Ownby 2003a, 2008). This class of indigenous Chinese movements has not been inspired by modern ideals of justice or freedom – or, indeed, much else that can be represented as being in harmony with either the liberal democratic political imagination or even the more familiar world religions (Masuzawa 2005). These characteristics set Falun Gong apart from the narrative of social movements-as-progressive, making it difficult to see how Falun Gong's protest activism conforms to our social science model of the modern social movement, or what I consider to be the "social movement-ness" of the Falun Gong case. Moreover, these same biases have caused us to generally underestimate the objective importance of Falun Gong for contemporary Chinese politics and history. I make this point in Chapter 3, where I discuss Falun Gong's importance to the rise of China's security state and the Article 23 controversy in Hong Kong.

If Falun Gong is not usually seen as a social movement engaged in contentious politics, then how is it typically categorized? The most common way is to see it as a kind of hiccup from the past. Imperial Chinese history, it is commonly noted, was punctuated by sectarian religious groups that occasionally emerged to become existential threats to the empire. As a sectarian uprising, and combined with the perception that Falun Gong's organizational form resembled that of the early days of the

---

[4] For a discussion of these New Age elements, see Benjamin Penny's book, *The Religion of Falun Gong* (2012), especially chapter 4.

CCP,[5] Chinese leadership saw the religious movement in 1999 with a kind of "historical resonance" (Perry 2001: 169), harkening back to the Taiping Rebellion that nearly felled the Qing Dynasty, or the Yellow Turban Rebellion that nearly did the same for the Han in 184 AD. This historical association helps to explain why the CCP reacted with such ferocity to what was, in fact, a nonviolent and semireligious community of enthusiasts for taichi-like exercises and spirituality. Elizabeth Perry, among others, argued that the central leadership's "real fear" of Falun Gong was "that the movement would turn into the sort of sectarian-inspired rebellion for which Chinese history is famous" (2002: xx).

Whatever the empirical plausibility of such a fear, the sectarian rebellion interpretation itself provides a different vantage point from which to appreciate the puzzle of Falun Gong's actual mobilizational form. The religious group did not become a violent rebellion. Instead, it became something that was undoubtedly impossible for a sectarian uprising to become in China's imperial age: a modern social movement using voluntary grassroots association, media, and nonviolent tactics to defend itself against repression and to widely advocate for an alternative vision of what Chinese society should be. This book will offer an explanation for just how a neo-traditional sectarian Chinese religious movement made this "social movement turn" and appropriated for itself the collective action repertoires of modern social movements.

The consequences of Falun Gong's social movement turn have been significant. Without exaggeration, Falun Gong might be the most well-organized and tenacious grassroots Chinese protest movement *ever* to challenge the CCP. Its participants have also paid dearly for their ideal commitments in terms of lives lost, traumatized survivors, careers ruined, and families separated. Without a doubt, Falun Gong ranks as one of, and by some measures perhaps the most, severely persecuted groups in the reform era. Moreover, multiple third-party sources have alleged that the CCP consistently singled out Falun Gong for extraordinary degrees of state violence and coercion (Chinese Human Rights Defenders 2015; Gao 2007; Human Rights Watch 2002, 2015; Matas and Kilgour 2009; Noakes and Ford 2015; UN Commision on Human Rights 2006; US Department of State 2007).

Yet in spite of this objectively remarkable history, the academic library shelf has surprisingly little to offer about "the Falun Gong problem," as

[5] I emphasize this was a perception and not a reality; the ethnographic studies of Falun Gong in diaspora provide little support for such a perception.

Chinese leadership initially referred to it. Falun Gong is known everywhere, but understood almost nowhere. We might say that Falun Gong suffers from an asymmetrical visibility dilemma: the CCP sees the Falun Gong through a lens of exaggerated threat, as if using binoculars to look at something nearby; and the Western academy, using the same binoculars but looking through the wrong end, sees Falun Gong only as distant, tiny, and peculiar in its aspect. One side sees Falun Gong too much, the other not enough. If there is a cautionary lesson is this, it could be told thus: woe be to any people who dare to both reject the hegemonic vision of the CCP *and* the liberal West's progressive alternative, for the dissenting group faces defamation and violence from the first and mute apathy from the second.

Along with the way that political and disciplinary sensibilities have converged to erase Falun Gong from view, practical and methodological issues add even more challenges. Researching the Falun Gong is a difficult task. At the most practical level, it is hard to collect data on a group that is thinly diffused across tens of countries around the world, severely repressed in China, skeptical of academic researchers and journalists, institutionally invested in shaping its public narrative, and rigidly private about some aspects of its organizational infrastructure, as are the leaders of the Falun Gong's only religious temple. Difficulties further compound when one considers that the literatures on Chinese religion, on the sociology of new religious movements, and on political social movements all can and should contribute to our understanding, but they are quite distinct from one another. Furthermore, to understand Falun Gong's diaspora mobilization requires grasping the movement in its own cultural and historical context that began in China, but then rearticulated and changed through migration and transnationalism across multiple national contexts. Any researcher committed to some variant of methodological nationalism, in which the research object is defined in reference to a single national context – e.g., "protest in China" or "Asian–American movements" – will necessarily fail to grasp the sweep of the case. There is no way to adequately grasp the Falun Gong case without fully embracing a global perspective. Terminologically, I address this difficulty by adopting the phrase "global China," which refers to the loose, but real, Chinese cultural unity that stretches across contemporary political and territorial boundaries. Empirically, I address the problem by looking broadly across the globe for sites of activism and by interpreting events in relation to one another, across national and territorial boundaries. I will say more about global China as a research frame in Chapter 2.

The existing literature on Falun Gong overcomes aspects of these various research challenges, but none have created a coherent narrative that accounts for the form and trajectory of Falun Gong's mobilization in reference to contentious politics. On Falun Gong, the three best scholarly books in English are David Palmer's (2007) study of qigong, which covers the movement in China, but does not follow it overseas; David Ownby's (2008) book on Falun Gong, which considers Falun Gong as a religion and as a political movement, both in China and overseas, but does not engage with any social science literature on contentious politics; and Benjamin's Penny's book (2012) on Falun Gong as a religion, which self-consciously tries to isolate the religious from the political, sometimes at the cost of obscuring their coevolution. In addition to these three book-length studies, there are many articles and one influential MA thesis published on the topic.[6] As a companion work on Falun Gong, UCLA political scientist James Tong's (2009) book, *Revenge of the Forbidden City*, examines the Chinese government's repression of Falun Gong. Tong's book says little about Falun Gong as a religion or movement, but it is the only book-length analysis concerning the repression in China. Recent scholarly work has begun to advance beyond Tong's book (Noakes and Ford 2015; Tong 2012). These demonstrate that, as of 2015, and counter to widespread assumptions, Falun Gong had not disappeared in China, repression remained active and ongoing, and Falun Gong continued to be a significant concern to the Chinese state.

Although several articles consider Falun Gong from the perspective of social movement literature, none of the book-length studies develop those themes and none construct a research program around the question of the relationship between Falun Gong as a religion and its formal adoption of social movement activism. In using the Chinese democracy movement as a contrast case, one finds many sources on Minyun in China, but little regarding the movement's less influential overseas efforts (but see Chen 2014; He 2014). As a result, this book also provides a brief narrative of the overseas Minyun history that cannot be found elsewhere in English.

Researching movements that are thinly spread around the globe, volunteer based, vigorously suppressed, and justifiably suspicious of outsiders

---

[6] Ackerman 2005; Bell and Boas 2003; Burgdoff 2003; Chan 2004, 2013; Chen, C. H. 2005; Chen, N. N. 1995, Chen, Abbasi, and Chen 2010; Edelman and Richardson 2003; Fisher 2003; Junker 2014a, 2014b; Lu 2005; McDonald 2006; Ownby 2003a, 2003b; Palmer, D. A. 2008, 2009a; Palmer, S. J. 2003; Penny 2002, 2003, 2008; Porter 2003; Thornton 2002, 2008; Tong 2002a, 2002b, 2012.

presents unique challenges. I have attempted to meet these challenges by using multiple methods, including comparative historical, ethnographic, and archival approaches, and then by triangulating data from the variety of sources to strengthen the validity of my conclusions. I have gathered data through interviews and observation in the USA, Japan, Taiwan, and Hong Kong; I conducted four months of participant observation in one US city; and I have extensively analyzed materials published by both Falun Gong and the democracy movement online and in print. I began field visits on the project in 2006 and maintained such visits periodically through 2015. My analysis of published activism narratives in both movements used the method of quantitative narrative analysis, for which I received a National Science Foundation Dissertation Improvement Grant (#0961624) from the Methodology, Measurement, and Statistics (MMS) Program. I synthesize these various materials into a comparative historical analysis that addresses the governing questions of the research. A more detailed methodological description is provided as an Appendix.

SUMMARY OF THE BOOK

The book is organized into three parts. Part I, titled "Thinking Comparatively," explains why it is beneficial to compare Falun Gong and Minyun as political protest movements. Chapter 1 introduces the cases and the governing research question, Why did Falun Gong outperform diaspora Minyun as a 'modern social movement'? Advocates of Chinese democratic reform in diaspora wanted their efforts to become a sustained and energetic political movement, and yet it failed to become one. Practitioners of Falun Gong, by contrast, only wanted to defend their religious community and stay out of politics, but what they became was a sustained and energetic protest movement. Why these different outcomes? And what might the answer imply for our theories of social movements? Chapter 2 in Part I explains the logic of comparing these two cases and will be of greater interest to readers concerned about comparative historical methodology; other readers may want to move immediately to the third chapter. Chapter 3 makes the strong thesis that, in terms of its impact on Chinese political history, Falun Gong is roughly analogous in importance to Minyun. To support the claim, I examine two episodes in which Falun Gong's real significance has been overlooked or forgotten.

Part II, titled "The Cases," consists of three chapters separately examining Falun Gong and Minyun in detail. Chapter 4 describes Falun Gong in largely synchronic terms – what it is, what its religious beliefs are, and what characteristics of the religious community made it especially adept at engaging in political protest? Chapter 5 is a diachronic account of Falun Gong's politicization, spanning from its earliest confrontation with the Chinese state in 1996 to its mobilization as a protest movement and finally to its dilution by millenarianism. Chapter 6 describes the overseas Minyun case in contrast to Falun Gong. Since there is little written in English about the 1989-era Chinese diaspora democracy movement, this chapter provides an original analysis and survey. A major implication of Part II is that, even though supporters of both movements attempted sustained campaigns against the Chinese government from overseas, the Falun Gong not only outperformed Minyun in terms of organizational intensity and tenacity over time and place, but in some ways Falun Gong's mobilization form had more "social movement-ness" than Minyun. This was true even though Minyun participants consciously imagined themselves as mobilizing in the form of a social movement and Falun Gong practitioners did not.

Part III, titled "Making Social Movements in Diaspora," consists of two chapters that seek to delineate how these different mobilization outcomes came to be. Chapter 7 uses quantitative narrative analysis to inventory and compare the tactical repertoires of both movements over analogous periods of two years. By looking at the different tactical repertoires, I show that the two movements oriented themselves to their publics in quite different ways. Falun Gong's activism depended on seeing the public as a source of political power, whereas Minyun's activism embodied an older, tribune-like protest model in which the public is passive and elites speak on their behalf. I argue, following Charles Tilly's analysis of the role of the public in social movements, that this different orientation on the public is a key reason that Falun Gong can been seen as having more "social movement-ness" than Minyun diaspora. Further, these different orientations on the public contradict our expectations regarding which movement is progressive and which conservative. The neo-traditional religious movement, at least in this respect, better fulfilled the inherent democratic potential of social movements because it emphasized the agency of the public and grassroots participation. By contrast, the democracy movement reproduced elite, paternalistic politics under the banner of democracy.

Chapter 8, the final, empirically focused chapter, examines the coevolution of the social movement form and the charismatic religious culture of Falun Gong. This transformation initially involved a proto-democratic turn through which movement participants defended their minority rights against the state through protest movement tactics. This turn to social movement activism was carried out in a diffuse, decentralized, and bottom-up way motivated by Falun Gong's religious ethic of activism. The charismatic leader did not direct the mobilization. Instead, the followers "led" by transforming themselves into a modern, nonviolent protest movement. Yet, the story did not end there. When the charismatic leader did reassert his interpretative authority over the movement, he "spiritualized" (Melton 1985) the framing of the repression and resistance movement. One of the various consequences of this spiritualized interpretation was that it diluted the movement of its focus on rights or other political arguments and reorganized the purpose of activism toward "saving" the souls of the public before divine punishment arrives. The apocalyptic turn in framing had the effect of both marginalizing the movement and diluting its political character.

The final chapter reappraises the findings in light of the original research question and draws out their implications for several areas of scholarship, including theories of religion, charisma, and contentious politics. I also reflect on what the Falun Gong case suggests about the complex and unstable relationship between a religious movement and progressive, democratizing change. Finally, I note directions in further research suggested by the study and pay a brief tribute to the practitioners who generously shared their experiences with me as I researched this book.

PART I

THINKING COMPARATIVELY

I

Protest Made in Global China

FALUN GONG AS A MODERN SOCIAL MOVEMENT

July 16, 2009, Washington DC: nearly 1,000 Falun Gong practitioners, known to each other as "Dafa disciples" sat in lotus position on the grass stretching between the Washington Monument and the Capitol Building. They formed long, uniform rows. At one end of the formation, dozens of practitioners positioned their bodies, as they held lit candles, to spell out the words "Falun Dafa" in English and "Orthodox Law" (*zhengfa*)[1] in Chinese characters (Figure 1 shows a similar image from 2015). Among these rows of mostly Chinese faces were many practitioners, dressed in white, who held portraits adorned with black crepe paper depicting mainland compatriots who had been "persecuted to death." As dusk set in, the candles they balanced in their fingers seemed to brighten; a hush spread as the protesters became a living luminaria. Each flickering light honored the decade of experience they had shared since the Chinese Communist Party (CCP) outlawed Falun Gong in July 1999: they allege that over 3,000 practitioners were killed from brutal coercion practices routinely used by state security and that tens of thousands of lives were derailed, jobs were lost, and families were split up. The candlelight flickered as if in defiance against a decade of state-led defamation and hatred, which has made a social pariah out of a once-popular spiritual community based on a doctrine of "truthfulness, compassion, and patience." But the decade had not only been one of victimization: For practitioners who made up the

---

[1] "Dafa" may be translated as "The Great Law" or "The Great Dharma." Within Falun Gong, *zhengfa* means both "orthodox dharma" and something like "rectifying the universe."

FIGURE 1 Falun Gong activists in Hong Kong use their bodies to spell *zhengfa* (正法) in July 2015

many small pockets of Falun Gong practitioners that were spread out across the globe outside of the People's Republic of China (PRC), in the global Chinese diaspora, the decade had also been ten years of protest, nonviolent resistance, collective action, marches, rallies, and vigils. Of petitions, white papers, lobbying, leafleting, lawsuits, and guerrilla theater. Of making nonprofit organizations, gaining legal recognition, starting newspapers and television stations. Of reaching out to the public. Of shaping themselves as a community with standing and resources to challenge persecution in their homeland and defamation around the globe. For a cohort of Chinese émigrés, many of whom had grown up in the authoritarian political climate of Mao's and then Deng's China, this vigil also marked a decade of first-hand experience in grassroots, social movement activism.

The candlelight vigil, held on a Thursday evening, was the first event of four days of activities for which Falun Gong activists, primarily from North America but also from places as far away as Europe and Taiwan, converged on Washington DC. On Friday, activists held a political demonstration in front of the Capitol, which featured speeches by

members of the US Congress and nongovernmental organizations. Then
they all marched, about 2,000 people strong, down Pennsylvania Avenue
chanting slogans and carrying signs in English and Chinese. Up and down
along the route of the march, Falun Gong "practitioners" or "Dafa disciples" distributed literature about the movement, engaged onlookers in
conversations about their cause, and gathered signatures of support from
the public.

After the march, I accompanied a contingent of about 60 practitioners,
a number of whom came from Taiwan for these events, to the Chinese
embassy for an hour-long silent protest vigil on the sidewalk directly
opposite the embassy's entrance. On the third day, Saturday, the Falun
Gong paused its protest schedule for an all-day "Cultivation Experience
Sharing Conference." In addition to the 3,000 or so in the audience,[2] the
movement's religious leader, Mr. Li Hongzhi, made a surprise appearance. Finally, on Sunday, activists returned to the National Mall to try to
garner support from non-Falun Gong organizations through campaigns
called "Million Minutes of Meditation" and "Freedom for Falun Gong."

These events in Washington DC illustrate changes that occurred within
a Chinese religious community that became politicized after the Chinese
government banned it in the July of 1999. By the time of the ban, the
religious movement had gained a considerable following among the diaspora population of mainland Chinese migrants throughout the world.[3]
Many of those who followed the movement in diaspora reacted to the ban
by publicly opposing it; their efforts quickly took shape as a transnational
protest campaign to oppose the persecution and defend the rights of Falun
Gong believers everywhere. The global community of Falun Gong

---

[2] This event was only open to practitioners, so I was unable to attend. For audience estimate
from the Falun Gong source, see http://en.minghui.org/emh/articles/2009/7/19/109313
.html#.T7PxpsWTW1k (retrieved on May 16, 2012).

[3] A quick clarification of terms will be helpful: throughout the book, I use several English
words that are best understood in reference to standard Chinese terms. I use "mainland"
(cf., *dalu*) to refer to the People's Republic of China, as distinct from Taiwan, Hong Kong
and Macao, and the Chinese diaspora. Also, in keeping with Chinese usage, I use the term
"overseas" (cf., *haiwai*) from the perspective of mainland China, thus meaning those areas
outside of China. Also, I use "overseas" and "diaspora" interchangeably. Although
"diaspora" can be defined in different ways, I follow Sheffer (1986), who states,
"Modern diasporas are ethnic minority groups of migrant origins residing and acting in
host countries but maintaining strong sentimental and material links with their countries
of origin – their homelands" (p. 3). Unless otherwise specified, I use the term "China" to
mean mainland China, excluding Hong Kong and Macao. Finally, I use the term "global
China" to recognize the loose but real Chinese cultural unity that stretches across these
political and territorial boundaries.

believers, a religious movement that started in 1990s mainland China, had somehow put to work the social technology of modern political protest – or "the social movement" – to defend itself against interference from the Chinese state. When put into context, this turns out to be sociologically remarkable.

To start, we can say that the capacity for any group to mobilize in the form of a social movement depends on a variety of conditions. The first is simply historical. Carrying out organized, coordinated, and sustained campaigns of political protest through demonstrations, petitions, and the like has not been an automatic or universally available possibility throughout history. The "social movement" is not timeless – it emerged as a distinct form of contentious politics around the late eighteenth century in Western Europe and North America. It was a secondary effect of larger social processes, such as the increasing role of representative parliaments in national politics, the expansion of print capitalism, and commercialization (McAdam, Tarrow, and Tilly 2001; Tarrow 2011; Tilly 2008a; Tilly and Wood 2013). It would be anachronistic, for example, to expect the Taiping sect from a century and half earlier in China to wage a social movement rather than wage, as it did, an insurrection and civil war. The "social movement" as an extra-institutional means for changing institutional politics was simply not yet a conceivable possibility for those who led that nineteenth-century rebellion.

And even when social movements are conceivable to actors, they are still often not possible. Social movements can only exist in places where democratic political institutions protect freedom of speech, assembly, association, fundraising, independent media, and the like. China today is home to much political contention and protest, but its legal infrastructure is hostile to social movements. A social movement involves collective actors who are voluntary, self-constituted, and autonomous. That kind of autonomy has yet to be synthesized with China's political infrastructure. Moreover, social movement actors challenge authorities by making claims upon them. China's model for managing dissent and conflict does not allow for self-constituted political actors to play the role of challenger and openly wage legitimate campaigns against the state. The civil society architecture necessary for sustained campaigning across time and space is also not part of the mainland Chinese system. As a result, collective protest in China occurs, but it is primarily episodic and localized rather than sustained, organized, and national (but see Sun and Zhao 2008).

The historical and institutional specificity of social movement protest is the first clue that the Falun Gong's protest mobilization deserves attention. Why was the Falun Gong community outside of China able to adopt the social movement form that is absent in China? Part of the answer is due to what Sidney Tarrow (1998) calls the "modularity" of social movements. Social movements involve a repertoire of protest practices – like marches, petitions, and forming associations – that can be shared and repeated across different sites, for different causes, and used against different authorities and targets. The diaspora of Falun Gong was able to avail itself of this modularity and thus learn, share, and repeat practices that many other movements have used before.

The fact of modularity means that social movements are a kind of social technology – a form or means to accomplish something – rather than a phenomenon limited to certain substantive cultural or political projects, such as raising wages, expanding civil rights, or expelling immigrants. In what particular ways did the Falun Gong adopt this historically specific social technology? To answer that question, we need to enumerate what formal elements comprise the social movement as a technology or model for action. Charles Tilly's work offers the most recognized framework for describing what is historically specific about the social movement (Tilly 2008a, 2008b; Tilly and Wood 2013). First, all contentious politics involve some actor making claims that bear on some other actor's interests in a politically relevant way. For the purposes of this book, I am only considering cases in which the Chinese government is the target of claims. These are cases in which a collective actor is a "challenger," meaning a political actor who does not have "routine access to government agents and resources" (McAdam, Tarrow, and Tilly 2001: 12) and who makes public claims that, if realized, would bear upon the interests of Chinese authorities.[4]

A challenger making claims against the state is a kind of contentious politics, but it is not necessarily a social movement. A social movement involves a synthesis of three signature elements: campaigns, the social movement repertoire, and WUNC displays (explained later) (Tilly and Wood 2013). One can recognize a campaign because it is a collective effort of public claim making that endures through time and (usually) spans many places. Campaigns are "repeated, coordinated collective claims concerning the same issues and targets" (Tilly 2008b: 121). Campaigns require resources, organization, and networks. In a social

---

[4] Movements can also target nongovernmental actors and even culture itself, but those are not the concern of this book. So, to simplify prose, sometimes I will speak of social movements simply as making claims on political authorities.

movement campaign, the people doing the campaigning do so not as officials in government or some other constituted authority. They act upon their status as ordinary members of the public, voluntarily and autonomously coordinating their efforts to make public claims against their targets.

The second signature feature of a social movement is that it involves a recognizable repertoire of collective practices associated with participatory, grassroots politics, such as creating special-purpose associations, mounting rallies and vigils, and signing petitions. The set of practices included in the list is more or less the same for different movements, although it is open-ended in a way that allows for contextual variation and invention. Fundamental to the social movement, however, is that its repertoire is primarily nonviolent.

Third, social movement activists make what Tilly called WUNC displays. WUNC is an acronym for public demonstrations of worthiness, unity, numbers, and commitment. A peaceful, orderly march of 10,000 people chanting the same slogan past city hall conveys that participants are worthy citizens (peaceful, orderly), are unified about a cause (expressed by chanting the slogan together), have broad enough support to warrant being heard (10,000 people), and are committed enough to follow through with all the effort of at least the march itself, if not much more.

WUNC displays are important as a formal marker of social movement activism, but their performative aspect also indicates another key feature of this social technology: WUNC displays are a performance and any performance only works if there is an audience. Social movements involve communicating claims through social relations that link challengers, the public, and targeted authorities. In social movement protest, the audience is usually the wider public. The public can be immediate bystanders who observe the march, and who sometimes become part of the performance, but the public also includes those people who hear the claims through mass media and other forms of propaganda outreach. Winning the public's sympathy and support is key to succeeding in a social movement campaign. A challenger who does not have public support will hardly be heard by authorities, let alone be able to pressure authorities to make concessions. Challengers attempt to leverage power over authorities through public support. Support comes in many forms, including new members, resources, and increased numbers of voices in support of the shared claim, especially as determined through opinion polling (Alexander 2006). In all polities, public opinion matters, but democracies have a formal mechanism to transform public opinion into kicking officials out of office and putting new people in. In summary, the performative aspect of WUNC displays reveal that a modern social movement depends upon an underlying set of *triadic social relations* involving challengers, publics, and authorities. Challengers use performance and persuasion to gain public support, which then can be leveraged against recalcitrant authorities.

At the Falun Gong events marking the tenth anniversary of the persecution, we could see many of the signature, formal features of modern social movement activism. We saw people cooperating for a common purpose on the basis of their ordinary status as citizens. Their collective action came from outside of institutional politics as a self-constituted challenger making claims against Chinese authorities, communicating messages to the public, and trying to garner support from the US government. The protest's participants joined in on a voluntary basis. For Falun Gong events, individual activists usually paid their own expenses and often endured hardships to make participation happen – like spending a night in a car to save money on hotel costs. Also at the protest events were various nonprofit, nongovernmental, voluntary special-purpose associations, such as the World Organization to Investigate the Persecution of Falun Gong. These organizations made public claims that bear on political authorities – albeit across transnational space to the distant homeland polity. In addition, the weekend events were part of much larger campaigns that had already extended over years and across global space. Finally, we saw activists making these claims through public performances that communicate WUNC. They displayed the Falun Gong community as worthy of recognition, united, numerically significant, and earnestly committed. Further, their displays used conventional forms of nonviolent protest – like the candlelight vigil, the street march, the sidewalk occupation, and public pledges of support from institutional allies, like members of the US Congress. All of these features of Falun Gong collective action conformed to the formal elements of a modern social movement.

The events of this particular weekend were only a snapshot of Falun Gong mobilization over what is now approaching two decades. Activists of the Falun Gong diaspora began protesting in 1999 and, as I write this book, are still protesting. One can find the Falun Gong active in many places, including North America, Europe, and Asia, especially Taiwan, Hong Kong, South Korea, Japan, Thailand, New Zealand, and Australia. Protest has encompassed an impressive variety of claim-making tactics and organizational forms. Marches and vigils are only the tip of the iceberg. Activism has also included creating a media conglomerate of newspapers, radio networks, and satellite television broadcasting; suing Chinese state leaders under international law in courts around the world; inventing and distributing web browsing software that people in China can use to evade Internet firewalls and censorship; hacking into mainland Chinese television networks to broadcast Falun Gong media; creating brochures and weekly updates on Falun Gong news that are tailored to locally specific regions in China by overseas practitioners and then distributed in those local mainland places by clandestine networks of practitioners; coordinating hundreds of thousands of telephone calls into China, some of which target ordinary members of the public and others targeting local bureaucrats engaged in policing Falun Gong; lobbying governments and international agencies around the world to decry the repression of Falun Gong as a human rights violation; systematically and daily seeking out PRC tourists to Hong Kong, Taipei, Tokyo, New York, and elsewhere to hand them leaflets and newspapers militantly critical of the CCP; and networking with adherents in China to monitor human rights abuses in China and broadly publicize information. Beyond these obviously political projects, Falun Gong activism has also spilled over into activities that might be considered primarily nonpolitical, like the Shen Yun Performing Arts dance and music performances that travel the globe in order to revive "the true, five-millennia-old artistic tradition of China."[5] These performances are promoted as apolitical and not related to Falun Gong, but the content of the shows contain homages to Falun Gong's religious beliefs and its charismatic leader; vignettes vilifying the CCP and its repression of Falun Gong; and a millenarian narrative that portrays human history beginning with divinities bringing Chinese civilization to earth and then ending in the apocalyptic destruction of communist-controlled China, followed by an age of Falun Dafa bliss.

How many Falun Gong practitioners are carrying out all this activism? Even after years of research, I cannot answer that question with certainty. The Falun Gong does not have official membership lists, congregations, dues, or other means of directly accounting for its size. Local activism is carried out in decentralized ways by intensely committed devotees, either in small cells or even as solitary individuals. My field research in various cities in North America and Asia, as well as my

---

[5] From the mission statement of Shen Yun Performing Arts, Inc., as reported on its 2012 IRS 990, available at www.guidestar.org/profile/20-8812402.

observations at large Falun Dafa events that attract practitioners from all around the world, points to the conclusion that the actual number of Falun Dafa practitioners outside of mainland China is quite small, perhaps under 40,000 in total, a third of whom live in Taiwan. Although there is reason to believe that the Falun Gong has a stable, if not increasing, population in China today (Noakes and Ford 2015), I see no evidence of its increasing popularity overseas – rather the opposite. These relatively small numbers of global adherents mean that all the activism earlier described is the product of a diffuse, thinly spread, and small global community. Not only has this community engaged in, especially relative to its size, an astounding variety of collective actions, it has maintained such efforts over a time period during which international media generally ceased reporting on Falun Gong and the Chinese state maintained or increased its efforts to crush the movement. Where are the "political opportunities" to which scholars often attribute the flourishing of a social movement? In a vacuum of any encouragement beyond the internal cultural dynamics of the community of believers, Falun Gong activists have pressed on, challenging the Chinese state with what is recognizably the social technology of a "social movement."

CAN A RELIGIOUS MOVEMENT BE A "SOCIAL MOVEMENT"?

In writing this book, I have sometimes encountered the criticism that Falun Gong may "walk and talk" like a social movement but that does not make it a real social movement, at least in the political sense identified by Tilly and others. Even though Falun Gong displays the *formal* criteria of a social movement, one might argue that a new religious movement lacks the *substantive* criteria for what ought to be included in the study of political social movements. This criticism raises a core issue in the intellectual boundaries surrounding the study of social movements and, even more generally, the place of religion in modernist social theory. Since the 1960s, social scientists, as Craig Calhoun has argued, have strongly associated social movements with democratization, modernity, and "progressive social change" (Calhoun 2012: 1). Working under the presuppositions of secularization theory, scholars commonly segregated the study of religious movements from political ones (Calhoun 2012: 37; Kniss and Burns 2004). The paradigmatic cases of the social movements field after 1960 were secular and progressive, especially the labor movement and then "citizenship movements" (Jasper 1997). Even the new social movements emphasized by European scholars and the cultural turn taken

within the American field[6] have generally continued to see religious movements, especially those invoking tradition and "reactionary" standpoints,
as something distinct from the subject matter of social movements.
As Calhoun argues, theorists have generally seen religious and nonpro-
gressive movements as "false starts and short circuits that expressed
human dreams and frustrations but had little to do with the overall course
of social change" (Calhoun 2012: 275). To the extent that modernity and
secularization are linked theoretically, Tilly's construction of the social
movement as a historically modern form of collective action has indirectly
reinforced the academic segregation of religious and political movements.

Swimming against the current, however, are studies (e.g., Calhoun
2012; Kniss and Burns 2004; Lofland 1985; Morris 1984; Smith 1991,
1996a, 1996b; Stamatov 2010; Wood 1999, 2002; Young 2006) that
demonstrate and theorize the confluence of religious and political activism. Some of that work operates within the framework of the overarching mobilization paradigm, which aims to explain mobilization as the
dependent variable and emphasizes strategic rationality. But some work
on religion and protests raises the spectre of the religious and political
categories collapsing into one another, such as protests operating as
"religious rituals" and even being a functional equivalent of religion for
those without formal religion (Jasper 1997: 13–14).

Given the range of ways that religion and social movements empirically
and theoretically intersect, in this book I eschew any substantive definition
of the social movement that necessarily ties it to progressive change,
thereby excluding a politicized new religious movement like Falun
Gong. Similar to Calhoun's (2012) *The Roots of Radicalism*, which
shows how religious, nationalist, communitarian, utopian, and other
nonlabor movements prior to the twentieth century properly belong to
the study of social movements, I explore social movement cases in this
book without assuming that the cultural contents of the movement have
some inherent relationship to their "social movement-ness," that is, to the
degree to which cases of collective action conform to the formal attributes
of the ideal typical social movement described earlier. Putting such traditionalist movements back into the mix also means that we can look for the
possibility of counterintuitive outcomes, such as conservative movements

---

[6] I find Jasper's (1997) summary especially useful as a critical review of the field. The biggest
  development since his 1997 book has been the emergence of the contentious politics
  framework, but that framework largely preserves the segregation of the religious and
  political according to earlier analytical models (but see Aminzade and Perry 2001).

having progressive consequences and progressive movements having conservative or reactionary consequences. Can traditional religion inspire social practices that embody ideals of democratic citizenship without championing those ideals directly? Can modern discourses about democracy actually impede the emergence of social movement practices and democratic subjectivities? What would such different path-dependent trajectories mean for social and historical change, empirically for China and theoretically for social movements in general?

These questions all focus on the relationship between the particular culture of a movement and how its participants use the technology of the modern social movement. Empirically, we can observe how different movements, such as religious and nonreligious, mobilize more or less in accordance with the observable features of the social movement. I am conceptualizing the social movement as if it were a continuous variable, in which we can see different degrees of social movement-ness.[7] More "social movement-ness" means more conformity to the ideal typical attributes of the social movement, i.e., making claims on authorities, waging campaigns, using the social movement repertoire, performing WUNC displays, and harnessing the underlying relations between actors, publics, and authorities.

VARIATIONS IN SOCIAL MOVEMENT-NESS

One of the contributions of this book is to argue that social movement modularity is conditioned not just by external factors – like the existence of repression or a social context favorable to social movements – but is also dependent on the within-group culture of the challengers. Within-group culture can facilitate the rapid and intensive adoption of social movement activism or it can hinder such modularity. The cultural features that determine facilitation or hindrance may not be ideological or related to differences in goal orientation, like progressive or reactionary, but are instead historically specific to the taken-for-granted ways of doing things that participants in a group share. Some movements, more than others, are better suited to adopting the distinctive modern social movement form. The cases in this study suggest that the conditions that determine this suitability are historically specific rather than essentially linked in any way to espoused political ideals.

---

[7] Roughly similar to how Tilly thought of democracy as democratization and de-democratization (2007).

Determining the relationship between Falun Gong's religious character and its social movement mobilization requires a research design that can isolate the effects of religious culture in the politicization process. Falun Gong is a Chinese salvationist movement, espousing a millenarian mission based on a syncretic mix of Buddhist, Taoist, Confucian, New Age, and folk Chinese ideas and practices. What relationship did this religious culture, like ideology and belief, ritual, and the obligations of Falun Gong spiritual practice, have to the modular appropriation of social movement technology? How do we separate the effects of external context, like repression and political opportunity structure, from the internal group processes that may play a role? This study uses two comparative historical strategies. First, I compare Falun Gong to a negative case, the Chinese diaspora democracy movement, because this case shared analogous external circumstances but had a different within-group culture. Second, I trace the specific ways that the within-group culture in both cases influenced how each movement adopted the ideal typical social movement form.

Why can the Chinese diaspora democracy movement serve as a good contrast case to Falun Gong? In the imperfect but illuminating way that historical case comparisons work, we can "control" for the independent variables of external context and focus attention on how within-group culture shaped the variation we see in mobilization outcomes. The diaspora Minyun movement, known as *haiwai minyun*, experienced a roughly analogous initial situation as the Falun Gong – repression in China and mobilization overseas – but did not take up the social movement model for protest with the dexterity or mobilizational success we see in Falun Gong. Minyun, like Falun Gong, began in China and met severe repression in the homeland. After repression, Chinese diaspora supporters around the world, but especially those in North America, tried to mobilize collective action to continue the cause and pressure the homeland authorities to reform. Overseas Minyun activists faced similar kinds of challenges as those faced by overseas Falun Gong adherents and often tried to solve those challenges with the same kind of strategies. But the outcomes – how much each achieved "social movement-ness" – were quite different.

Although in-depth comparison of strategies and protest tactics will be examined in later chapters, let me provide a vivid illustration of Minyun mobilization in light of the Falun Gong example that opened this chapter. Only about six weeks prior to the Falun Gong vigil previously described, Minyun diaspora activists also held protest events in Washington DC and also to commemorate a major anniversary: it had been 20 years since June 4, 1989, when tanks in Beijing crushed the student-led democracy movement. The Minyun protests, like those of Falun Gong, spanned several days and also began with an evening candlelight vigil. The vigil, which I observed, took place at a small triangular park dedicated to the "Victims of Communism." The event attracted about 150 participants. We all held flickering candles and listened to speeches from famous Chinese dissident exiles, like Zhang Boli, who had been a key figure in the hunger strike and occupation in Tiananmen Square and then spent the following year hiding in the wilderness along the Chinese border with the USSR. We applauded the recently arrived immigrant Fang Zheng, who lost both legs to a tank on June 4, 1989 as he saved the life of a fellow protestor. The commemoration ended, curiously enough, during an intense downpour of rain throughout which Zhang Boli, accompanied by a group of male singers, defied the deluge by singing Christian hymns in Chinese at top volume into the microphone.[8]

On the day after the candlelight vigil, several hundred Minyun supporters convened on the West Lawn of the Capitol Building for a rally that focused on more speeches by Minyun leaders, members of the US Congress, and leaders from allied nongovernmental associations. The crowd, dwarfed by the size of the Capitol Building lawn, was divvied up into several brigades of protestors. One brigade, representing the Chinese Democracy Party, wore blue vests and held blue and red flags. Another brigade wore black shirts with red and white logos and carried a red and white flag; they too claimed the name of the Chinese Democracy Party. Wearing still different colors and bearing a yet different flag was a third and smaller group called the Chinese Freedom Democracy Party. I wandered between the groups asking participants if those in black differed from those in blue, and so forth. At first, everyone insisted that there were no differences, because they had the same purpose: democracy in China. But when I pressed the matter, people admitted that each belonged to different organizations with different leaders. As I tried to understand what separated the organizations, my further questioning exposed that the participants were not sure themselves. Conversation was revealing in another way as well: most people in these separate democracy battalions struck me not as the readers and authors of the

---

[8] According to his memoir (2002), Zhang had become a Christian after he was saved by Jesus on Christmas day 1989, when he was on the run from the Chinese police and had become lost in a blizzard in the forbidden zone just inside the Soviet Union's southern border.

elite democracy journals that I had been reading as part of my research on Minyun. Instead, their accents in Chinese and their inability to communicate well in English suggested that many were not the cosmopolitan, educated elite who comprise the majority of post-1978 documented mainland Chinese immigrants to the USA. Also surprising to me was that few seemed especially fervent about their political mission. I revisit these anomalies in Chapter 6.

The contrast between these two moments of Chinese diaspora protest events is instructive: both Falun Gong and Minyun events were the products of transnational social movements making claims on homeland Chinese authorities from the political sanctuary of diaspora; both involved solemn candlelight vigils to mark the anniversaries of repression events in China followed by conventional political rallies next to the Capitol Building; both movements chose Washington DC as the stage from which to mount their claims; and both were efforts to preserve the collective memory of their movements in the face of their erasure in China. Yet, as an observer, it was difficult for me to avoid the conclusion that the Falun Gong's efforts not only demonstrated a much more vigorous scale of mobilization, but that its form of collective action somehow better realized an implicit dream of any social movement, which is to assert "the right of ordinary people to public voice" and signal "that people united around a set of claims have the capacity to act together consequentially" (Tilly 2008b: 123).

If we just compare the candlelight vigils, for instance, we see that, in size, Falun Gong participants outnumbered Minyun several times over. In symbolic gravity of place, the National Mall outperformed the Victims of Communism memorial park. And, in regard to how participants performed protest, Falun Gong practices employed more visually striking displays. Falun Gong activists used their bodies to spell out words affirming their legitimacy as a public actor, and staged a photo shoot that appropriated the Capitol Building as part of dramatic display of WUNC. Images like these are appealing for the media and communicate in a glance what 30 minutes of speech making might still fail to convey. At the Minyun candlelight vigil, by contrast, the protest form concentrated on speeches by celebrated exiles and the brief presentation of memorial wreaths. People held candles in no particular arrangement. Some participants wore matching t-shirts, but many did not. Overall, if you were an uninformed member of the public passing by or glancing over a newspaper story about the event, the images coming from the Minyun vigil would not symbolically communicate the movement's purpose and collective standing. It was a weak performance of WUNC.

These two moments of protest and commemoration in Washington DC captures a contrast that could be illustrated by innumerable other examples. The Falun Gong somehow tapped into a grassroots Chinese community and transformed its members into activists in a way that Minyun attempted but did not deliver. In matters of scale and duration, the Falun Gong sustained greater mobilization, internal unity, and "artful creativity" (Jasper 1997) over time and far-reaching global space. Although the memory of the 1989 Tiananmen suppression remains highly sensitive in Chinese politics, it has often been said that the CCP has feared the Falun Gong more than Minyun.

The irony of Falun Gong outperforming Minyun as a protest movement, and its ensuing puzzle, becomes even starker when one learns more about Falun Gong. Not only is Falun Gong a new religious movement, it is also a case of charismatic community led by the heroism of a faith healer turned messianic preacher. The teachings of Falun Gong include a thicket of syncretistic religious discourses. They eclectically synthesize Chinese folk religion, Buddhism, and New Age ideas. Theology ranges from conservative but mainstream moral ideals to magic, pseudoscience, and millenarian claims that the end of history is happening now. Yet nothing in this bricolage has anything much to say about democracy. In contrast, Minyun journals and speeches are packed with sophisticated arguments, theories, and plans for creating a democracy movement and a democratic China. Yet, it is the Falun Gong that made mainland Chinese immigrants around the world into political activists. Falun Gong activism, not that of Minyun, quickly and intensively embraced the social movement form. Why was the Falun Gong able to mobilize using this modern social technology where Minyun fell flat? How did Falun Gong's religiosity, its bonds of faith, ideas about salvation, and charismatic authority transform immigrants from authoritarian China into a small army of social movement activists?

2

Comparing Falun Gong and Minyun as Movements

Obviously, Minyun and Falun Gong are themselves quite different sociological phenomenon. On what basis and for what purpose can they be compared? In both cases, members of the Chinese diaspora voluntarily mobilized to protest against homeland Chinese authorities. In comparing these diaspora mobilizations, I compare how much mobilization each accomplished and what form that mobilization took. This means, I hasten to add, that I am not comparing how well each movement succeeded in reaching its goals of changing state policy in China. Both movements were unsuccessful in this respect. In fact, their confrontational tactics may even have spurred the CCP to harden its authoritarian tendencies and more vigorously repress dissent of all kinds in China. Rather than movement success, I compare success in creating a social movement that adheres to the definition discussed in Chapter 1. How did Minyun and Falun Gong more or less embrace, put to work, and conform to the modern social movement as a form of collective action?

I consider their differences in both quantitative and qualitative dimensions. In its quantitative aspect, the Falun Gong's overseas mobilization vastly outperformed that of Minyun. Whereas 1989-era Minyun largely disintegrated as a movement within two years of its peak in the summer of 1989, the Falun Gong protest mobilization now is approaching two decades of sustained action. This quantitative difference is not only temporal, but also spatial: Falun Gong activism has been more extensive and intensive around the globe. Some of this quantitative difference can be accounted for by the ten years of out-migration from China that elapsed between the movements, because there were absolutely more mainland Chinese living outside of China in

1999 than 1989, but that difference is almost certainly not enough to account for the disparity. In addition to quantitative variation, the qualitative character of each movement's mobilization – that is, the specifics of how people protested – also differed in important ways. These qualitative differences point to how the within-group culture of each movement, meaning the religious culture of Falun Gong versus the non-religious, elite culture of Minyun, differently influenced each case.

To clarify why and how we can compare Minyun and Falun Gong, this chapter offers a brief sketch of the historical arc of each case. Readers will find fuller histories when I examine the cases in depth in Part II. Although comparison requires separating the cases, they are, of course, not fully independent of one another. For example, everyone participating in Falun Gong more or less knew about the 1989 democracy movement in China, which was put down by tanks on June 4. Moreover, the CCP learned from its experience of 1989 in ways that shaped its response to Falun Gong a decade later. Both movements occurred at different points in a common but evolving historical context. In this chapter, I consider three elements of that context as they pertain to each case: one, China's increasing out-migration and transnational mobility; two, the global revolution in digital communication technology represented by the Internet; and, three, the extent to which domestic Chinese contentious politics had become transnational and global. These differences in context, however, are not sufficient to account for the differences in mobilization quantity and quality that this study documents. Instead, the cultural constitution of each movement, stemming from the dynamics of its own tradition, shaped the outcomes in ways that are analytically distinct from the changes in historical context.

Finally, I conclude the chapter by considering two alternative explanations for the different case outcomes based on social movement literature, namely resource mobilization and the structures of political opportunity.

MINYUN AND FALUN GONG: RESURGENT TRADITIONS AFTER MAO

Scholars and journalists have regularly referred to the democracy movement of 1989 and to the Falun Gong as exemplars of the most politically sensitive topics in China.[1] Both movements have deep historical roots.

---

[1] In Yang Guobin's study of the Internet in China, he identifies the three most taboo topics to be the 1989 Tiananmen demonstrations, the Falun Gong, and independent political parties (Yang 2009: 53).

Minyun dates back to the May Fourth Movement of 1919, in which Chinese elites rejected traditional culture in favor of "science," "democracy," and a secularist view of modern state-building. Chinese democracy activism throughout the 1980s followed in this tradition: it was primarily enacted by youthful elites and was oriented towards the twin goals of democratization and building a powerful nation. The 1989 student demonstrations in Tiananmen Square extended this tradition, but were also a response to a host of economic and political pressures that accompanied China's post-Mao transition (Calhoun 1995; Esherick and Wasserstrom 1990; Goldman 1994; Leijonhufvud 1990; McAdam, Tarrow, and Tilly 2001: 207–218; Nathan 1985; Schwarcz 1986; Spence 1999 [1990]; Wasserstrom 1990; Zhao 2001). Even though 1989-era Minyun has historical precedents, and there are activists and organizations that have sought to maintain its cause over recent decades, this study focuses rather narrowly on the 1989 era, whose heyday of overseas activism had clearly passed by 1991. To keep the text unencumbered, and unless otherwise indicated by context, I use the term "Minyun" to refer to this 1989 era, including in reference to the overseas movement, which is properly called *haiwai minyun* in Chinese.

The reforms of the 1980s did not only inspire political movements, they led to other kinds of movements as well. Among these was a faddish rage for qigong[2] exercises. Qigong consists of many different slow-moving meditative exercises that are supposed to promote health, cure disease, prolong life, and even confer supernatural powers. Starting in the mid-1980s, charismatic qigong preachers appeared and offered mass teachings in urban parks, leading to the formation of many different groups of qigong enthusiasts. Falun Gong was a relative latecomer to the qigong scene. It was founded by Mr. Li Hongzhi in 1992, which was after the repression of the democracy movement and before the coming economic prosperity had really taken off. Li rose from obscurity to fame as a qigong master through a combination of his successful charismatic and faith-healing performances, as well as through considerable early support from the Chinese state. But in 1996, the Falun Gong's relationship with the authorities turned sour. The state closed the Falun Gong's official national organization and restricted the group's publications. Around the same time, Li immigrated to the USA, from where he continued to travel and preach. In 1999, activists in Beijing mounted a demonstration involving perhaps over 20,000 protesters with the aim of winning back the

[2] Pronounced "chee gong."

qigong movement's legal standing as a community. The state responded by banning the movement and subjecting it to vigorous repression. The Falun Gong, both inside and outside China, responded to this repression by collective resistance through protest. Over the years, the Falun Gong's ideological position relative to the CCP has evolved toward increasing oppositional militancy. Nevertheless, Falun Gong teachings explicitly forbid violence, which has thus far constrained opposition efforts to nonviolent tactics (Chan 2004; Chen 1995; Ownby 2003a, 2003b, 2008; Palmer 2007, 2009a; Tong 2002a, 2002b, 2009).[3]

Even though Falun Gong began as a qigong group, it is widely regarded as a new religious movement. In fact, one of the reasons the Falun Gong clashed with authorities as early as 1996 was because the movement had already begun evolving in a religious direction (Palmer 2007: 224). It should be noted, however, that whether or not Falun Gong is a religion has been a matter disputed by movement participants. In some public contexts and in many of my interviews, Falun Gong practitioners have denied that the community is a religion, citing that the Falun Gong does not have churches, membership roles, formal clergy, and other institutional features of a religion. These denials, however, should be put into their discursive context. The Chinese government only permits five religions to operate in China; so, in the Chinese context, if the Falun Gong self-identified as a religion, it would be representing itself as a regulatory outlaw and help legitimate the government's anti-Falun Gong policy. Nevertheless, in the American context, Falun Gong fits both legally and culturally into the social landscape as a religion. For example, practitioners have built a large temple complex with Buddhist-style statues and hundreds of dormitory beds in the town of Deerpark in rural New York. The community's property is registered as a church to Dragon Springs Buddhist Inc.[4] Not only does this legal status confer tax benefits, but practitioners frequently use Falun Gong's religious identity to negotiate the institution's place in the wider community. For instance, in 2008, a volunteer construction worker, Mr. Liu Janin (as spelled in the local newspaper report), died from a fall when working at Dragon Springs. The regional newspaper reported being rebuffed on religious grounds when trying to gather information: "'We are a religious

---

[3] For the early history of Falun Gong and the qigong fad, Palmer's work (2007) is the best documented and most authoritative.

[4] Based on a search of the National Center for Charitable Statistics, retrieved on June 12, 2017.

community,' said a Dragon Springs man yesterday, who wouldn't identity [sic] himself. 'We do not give information to the public'" (Sacco 2008). Regulators from the town and state have also been denied access to the temple and its many construction sites based on the justification that it is a religious site that does not permit visits from nonbelievers. In my visit to Deerpark, religious grounds were cited among the justifications for refusing my entry to Dragon Springs.

If Falun Gong is a religion, what kind of religion is it? Seen retrospectively in Chinese history, Falun Gong ideology bears a family resemblance to many centuries of sectarian religious communities in China (Lu 2008; Madsen 2000; Ownby 2003a, 2008; Penny 2012; Perry 2001).[5] Its teachings are socially conservative, fundamentalist, millenarian, and require exclusive allegiance. The community has been deeply shaped by its living charismatic founder, who has preached his absolute authority in matters of morality and the cosmos. Falun Gong has no formal clergy. Officially, there is only Master Li and the community of practitioners, although various structures of authority exist throughout the Falun Gong network of organizations, such as Falun Dafa Associations, Shen Yun Performing Arts, *The Epoch Times*, Dragon Springs Temple, Fei Tian College, Universal Communications Network, and so forth. I have been frequently told that there are no ritualistic, administrative, or financial mechanisms for identifying, registering, or keeping track of members. One is free to come and go from the movement as one pleases, it is commonly said.

Being a "practitioner" may be entirely voluntary and have no administrative or legal meaning, but it carries many consequential meanings for participants. To be a practitioner, or "a disciple of the Fa," as is it sometimes called, requires fulfilling a set of demanding expectations for daily life, including ritual prayers and exercises, studying of Li Hongzhi's teachings, and carrying out "clarifying truth" activism on behalf of Falun Gong. The latter expectation, which is a major concern of this book, is also the one that is usually most demanding of time and money. Among the committed activists who I met, many dedicated enormous amounts of their time and personal resources toward the Falun Gong cause of "clarifying truth."

---

[5] Penny qualifies this comparison and argues that Falun Gong also represents something distinctively new (Penny 2012).

GLOBAL CHINA AS CONTENTIOUS CONTEXT

In spite of their sociological differences, history has put Minyun and Falun Gong together into one category because they share a common pattern of contentious interaction with the Chinese state. They are the only Chinese protest movements to emerge in the reform era that (1) began urban; (2) spread across social divides such as province, occupation, class, and ethnicity; (3) mounted coordinated, national claims against the central state authorities; and (4) generated enough mobilization to spur the state to enact nationwide repression campaigns involving massive propaganda, arrests of leadership, and violence. Protests have increased in China many times over since the 1980s, but almost all of these protest incidents have concerned local grievances and targeted local authorities; few dare to directly challenge the central authorities in Beijing. Minyun and Falun Gong are unique, however, for mobilizing participation across multiple social divisions and for explicitly targeting national leadership.

Minyun and Falun Gong share another feature, which is that they are engaged in transnational contentious politics. In recent years, a considerable body of work has identified ways in which social movement activism has taken on new transnational forms. The new transnationalism in social movements involve previously unconnected activists from different places in the world forming coalitions that jointly respond to globalization and to the internationalization of global governance (Della Porta and Tarrow 2005; Keck and Sikkink 1998; Smith 2008; Smith and Johnston 2002; Tarrow 1998, 2005). If coalitions and globalization define the "new transnationalism," then the transnational activism of Minyun and Falun Gong would seem to belong more to the "old transnationalism," such as when Sun Yat-sen raised money and support in diaspora for a republic of China. Overseas, Minyun and Falun Gong have been transnational efforts waged by migrants, sometimes exiles, in attempts to harness the free political space outside of China to influence homeland politics. Unlike anti-globalization coalitions, Falun Gong's global network is constituted by a single, solidary community – all co-believers in the religious movement. Even the Minyun diaspora in 1989, when it was most active, still can be understood as a single solidary community – a sort of extra theater of action to supplement the national one in China. It was not a coalition of diverse constituencies, as found in the "new transnationalism." In this sense, Minyun and Falun Gong are more similar to the Hindu nationalist diaspora movements studied by Prema Kurien (Kurien 2004, 2007), but since China, unlike India, does

not permit independent movements and political parties, the actual relations of Minyun and Falun Gong to homeland politics are quite different.

The form of transnationalism in operation for these Chinese movements is specific to China and the particular field of transnational contentious interaction that has become possible after 1978. For both
Minyun and Falun Gong, events that occurred in China influenced the
movements outside of China, and, with less regularity, overseas campaigns and efforts influenced events in China as well, although rarely
with the long-term effects desired by diaspora activists. From the point
of view of contentious politics, domestic China (*guonei*) and the overseas
space (*guowai*) have been for these movements a contiguous theater of
interaction, even though any particular context is also nationally specific.
Spanning the *guonei/guowai* are common culturally Chinese signifiers,
identities, and interpretive frameworks. Of course, many of those signifiers, like "being Chinese" or "patriotism," are construed differently by the
opposing camps. But the interactive battle over signification and the use of
common language and terms in the play of contention means that there is
a contiguous, transnational cultural space through which interaction and
contention unfolds. Thus, we can construe the field of contentious interaction as a single space, "global China." That space is further broken up
into various national-level (and other) institutional regimes and fields of
action. To identify actors and action I will regularly speak of "overseas,"
"diaspora," and "within China," but those distinctions do not contradict
the usefulness of seeing all actors together operating within a common
global Chinese theatre.

Global China, as a transnational space of contentious politics, emerged
from new patterns of out-migration that occurred after 1978. Between
1949 and 1978, mainland Chinese migration to Western democratic
countries basically did not occur. Since 1978, there has been a sustained,
and increasing, stream of students and migrants out of China into democratic countries. Chinese out-migration has a long history and strong
regional variations; immigration to Southeast Asia was different from
immigration to Western countries (including Australia and New
Zealand), and both of these still differed from immigration to destinations
of predominantly Chinese populations, such as Taiwan, Hong Kong, and
Singapore (Kuhn 2008; Wang 1991, 2000). In the contemporary period,
these region-specific variations have remained significant, but the most
important development for the present study has been the new wave of
emigration from socialist China into settings where waging protest movements is routine and protected.

China's post-1978 new wave of out-migration has been steadily increasing in scale since the 1980s. Overall, Chinese migrants' favored destination has been the USA, but the pattern of increasing out-bound mobility generally holds for Canada, the Philippines, Australia, New Zealand, Singapore, South Korea, and Japan. Figure 2 provides an overall picture of this trend based on estimates of migrants from China compiled from the United Nations Global Migration Database (UNGMD) from 1990 to 2015. The graph vividly demonstrates the importance of North America, and the USA in particular, for post-1978 global China. A closer look at the UNGMD further demonstrates that the USA has been the favored country of destination for mainland Chinese migrants since 1980.[6] As a single country, the USA absorbed the plurality, between 30 and 36 percent, of all outbound migrants from China between 1990 and 2015, with the peak being in 2000 at about 36 percent. Although, since then, migration to East Asia increased to about 20 percent of the total, the USA and Canada have still enjoyed an absolute increase year after year in migrants from China. Migration to the USA was greater than that of any other major region, let alone single country, excluding Hong Kong. Together with Canada, North America has absorbed at least four out of every ten Chinese migrants since at least 1990. One way this trend is reflected in the cases here is that both overseas Minyun and Falun Gong, as social movements, were centered in North America and, in both cases, New York featured as a primary base of operation.

Along with migration during this period, changes in global communication, and especially the Internet, have revolutionized how people share information and coordinate with each other across the globe. In effect, the Internet collapsed many spatial and financial barriers to transnational mobilization. Developments in communications technology, however, had quite different impacts on the two diaspora movements. In 1989, for example, the fax machine and satellite television broadcasting played a big role in allowing the protests in Beijing to reach a global audience. The Internet did not exist in China in 1989; it became publicly available in 1995 and by 1999 was in full swing. Falun Gong activism heavily relied on the Internet, especially after repression, and so some of the quantity and quality of Falun Gong activism was due to

---

[6] Figure 2 data comes from the UN Department of Economic and Social Affairs Population Division estimates that are available only to 1990. The author compiled data using the UNGMD database as far back as 1980. Even in 1980, the USA was already absorbing the plurality of mainland Chinese migrants.

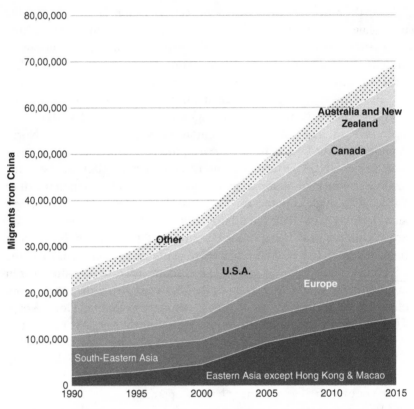

FIGURE 2 Estimates of migrants from mainland China by destination (excluding Hong Kong and Macao).
Retrieved from "International Migrant Stock 2015," UNGMD, United Nations Department of Economic and Social Affairs Population Division © United Nations in June 2017

having this revolutionizing communication tool. But, as it happened, 1989-era overseas Minyun activists also used digital media to coordinate protest. The Chinese foreign students and scholars who mobilized to support their Minyun compatriots in China in 1989 heavily relied upon electronic mail and LISTSERVs, which were precursors of today's Internet and social media. Their newsgroups and online magazines, accessible through university-based networked computers, provided to the emergent mainland diaspora a kind of space-transcending, inexpensive, and immediate imagined community. Although the 1989 LISTSERVs were rudimentary in comparison to what was to become available later, they played a key role in coordinating diaspora activism. According to Yang Guobin, the Chinese diaspora of the late 1980s was home to the "earliest Chinese online communities" (Yang 2009: 159). As we will see in Chapter 5, these online communities played a major role in coordinating overseas Minyun activism in the 1989 era.

By the time Falun Gong moved overseas, Internet bulletin boards (BBSs) and soon thereafter websites as we use them today emerged. Overseas, the Falun Gong was quick to take advantage of these communication instruments. One of Li Hongzhi's earliest and most influential supporters, Mr. Ye Hao, was particularly active in creating Falun Gong's global Internet presence. According to Internet reports, Ye graduated from China's second most prestigious university, Tsinghua, in 1959, spent a career working in China's Ministry of Public Security, including for his final 15 years before retirement in 1996 at the Eleventh Bureau of the Ministry of Public Security, which was in charge of cyber security. Ye Hao immigrated to Canada after he retired and went on to coordinate from Canada and New York the Falun Dafa Research Society's Foreign Liaison Group. This work involved running the Falun Gong BBS websites and eventually the establishment of the key Falun Gong website, Minghui, in 1999.[7]

Thus, the Internet, along with the sweep of other changes carried on by globalization at this time, structured the opportunities and resources for political movements in the emergent new global China. In particular, as barriers to communication and travel fell, and more and more people overseas could concern themselves with events in China in real time, China, as both an imagined community and as a network of people linked linguistically, socially, and economically, became more global. These common contextual factors – migration and the Internet – influenced the two cases differently due to the decade of time that elapsed between them, but they also created a shared context for both movements. I defer

---

[7] Information gathered from "*Ye Hao de jiben qingkuang*" (Basic Information on Ye Hao) http://boxun.com (retrieved on May 9, 2013); "*Renwu: Ye Hao – Tianjianweiji*" (People: Ye Hao – Tianjian Wiki) from www.wiki.tianjian.cc (retrieved on May 8, 2013); "*Ye Hao – Falungong zhi wang*" (Ye Hao, Falun Gong's King) from www.rbw.org.cn /article.aspx?i=Bks&ty=uuB (retrieved on May 8, 2013); also see "Falun Dafa's Transmission on Internet Notice" from June 1997, retrieved on July 25, 2013, from www.web.archive.org. Ye Hao was identified as one of two contact people, the other being Li Chang, who remained in China and was sentenced to 18 years in prison on December 26, 1999, for being a leader of Falun Gong.

discussion of how the two cases were differently shaped by this context until Part II.

MONEY MATTERS AND OTHER CONVENTIONAL EXPLANATIONS

Having outlined a case comparison based on social movement-ness as the dependent variable, let me consider two conventional perspectives that one might use to explain the Falun Gong's more sustained, intensive, and "social movement-like" mobilization: resource mobilization and political opportunities. The resource mobilization perspective, initially laid out in a seminal article by McCarthy and Zald (1977), holds that social movements succeed when they can acquire a steady supply of resources from constituents. This economistic model of movements holds that any social movement organization, or "firm," is in competition for resources with similar firms in the same "social movement industry." In addition, the total amount of resources potentially available is limited by the overall wealth of society and the particular constituencies available to the social movement "firms."

How does resource mobilization theory apply to these cases? Even a very superficial look at these two cases reveals that the Falun Gong has been extraordinarily successful at accumulating resources and deploying them for communicating its messages to the public. In doing this research, over and over again people have asked me: where does the money come from? Behind this question is often the suspicion, encouraged by mainland Chinese anti-Falun Gong propaganda, that the Falun Gong receives money from "anti-Chinese forces" like the CIA or Taiwan. Although I have had no access to insider information, a few observations can be made based on my research. The first is that I have never seen credible evidence for covert support to the Falun Gong from the USA or the government of Taiwan. Speaking speculatively, even if at some point Falun Gong activists did in fact receive such support, such as in the early 2000s, it is very unlikely that such support would have been maintained over time, given that the Falun Gong's political efforts are deeply entwined with its particular religious vision, the latter of which sets it in high sociocultural tension with its environment, including conventional political authorities. Moreover, we do not need covert state action to explain Falun Gong's appearance of affluence. The accumulation of such resources is plausibly accounted for by available facts.

First, let's consider how and which resources the Falun Gong acquires and from which constituencies, and compare these to Minyun. Following the resource mobilization perspective, we should expect that the total amount of wealth available to be garnered from constituencies in the Chinese diaspora was considerably more in Falun Gong's era than in the early 1990s. There were more Chinese overseas and there was much more overall Chinese wealth in 2000 than 1990, for example. Nevertheless, Falun Gong's most dependable constituency is in fact quite small – only the community of believers. Minyun constituencies of the 1989 era, by comparison, were much greater in number, even though the total diaspora population was smaller and poorer. Furthermore, the "conscience constituencies" of Minyun, which McCarthy and Zald highlight as especially important, included everyone who wished to see democracy emerge in China, and certainly included the governments of the USA, Taiwan, France, and elsewhere. In fact, according to one interview with a Minyun leader from the 1989 era who was involved,[8] the US government offered to fund a foundation of Minyun leaders to collectively distribute grants. Because of so much infighting among the members, the foundation never got off the ground. A willing and wealthy conscience constituency was there for Minyun, but internal movement factors, which will be considered in greater detail in Chapter 6, derailed the process.

Falun Gong's constituency was much narrower than that of Minyun, but as a religious movement with a charismatic leader and transcendent and totalizing ideology, the Falun Gong has intensively gleaned resources from its members. In some important cases, this appears to have meant donations in money or investments into Falun Gong projects by wealthy individual believers. One well-informed interviewee, for example, specifically mentioned that wealthy individuals from Taiwan had played an important role in providing funds for Dragon Springs.[9] In my field research, which focused on more ordinary participants, most resources were donated in the form of participants directly paying for the expenses of the immediate effort they were engaged in (see Chapter 4 for more detail). And perhaps the biggest resource mobilized within the movement has not been dollars but volunteer hours. This observation, evident in field research, is also supported by looking at Internal Revenue Service (IRS) tax reports submitted by Falun Gong-related organizations to the US IRS.

[8] Interview, December 2, 2009, New York City.
[9] Interview, June 7, 2016, Orange County, New York.

These report that the vast majority of labor for even formal organizations like the newspaper *The Epoch Times* has been voluntary. In addition to donated time and money from practitioners, the Falun Gong movement from its earliest days cultivated revenue streams, such as sales of books and videos, and later through selling advertising in its media productions and from ticket sales at the Shen Yun concerts. Shen Yun appears to be the most profitable of the Falun Gong-related non-profits. In 2015, it collected $15 million in program revenue, $100,000 in investment income, and had amassed over $60 million.[10] Finally, another key basis for Falun Gong resource mobilization is the tax regime in the USA, which is favorable to non-profit organizations, and especially beneficial to churches, which, unlike non-profit organizations, do not even need to publicly disclose their assets and expenses. At least one major Falun Gong organization, Dragon Springs, is registered as a church. Given Falun Gong's intensive volunteer mobilization, the totalizing commitment its culture demands of practitioners, and the income streams from efforts like Shen Yun, the movement's total wealth appears *prima facie* to be in proportion to its resource mobilization efforts.

A second reason that the resource mobilization does not provide an adequate explanation for Falun Gong's greater social movement-ness relative to Minyun is that resource mobilization is one of the outcomes, rather than a cause, of successful social movement mobilization. Why the Falun Gong has been able to glean so much time and money from its participants is one of the dependent variables in need of explanation.

Another conventional approach to explaining the different outcomes between Minyun and Falun Gong concern political opportunity. Did broader political conditions that were beyond the influence of movement actors cause Minyun's demobilization and Falun Gong's sustained mobilization? Did the broader political context favor Falun Gong and disfavor Minyun? In fact, neither movement enjoyed much in the way of political opportunity after their homeland movements faced repression in China in 1989 and 1999, respectively. Nor did either movement succeed in changing Chinese state policy according to movement goals. Objectively speaking, neither movement has had any compelling reason to believe that such success was within reach. The logic of comparing political opportunities simply does not account for the differences in mobilization quantity and quality, because neither movement enjoyed much political opportunity, but the Falun Gong kept on mobilizing anyway.

[10] Based on IRS Form 990, retrieved from www.guidestar.org.

3

The Forgotten Importance of Falun Gong

This chapter takes up the Minyun/Falun Gong comparison from another perspective: is Falun Gong important enough as a case to compare against the 1989 democracy movement? Undoubtedly, the 1989 democracy movement is widely considered a threshold historical event that shaped China's reform era, influencing factional alignments in the CCP, education and domestic security policy, generational identities, and more. To use the language of Dan Slater (2010), who argued for seeing contentious politics as a cause rather than only an effect of political structures, the Tiananmen event, in its totality, "re-ordered" power in China in ways that has reverberated for decades. By comparison, Falun Gong is often seen as an historical anomaly without lasting consequence for Chinese politics. Its "ordering" effects for Chinese politics and institutions are widely underappreciated or forgotten. In this chapter, I analyze two historical episodes that illustrate how the repression of Falun Gong and ensuing contention had enduring, path-dependent consequences that reverberate far beyond the Falun Gong case. The first example of Falun Gong's importance concerns the evolution of security institutions in China after 1999, a period during which China shifted to using security and policing, rather than legal institutions, to manage "social stability." The second episode I examine concerns the place of Falun Gong in motivating the timing and pace of Article 23 legislation in Hong Kong, which triggered a wave of protest and initiated a new era of democracy activism in Hong Kong. Both examples illustrate the underappreciated significance of Falun Gong's contentious history with the CCP.

FALUN GONG AND THE RISE OF THE CHINESE SECURITY STATE

The student democracy protests of 1989 and the crackdown that followed are well recognized to be a pivot by which the CCP regime consolidated its contemporary approach toward political liberalization and fused authoritarianism with state-driven capitalism. Throughout this era, as throughout the CCP's history, party and state institutions for managing domestic security evolved in interaction with political processes (Guo 2012). I engage here directly with the provocative thesis that, after 1989, China's bureaucracy evolved into "a security state," meaning that the party state came to rely primarily on domestic security and policing rather than rule of law to manage dissent and popular contention. Following this thesis, as argued persuasively by Wang Yuhua and Carl Minzner (Wang and Minzner 2015) in *The China Quarterly*, after 1989 Chinese leadership came to see "stability" and "domestic security" as the most essential basis for ensuring single-party rule. Over time, political emphasis on stability and control led to a new field of administrative and police activity known as *weiwen gongzuo* ("stability maintenance work"). Since the mid-2000s, the government has come to favor *weiwen* ("stability maintenance") over the judicial system and "rule of law" as the primary mode by which it manages social unrest (Wang and Minzner 2015; Xie 2012). Becoming a security state, according to this interpretation, included "the rise in the bureaucratic stature of the police, the emergence of social stability as a core element of cadre evaluation mechanisms, [and] the expanded responsibility for political-legal authorities for coordinating state responses to social unrest across all fields of governance" (Wang and Minzner 2015: 355). In Wang and Minzner's historical account, the rise of the security state began as a response to the pivotal events of 1989, including the student protests of Minyun and the collapse of communism in Eastern Europe. Thus, in their account, Minyun features prominently in the story of the rise of the security state; by contrast, Falun Gong is nearly absent.

A more complete account of the rise of the security state should include the state's frustrated attempts to eliminate Falun Gong. The repression of Falun Gong, which was a top priority of central leadership in late 1999 and into the early 2000s, had major consequences for the security apparatus described by Wang and Minzner. Its omission from their narrative is emblematic of the way social scientists working within our most trusted paradigms find it difficult to see Falun Gong. Relying on secondary literature, I argue that the repression of Falun Gong is essential for explaining the new *weiwen* security infrastructure and the intensification of policing over "rule of law" that occurred in the mid-2000s. My interpretation better accounts for the focus on *weiwen* work starting in the 2000s, suggesting that the two protest episodes, the 1989 movement and Falun Gong, each played a role in "ordering" (Slater 2010) how the security state wielded power.

China's security infrastructure greatly expanded in the decades following 1989. By 2010, three separate CCP organizations had come to jointly enforce domestic security: the Political-Legal Committee (PLC), the Committee for Comprehensive Management of Public Security (CMPS), and the Central Small Leading Group for the Preservation of Stability ("the Leading Group") (Xie 2012). This three-part structure is replicated at all levels throughout the party state institutional pyramid; CMPS agencies and the Leading Group, in the form of "stability maintenance offices" (*weiwen ban*), reach all the way down to the township level or below and are tightly integrated into the party leadership structure at each tier.

Why did this expansion of the security infrastructure occur? Part of the answer is that more protests and other disturbances were occurring. Yet, the emphasis on policing dissent through repression, some argue, set into motion a reinforcing cycle of more protests and more policing. As state officials increasingly used a public security framework to manage dissent, more mass incidents occurred. Of course, we know that repression itself can escalate protest, but, in the Chinese case, a more nuanced process seems to have unfolded. As the state shifted to repression as its primary dissent management tool, the government explicitly tied the career advancement of officials to their performance records relative to preventing social unrest and achieving official *weiwen* targets. The unintended result of linking career advancement to achieving local stability targets was to give citizens a new source of leverage over officials. Local activists learned to use protest to "game the system" and extort local officials whose careers could be destroyed by failure to meet *weiwen* targets (Wang and Minzner 2015: 355; Xie 2012). Thus, the institutional logic of *weiwen* policy inadvertently created conditions for more protests (Xie 2012), at least at the local level,[1] which, in turn, spurred more state investments in the *weiwen* apparatus. The cumulative result of the

---

[1] I note that this appears true for protests about local grievances. The *weiwen* system may be successful at discouraging protest targeting national authorities.

reinforcing dynamic has been "securitization," or *weiwenhua,* of the Chinese state. Securitization has led to an increasing number of social issues being addressed through the lens of domestic security, the "pluralization" of the government agencies carrying out *weiwen* work, the "ballooning" of the *weiwen* apparatus itself, and the elevation of security-related officials within the party hierarchy (Wang and Minzner 2015).[2]

Wang and Minzner provide a historical account of the securitization process in which they emphasize the importance to decisions taken in the early 1990s. Thus, their account views the 1989 democracy protests as being central to shaping the policy turn, because a new security regime emerged in reaction. To make this point, they point out that shortly after the 1989 protests, the party re-established the central PLC, which had been eradicated by reformer Zhao Ziyang before he was purged due to his tolerance of the student protestors in May 1989. Next, the party also created the second key domestic security organization, the CMPS. The function of CMPS is to integrate non-security-related leadership into domestic security work. After CMPS came into being in 1991, Wang and Minzner depict a fairly steady evolution in securitization as a consequence of these early 1990s policy choices.

Although the overall securitization thesis is compelling, the historical narrative does not account for the invention of the party's third organization for domestic security, namely "the Leading Group," which has a vast network of local social stability offices. Wang and Minzner emphasized the advent of CMPS as the major institutional innovation of the *weiwen* era and depicted the creation of the Leading Group as a secondary consequence, which, for reasons they do not specify, was established by the party leadership "in the late 1990s" (2015: 315). But what is the Leading Group and why did it emerge when it did? On this point, Xie is more precise: the Leading Group, and its vast pyramid of offices, was originally established in response to the imperative of "annihilating Falun Gong" (Xie 2012: 18–19).

Following James Tong's analysis of the Leading Group's emergence, before April 2002, the Leading Group was called the Small Leading Group to Deal with Falun Gong (*chuli falungong lingdao xiaozu*); its executive agency was known as the 610 Office (read: "six-ten" or *liuyaoling*), in reference to June 10, 1999, the date that the politburo Standing Committee first established a formal organization exclusively to deal

---

[2] As Xie (2012: 3) put it: the more that government "seeks to suppress instability, the worse instability grows" (*yue wei, yue buwen*).

with Falun Gong (Cook and Lemish 2011; Tong 2009). The central leadership, including Jiang Zemin, Zhu Rongji, and Luo Gan, perceived Falun Gong to be such an acute threat that the existing institutional mechanisms – namely, the PLC and CMPS – were deliberately sidelined. In Tong's account, three reasons motivated their decision to create a new party entity to exclusively address Falun Gong: first, the PLC had too many competing tasks to focus adequately on Falun Gong; second, CMPS, which included PLC representatives as well as many non-security representatives, was functionally too diffuse to nimbly attack Falun Gong; and, third, the top leaders wanted to circumvent the state's unwieldy bureaucratic apparatus and manage the "major" threat of Falun Gong directly from the politburo Standing Committee (Tong 2009: 136–137). Cook and Lemish suggest that establishing the Leading Group was also an attempt to protect against infiltration in existing agencies by those sympathetic to Falun Gong (2011: 7). Although the Leading Group was initially *ad hoc*, it was soon made a permanent feature of the domestic security landscape (Tong 2009: 137, 140). Cook and Lemish estimated the agency retained in 2011 "at least 15,000 officers." Its mandate initially expanded to the eradication of other "heretical" groups. Later still, it was either renamed or used as a template[3] for the formation of the Central Small Leading Group for the Preservation of Stability in order "to handle the increasing incidents of local protests triggered by forced land acquisition and tenant eviction by local governments" (Tong 2009: 156). The historical pathway from repressing Falun Gong to the *weiwen* apparatus is quite clear.

Although Wang and Minzner omitted this part of the securitization story, its details strongly affirm their broader claim, also advanced by Xie, of security replacing rule of law reform as the regime's primary mechanism for dealing with social unrest. The Small Leading Group to Deal with Falun Gong, unlike the central party PLC and CMPS, conspicuously excluded representation from the three agencies of criminal justice, namely the Ministry of Justice, the Supreme People's Court, and the Supreme People's Procuratorate; it also excluded representation from the legislative wing of government, the National People's Congress (NPC) (Tong 2009: 135). The new 610 agency focused on domestic security and policing, rather than the courts and legislation, to manage

[3] Tong's analysis suggests a direct renaming and outgrowth, whereas Cook and Lemish suggest that 610 served as a model, since the 610 apparatus has continued to exist alongside the *weiwen* apparatus, sometimes sharing office space and staff.

the perceived threat of Falun Gong (Tong 2009: 155). Later, the agency was generalized from repressing cults to all manner of *weiwen* tasks. Like Wang and Minzner, and Xie, Tong also identified a policy shift towards "the predominance of public security concerns" (Tong 2009: 155), which supports the securitization thesis. But the origins of the *weiwen* infrastructure in the suppression of Falun Gong is at odds with an historical narrative that only sees as pivotal the democracy-related events of 1989 and renders invisible the Falun Gong case. Instead, the repression of Falun Gong led to the formation of the most conspicuously security-oriented apparatus within China's field of domestic security.

The disappearance of Falun Gong from the story of China's securitization fits the wider pattern of how modernist social scientists see religion – especially new religious movements – as a side effect and not a cause of history. Such a view might have been accurate if Jiang Zemin had come to the same "social scientific" conclusion, leading him to pursue a less severe policy, perhaps through co-opting Falun Gong, rather than annihilating it. But such was not the case. In 1999, the CCP leadership rallied to a definition of the situation that cast Falun Gong as the party's most immediate existential threat. Falun Gong responded with tenacious resistance, which was sufficiently sustained for at least fifteen years so as to warrant continued and costly repression efforts by the CCP (Noakes and Ford 2015; Tong 2009, 2012). The consequences of seeing Falun Gong as an existential threat to the CCP reshaped the institutional structure of domestic security in China, especially through the invention of the 610 and *weiwen* offices.

The securitization example is by itself sufficient to substantiate the argument that Falun Gong's historical significance has been underappreciated; but this is not the only example. An equally strong case can be made for seeing the path-dependent imprint of Falun Gong on major political events in Hong Kong.

FALUN GONG AND HONG KONG'S ARTICLE 23

The first fifteen years of Hong Kong's political history after the 1997 handover can be divided into two periods: before and after the Article 23 security legislation debate.[4] Article 23 of Hong Kong's Basic Law,

---

[4] Unless otherwise cited, my sources for this historical analysis are Suzanne Pepper (2008) and Christine Loh (2010). It may now be appropriate to identify a third period of post-handover Hong Kong history, marked by the Umbrella Movement and its aftermath.

which is the constitutional document of the Hong Kong Special Administrative Region (HKSAR) and the legal structure for the "one country, two systems" regime, requires the Hong Kong government to pass legislation to protect against acts of "treason, secession, sedition, [and] subversion against the Central People's Government." The legislation must include the proscription of hostile foreign political organizations operating in Hong Kong and local organizations "establishing ties with foreign political organizations or bodies."[5] In October 2002, Hong Kong's Chief Executive, Tung Chee Hwa, released to the public his government's draft for Article 23 legislation. It was open to public comment for three months, further revised, and then scheduled for a final vote by the Legislative Council on July 9, 2003. Popular resistance to the proposal incited the largest protest demonstration in Hong Kong since 1989, rallying more than 500,000 demonstrators on July 1, 2003, which was the sixth anniversary of the handover of Hong Kong from Britain to China. In spite of popular opposition, the Tung administration pressed ahead with the scheduled vote on July 9 until when, in the eleventh hour, the Liberal Party withdrew support and left Tung without the necessary votes in Hong Kong's legislative body. The defeat tabled Article 23 and eventually cost Tung his position.

These events were a major turning point for Hong Kong. Before the Article 23 debate, Beijing had taken a largely hands-off approach to Hong Kong politics. According to Ma Lik, a leader of the most influential pro-Beijing political party in Hong Kong, "the passing of the Article 23 legislation was the only specific task assigned to the HKSAR government by the Central Authorities in the six years after reunification" (Loh 2010: 221). After the bill failed, Beijing adopted an interventionist stance in Hong Kong, especially regarding electoral politics. The Article 23 debate also precipitated a seismic shift in popular politics. Before the debate, there had been relatively little popular support for challenging the central government in Beijing on issues of constitutional significance. After popular opposition halted Article 23 legislation, more ambitious popular demands quickly emerged, with activists calling for universal suffrage for the election of the chief executive, Hong Kong's highest office. Moreover, protest against Article 23 prompted the formation of influential new social organizations, such as the Civil Human Rights Front and (indirectly) the Civic Party. Finally, the July 1 protest became an annual counter-commemoration of Hong Kong's return to mainland Chinese

[5] See www.basiclaw.gov.hk/en/basiclawtext/index.html.

sovereignty and helped foment the 2014 Occupy Central and Umbrella Movement for "true" universal suffrage. Thus, the Article 23 episode, which began in the autumn of 2002 and ended the following July, was a turning point for both the CCP's management of Hong Kong politics and for the establishment of a sustained popular protest movement.

With the benefit of hindsight, it is obvious that the Article 23 episode was a disaster for Beijing. Many things that could have gone wrong did, including the manner in which one of the primary proponents of the legislation, Secretary for Security Regina Ip, haughtily offended the public, and how the cover-up of the severe acute respiratory syndrome (SARS) epidemic in China in the spring of 2003 gave the Hong Kong public a frightening, and economically painful, object lesson in Beijing's willingness to engage in deception. Christine Loh's analysis suggests that the timing and pace of the proposal also caused things to go wrong, especially the way Tung pushed Article 23 legislation "despite widespread demands for more consultation time" (2010: 210). Whatever Tung's own decision making, it was Beijing that first put Article 23 on the agenda in February 2002 (Yeung 2002).[6] The central government had ultimate say over the timing of the bill's introduction, the extent of its consultation period, and whether or not to pursue the bill after the largest protest since 1989 demonstrated clear public opposition. Throughout, Beijing was "pushy" (Wong 2006) and charged ahead, as if some urgent matter pressed for a speedy conclusion of the legislation. The question is, why?

Both Suzanne Pepper's and Christine Loh's accounts of the episode avoid explaining Beijing's motivations for the timing and pace of the Article 23 bill. Loh's passive tense grammar is perhaps emblematic of a common fatalistic regard of the central Chinese government: "That time arrived in 2002 when Tung Chee Hwa announced that it needed to be done" (2010: 219). By contrast, opposition voices argued that existing law was already sufficient and that "no real threats existed in Hong Kong, including Falun Gong only protesting peacefully" (Wong 2006: 81–82). Political scientist Wong Yiu Chung (Wong 2006: 75) attributed Beijing's motivations primarily to concerns about Taiwan and its pro-independence discourses attracting support in Hong Kong; but Wong also wrote that the "most sensitive and complicated" Falun Gong issue

---

[6] Just a few days after the NPC meeting that officially put Article 23 on the immediate agenda, Hong Kong local delegates to the Chinese People's Political Consultative Conference called for new restrictions in Hong Kong on Falun Gong, suggesting that the two concerns were simultaneously on the minds of authorities in Beijing (Li 2002).

could be another reason for Beijing's urgency. Wong, however, did not pursue the point very far and only mentioned one minor, if well publicized, incident pertaining to the Falun Gong renting Hong Kong City Hall in 2001. In fact, just at the time when Tung Chee Hwa introduced Article 23 legislation, the CCP was engaged in one of its most intense battles against Falun Gong, and this battle was being fought domestically in China and overseas, in Hong Kong, and throughout the Chinese diaspora. Although Beijing had many compelling motivations to press for the implementation of Article 23, when the broader context of the CCP's battle with Falun Gong at the time is taken into account, it becomes apparent that repressing Falun Gong in Hong Kong was the most likely immediate application for security legislation and, thus, was probably the most acute proximal motive behind Beijing's timing and urgency.

To appreciate the context, it is not enough to only consider Falun Gong in Hong Kong. In fact, relative to Taiwan or New York, the Falun Gong in Hong Kong was a small group and was not popular. When the movement was banned in China, the Hong Kong community only had a population of about 1,000 followers, of whom "about 200 were 'active'" (Chan 2013: 9). Human Rights Watch (2002) estimated a 2001 Falun Gong population in Hong Kong of 500. These small numbers have, in part, led to the impression that the Falun Gong was too small in Hong Kong to significantly influence Beijing on a matter as weighty and consequential as Article 23.

Yet, in the mainland, Falun Gong was more than a minor headache. Contention with Falun Gong had been escalating from the earliest days of the July 1999 ban. A turning point was reached in the winter of 2001, during which the central government committed itself to further escalating repression. As described by Noakes and Ford, Jiang Zemin "convened a rare 'central work conference' in February 2001 – the first such meeting since 1988 – and called on the assembled Party officials to unify their thinking and redouble their efforts to eliminate Falun Gong" (Eckholm and Rosenthal 2001; Noakes and Ford 2015: 662).[7] All seven members of the politburo Standing Committee – the seven most powerful men in China – "stood up one by one to endorse the anti-Falun Gong campaign as an urgent necessity and to justify the 1989 crackdown." One official at the meeting reported that leaders justified the policy by claiming Falun Gong had "become a tool of hostile Western forces, directly nurtured and

---

[7] The Tiananmen Massacre had resurfaced as a divisive issue with the publication of *The Tiananmen Papers* (Nathan and Link 2001).

protected by, among others, the C.I.A." In the same article, Jiang was also reported to have called for the full eradication of Falun Gong by the time of the sixteenth Communist Party Congress, in the fall of 2002 – a goal that we know, in hindsight, was not met.

Within months of the meeting, the central government approved violence against the Falun Gong and "directed a policy of 'using all means' to suppress the movement completely" (Lum 2003: 4; Noakes and Ford 2015). Throughout 2001 and 2002, adherents in China continued to defy the ban on Falun Gong by distributing Falun Gong literature, meeting secretly, and coordinating with Falun Gong networks headquartered in New York. Incarcerating and attempting to de-convert Falun Gong practitioners was a vexing, resource-intensive, and often futile task for Chinese authorities (Noakes and Ford 2015; Tong 2009, 2012). One indicator of the scale of the problem is the number of practitioners detained in the Re-education through Labor (RTL) system during 2002. My conservative estimate of the number is between 52,000 and 130,000 people.[8] Whatever the actual number, Falun Gong in 2002 was absolutely a major issue on the domestic security agenda.

In Hong Kong, the small Falun Gong community had become intensively mobilized. When Falun Gong was banned in China in July 1999, practitioners in Hong Kong – much like practitioners in North America and many other places – met in urgent, *ad hoc* meetings, where they decided how to respond and quickly became mobilized for protest (Chan 2013). From 2000 to 2002, stalwart Hong Kong practitioners developed their own repertoire of routine protest activities, like handing out leaflets in public places and setting up photo displays of allegedly tortured practitioners. They also held many special, larger activities like marches, sit-ins, candlelit vigils, hunger strikes, and counter demonstrations to CCP United Front-sponsored "anti-cult" events. Whereas

---

[8] I derived this estimate as follows: According to *The Economist* (December 19, 2002), the Ministry of Justice reported that the RTL system in 2002 contained around 260,000 detainees in total. At the single Beijing RTL facility in that same news story, 28 percent of the detainees were Falun Gong practitioners. The US State Department in 2008 reported estimates by foreign observers that at least half of all RTL detainees were Falun Gong practitioners. The 2015 Human Rights Watch report on RTL also suggested that at least a plurality of the RTL population, even a decade after 2002, was composed of Falun Gong activists (Human Rights Watch 2015). My estimate multiplied the total reported 2002 RTL population by a range of 20 to 50 percent. The estimate is conservative, especially because the Ministry of Justice may have underreported the total RTL population for 2002. For another discussion of the population of Falun Gong practitioners in RTL, see Noakes and Ford (2015).

leafleting appears to have occurred almost anywhere, from highly trafficked venues to neighborhood apartment buildings, major demonstrations and public events were staged at venues like Victoria Park, Chater Garden, the Hong Kong University Student Union, the Tsim Sha Tsui waterfront, and so forth. Among these places, China's Liaison Office, which represents the CCP in Hong Kong, was an especially important demonstration target, being the object of both routine and special event protests. In January 2002, Falun Gong practitioners also began to systematically target mainland tourists for leafleting at places through which tourists had to pass, like train stations, or where tourists spent time in less structured ways, as in shopping malls.[9] In fact, in March 2002, Hong Kong delegates to the Chinese People's Political Consultative Conference in Beijing cited the Falun Gong's tactic of targeting mainland Chinese tourists for propaganda to justify implementing legal restrictions against Falun Gong in Hong Kong (Li 2002).[10]

Given the CCP's antipathy toward Falun Gong and the giant campaign against it in the mainland, all of this Falun Gong protest and visibility on China's own soil must have been – at the very least – an irritant to Beijing. In February 2001, following Jiang Zemin's special meeting on eradicating Falun Gong, Beijing initiated a drive to finally shut down Falun Gong in Hong Kong (Human Rights Watch 2002). Tung Chee Hwa and Security Chief Regina Ip both took public anti-Falun Gong positions, mimicking the CCP rhetoric of calling the group "devious," "heterodox," and "an evil cult." All of this was said, even though Ip also acknowledged the group had broken no laws in Hong Kong; in fact, the Falun Gong was well known by police to operate "irreproachably, scrupulously … within the limits of the law" (Human Rights Watch 2002). The drive to move against Falun Gong backfired, because it raised public concern about the integrity of "one country, two systems" and by May of that year, Ip and Tung both dialed back their public invectives. As if to signal of defeat, President Jiang Zemin shortened his visit to Hong Kong in May 2001, from three days to one, which analysts at Human Rights Watch attributed to his concerns about the Falun Gong protesting his visit (Human Rights Watch 2002).

[9] "*Zhuajin shijian xianglai Xianggang lüyou de dalu lüke jiangqing zhenxiang*" (Seize the chance to clarify truth to mainland tourists visiting Hong Kong), retrieved on September 8, 2015, from www.minghui.org/mh/articles/2002/2/8/24544.html.

[10] My synopsis of activism during this period comes from reading Minghui reports from 1999 through to 2002 that describe activism in Hong Kong. The Minghui source is discussed in the Appendix.

The year 2002, during which Tung began the push for Article 23 legislation, was not only a period of increased repression by the CCP against Falun Gong, it was also a period of increased innovation and resistance by the global religious community. In 2001, Falun Gong had been essentially driven underground in the mainland, but many activists remained defiant and covertly mobilized. On March 5, 2002, a small band of Falun Gong practitioners carried out what was perhaps the movement's most provocative act of defiance ever: they hacked into television broadcast cables in Changchun City and successfully aired on eight channels to potentially 300,000 viewers nearly an hour of the Falun Gong's own videos (Gutmann 2014; Tong 2009). According to Falun Gong accounts – perhaps apocryphal on this point – people thought the ban on Falun Gong had been lifted and practitioners were openly congratulated on the street. The broadcast coincided with national and provincial leadership meetings in Beijing, which also were marred by a group of foreigners who staged a surprise protest in support of Falun Gong in Tiananmen Square. Authorities responded to the broadcast hack with severity: 2,000 Falun Gong practitioners in Changchun were detained, 150 sent to RTL, and leading officials in Changchun and the surrounding area were fired (Associated Press 2002). Tong (2009) describes intensive national efforts to prevent future broadcast hijacking, including elaborate monitoring teams made ready at any moment to shut down transmissions, and a national conference in September 2002 on how to prevent Falun Gong broadcast sabotage. Also in September, authorities announced the sentencing of fifteen people for up to twenty years in prison for the Changchun broadcast hacking (Pan 2002). Falun Gong sources report that six of the original broadcast activists died due to police brutality (Gutmann 2014). In spite of government efforts to prevent reoccurrences, Falun Gong activists succeeded in hacking perhaps two dozen more, if much briefer, broadcasts (Tong 2009).

Only eleven days after the first Changchun broadcast, on March 16, Hong Kong police upset the fragile toleration granted to Falun Gong protesters and unexpectedly arrested sixteen Falun Gong activists who were beginning a three-day hunger strike outside of the Liaison Office. This event is significant in at least two ways. First, its timing suggest that escalation may have been a result of pressure from Beijing connected to the Changchun incident. Certainly, the two events unfolded in close succession. Second, within Hong Kong politics, these arrests were quickly interpreted as a sign that the repression against Falun Gong had finally arrived in Hong Kong and that "one country, two systems" was in danger.

When the case went to court on August 16, the courtroom was packed with onlookers, including government representatives from the USA, Britain, and Canada (SCMP 2002). Falun Gong had become the canary in the coalmine for Hong Kong's democratic freedoms. The lower court judge in 2002 found the practitioners guilty, which fed the perception that constitutional freedoms were finally being threatened in Hong Kong. The verdict was eventually reversed by the high court in 2004, well after the Article 23 debate ended.

The Changchun incident was not the only extraordinary example of the Falun Gong escalating its battle with the CCP. Activists in democratic countries started to use foreign legal systems to put new pressure on Beijing. In 2002, diaspora activists initiated a series of lawsuits, which alleged crimes like torture, murder, rape, and genocide against individual Chinese leaders who could be charged in foreign courts when they traveled abroad. On August 27, 2002, for instance, Sichuan Party Secretary Zhou Yongkang, who later became the CCP's top security official, was served with lawsuit papers during a visit to Chicago. The mayor of Beijing and a deputy governor of Liaoning Province both encountered the same treatment when attending the Winter Olympics in Utah in February 2002 (Pomfret 2002). Then, in October 2002, President Jiang Zemin himself was served such papers in Chicago. Like the Changchun broadcasts, the Falun Gong was challenging the CCP with unprecedented – and even personally humiliating – forms of resistance.

When we put Article 23 into the context of Beijing's hot battle with Falun Gong, it becomes a highly plausible interpretation that Beijing was looking for more leverage to suppress Falun Gong in Hong Kong, and that the primary obstacle to its success was legal constraint. Even in 1999, the Commissioner of China's Ministry of Foreign Affairs, who had usually avoided comments that could be interpreted as meddling in Hong Kong's internal affairs, "warned that Hong Kong should not be used as an 'operation base' by the Falun Gong" (Loh 2010: 204). Although Article 23 would not have given the government authority to directly ban Falun Gong in Hong Kong as an "evil cult," the HKSAR government could have criminalized the group on the basis of its ties to hostile foreign political organizations – meaning the highly networked transnational Falun Gong religious community stretching from New York to Taipei. There was also suggestion that chanting slogans such as "Down with Jiang Zemin," common at Falun Gong protests, could be criminalized as subversion (Hon 2002). More than any other group, the Falun Gong was probably considered by Beijing the most immediate and pressing application for new security legislation and was quite likely an important element shaping CCP perceptions and decisions regarding the urgency and timing of Article 23.

Although this analysis is limited by the circumstantial nature of the evidence, it is better substantiated and serves as a corrective to the common and unexamined *assumption* that Falun Gong was a relatively minor and sideshow issue. Eradicating Falun Gong was a major policy objective for the CCP during the two and a half years prior to July 2003. Much of this historical context is easy to forget after the time has passed, especially given the confluence of CCP propaganda and modernist social science presuppositions, as argued in the introduction. In addition, the Hong Kong episode illustrates the importance of looking at transnational (or trans-territorial) interactions among contentious actors to make sense of what might otherwise appear to be locally specific events. If Hong Kong is examined as a closed theater of politics, the analytical frame itself obfuscates the global contentious dynamics between the Falun Gong and the CCP, which involved actors in the mainland, North America, Taiwan, and elsewhere. The CCP's frustrated policy objective of eradicating Falun Gong was quite plausibly a major incentive goading Beijing's approach to the timing and urgency of Article 23 legislation.

We have, then, two major developments in recent Chinese history that were significantly shaped, in path-dependent ways, by the contentious interaction between the CCP and the Falun Gong. But the role of the Falun Gong in these events has been largely overlooked by scholars and journalists, whereas the importance and influence of the Minyun events of 1989 remain a fundamental building block of historical interpretation. Both these historical episodes point to how the dynamics of contention between the Falun Gong and the CCP cascaded in ways that shaped the downstream history that followed. The overall pattern coincides with recent literature that explores how contentious politics can cause durable changes in state institutions and factional alignments (Slater 2010; Tarrow 2012). The dynamic and contentious interactions between the Falun Gong and the CCP in these two episodes influenced, on the one hand, party and state institutional formation in China and Hong Kong and, on the other hand, the trajectory of Hong Kong's post-Article 23 democracy movement.

Nor do these two episodes exhaust the possibilities for how CCP–Falun Gong contention has shaped Chinese politics. Slater emphasizes how contentious politics, particularly conflicts emerging from within the polity, "powerfully and persistently shapes how political alliances and rivalries will be defined" (2010: 276). It is widely recognized that Xi Jinping, who came to power in 2013, was in a factional battle with political rivals linked to Jiang Zemin, including Bo Xilai, Zhou Yongkang, Xu Caihou, Li Dongsheng, and others. Falun Gong sources have traced how the careers of these individuals in the Jiang faction have also been especially invested in the anti-Falun Gong policy.[11] To what extent factional identification and interests were shaped by the anti-Falun Gong policy remains in need of research but may ultimately prove to be an influential variable in shaping early twenty-first century elite CCP factional alignments. Such research, however, is beyond the scope of this study.

Falun Gong's importance for the rise of the security state and for Hong Kong politics also provides evidence for two other positions I take in this book. In both cases, scholarly interpretations of the events fit a pattern of overlooking the significance of Falun Gong, (presumably) because our well-established paradigms of political and historical interpretation view religious movements as epiphenomena rather than as causes of history. Moreover, the Hong Kong example also shows the advantages of a "global China" analysis over one in which the field of analysis is limited to national (or in this case "special administrative") boundaries. Although the Falun Gong in Hong Kong was numerically weak and attracted more hostility than popular support, the Article 23 controversy can be more fully understood if the global context of the CCP's battle with the Falun Gong is taken into account.

Together, the path-dependent significance of the Falun Gong's contentious interactions with the CCP in these two episodes also demonstrates the need for a better sociological account of the Falun Gong mobilization. How did a neo-traditional Chinese group of qigong enthusiasts come to play this outsized role in contemporary Chinese history? Much of the answer has to do with the Falun Gong's mobilization as a transnational protest movement, which is the topic to which I turn next.

---

[11] *"Shibada hou yu gaoguan duo shi pohai falungong de xiongtu"* (Since the eighteenth NPC, many of the purged high-level officials are persecutors of Falun Gong), retrieved on May 10, 2015, from www.epochtimes.com/gb/15/3/11/n4384692p.htm.

PART II

THE·CASES

4

Falun Gong: Qigong Fad, New Religion, Protest Movement

The following two chapters describe Falun Gong, its initial historical context, its characteristics favoring mobilization as a protest movement, and how its contentious relationship unfolded with the Chinese government.

FALUN GONG AS QIGONG FAD

Since the political and economic reforms of the early 1980s, China has experienced a resurgence of many sorts of religious faith and activity (Ashiwa and Wank 2009; Goossaert and Palmer 2011; Johnson 2017; Lian 2010; Overmyer 2003; Palmer 2009b; Stark and Liu 2011; Yang 2006). One chapter of this resurgence was the "qigong craze" (*qigong re*), which began in the early 1980s and lasted until 1999 (Palmer 2007, 2009a; Zhu and Penny 1994). The "craze" was a kind of semi-religious revival based on the popular practice of qigong, which refers to slow-moving exercises related both to martial arts and traditional Chinese medicine. For American readers, the most well-known form of qigong may be *taichi*. At its peak, the qigong craze is estimated to have involved 20 percent of the urban Chinese population (Palmer 2007: 6) and by some accounts was "probably the greatest mass movement in modern China that was not under direct government control" (Palmer 2007: 15; Zhu and Penny 1994: 3). Many different qigong groups emerged and competed. By 1996, Falun Gong had become one of China's largest and most popular qigong groups.

Qigong is a blend of traditional and post-1949 discourses and practices, which purports to improve health and deliver supernatural benefits (Ownby 2003a, 2008; Palmer 2007, 2009a; Xu 1999). In the early 1980s, societal and political changes in China favored the opening of social space for charismatic entrepreneurs of qigong and the popular diffusion of qigong as a specifically Chinese form of health promotion and science. Palmer's book (2007) about the qigong craze shows the complex ways that state institutions, political elites, academics, charismatic entrepreneurs, and popular qigong enthusiasts all contributed to the formation of the social and institutional "milieu" of the qigong fad. Although the Falun Gong is today the most internationally known qigong group from this era, Palmer maintains that the largest qigong group ever may have been the Zhonggong, which was the first group to combine charismatic leadership with an effective mass organization. Unlike the Falun Gong, however, the Zhonggong evolved in the direction of a commercial and bureaucratic organization, rather than as a religious sect. When the Zhonggong was in decline between 1996 and 1999, the Falun Gong was in ascendance (Palmer 2007: 208–219).

Falun Gong, or Falun Dafa, began in 1992, well after many prominent qigong groups had established themselves. It gained popularity very quickly. Although estimates of Falun Gong's peak membership in China vary by source and by definition, the most probable range is set between three and twenty million (Palmer 2007: 260). Chinese official sources from a state security investigation conducted in 1999 allegedly documented 2.3 million Falun Gong believers, nearly 360,000 of whom were members of the CCP (Penny 2012: 67). Falun Gong sources frequently have claimed 100 million members.

Falun Gong was founded in the northeastern city of Changchun by Mr. Li Hongzhi, who was around 40 years old.[1] Mr. Li's educational and work accomplishments were modest and ordinary, containing nothing to foretell his rise to fame as a charismatic qigong entrepreneur. Li's particular form of qigong is named after the "dharma wheel," or *falun,* which he claimed to put into each practitioner's body. Li's version of qigong is based on a set of easy-to-do exercises and eclectic teachings about morality, health, and the supernatural. In the first two years that Li taught Falun Gong, he traveled around China conducting nine-day workshops on his method of qigong. Each day of these workshops involved a long charismatic lecture by Li, the transcripts of which became the sources for Falun Gong's most influential publications, *China Falun Gong* and *Zhuan Falun* (or *Turning the Law Wheel*) (Penny 2012: 93–100). In these workshops, and at other public appearances, Li also became known for healing illnesses.

---

[1] His birthdate is a source of dispute.

After two years of qigong instruction and faith healing, Li Hongzhi began to lead his movement in a more explicitly religious direction than taken by other major qigong groups. Lu Yunfeng has argued that this religious turn was motivated by the pressures of the competitive economy of qigong groups during the early 1990s – i.e., Li perceived an available market niche that he felt able to fill (Lu 2005). Palmer describes Li's religious shift as follows:

... around the end of 1994 and beginning of 1995 Li Hongzhi introduced new elements which would subtly but profoundly change the nature of Falungong, until ideology replaced body training as its chief object.

In the autumn of 1994 he began to stress that Falungong was not a form of qigong but a higher universal Dharma or *Fa*. He compared the leaders of practice sites to temple abbots, whose role was to guide adepts to salvation. He forbade practitioners from healing others. He changed his birthday registration to May 1951, which in that year was the 8th day of the 4th lunar month, traditionally celebrated as the birthday of Sakyamuni Buddha. (Palmer 2007: 224)

As time went on, Li's preaching rejected "key points of the qigong discourse" in favor of a religious discourse focusing on cultivating one's "spiritual nature," reaching salvation, and what Palmer characterizes as a "paranoid fundamentalism" (2007: 225).

As part of this shift to a religious discourse, Li changed the style of his charismatic performance. He stopped his face-to-face nine-day mass workshops, in which he was said to have performed miracle cures, and engaged in a more heavily mediated form of evangelism, relying on publications, videos, and audio recordings. At the center of this new approach was Li's book, *Zhuan Falun*, published just days after the final lecture series he gave in China in December 1993. The chapters of *Zhuan Falun* are edited transcripts of Li's lecture series; reading the book is supposed to have the same effects on the reader as one would experience attending Li's workshops and interacting with him in person (Penny 2012: 97–99).

FALUN GONG AS NEW RELIGION

The religious contents of Falun Gong took shape around a combination of charismatic authority, qigong exercises, new collective identities, and a syncretistic blend of ideas from qigong, Buddhism, Taoism, New Age, and other sources.[2] Practitioners are expected to do five particular Falun

---

[2] Penny traces the sources of Li's influences not just to Buddhism and Taoism, but also New Age myths about Atlantis, the prehuman origins of the Egyptian pyramids, and even the television show *The X-Files* (Penny 2012: 130–131).

Gong exercises on a daily basis, accompanied when possible by a recording of Li Hongzhi narrating the exercise's instructions. The exercises, which include sitting meditation, require about forty-five minutes to complete. Followers, especially beginners, are strongly encouraged to regularly practice together in groups, as was common in China for most urban qigong groups in the 1980s and 1990s (Chen 2003). Although the exercises are supposed to bring health improvement, by 1994 the emphasis had shifted to morality, salvation, and improving one's spiritual nature, called *xinxing*. Li teaches that the universe is constituted by three principles: *zhen* (truth), *shan* (compassion), and *ren* (translated variously as patience, tolerance of suffering, and forbearance). Cultivation of one's *xinxing*, which is the central practice of Falun Gong, requires harmonizing one's life with these three elemental principles of the universe. *Zhen, shan,* and *ren* are to be understood not only as moral abstractions, but also as physical realities that materially constitute the universe. Since the universe is materially composed of moral principles, Falun Gong teachings involve a religio-cosmic notion of the universe, referred to by Li as the Great Dharma, or *dafa*. In this usage, the word *fa* carries a Buddhist connotation, meaning "dharma" or "holy law," as in the standard translation of *falun* as "wheel of law." The term *falun* pre-dates Falun Gong, but the meaning is different.

Falun Gong discourse is generally socially conservative in issues such as race, marriage, and sexuality. In addition, Li's teachings have always involved a millenarian view of historical time, but the persecution of Falun Gong by the Chinese state, as will be considered in Chapter 8, prompted the movement to radically amplify its millenarian themes and interpret the repression as an "end of days" battle with the forces of evil. In the long arc of Falun Gong's development, it has gone from a movement of individuals "cultivating" together their own individual healing and redemption to become a collective effort to change the social world around them by "saving" the souls of non-practitioners and stopping the persecution of Falun Gong. External repression, thus, spurred the movement to shift goals from individual ones to supra-individual, social goals (for more on this, see Chapter 8).

Falun Gong is considered by participants to be a spiritual practice and discipline that reshapes a practitioners' moral, physical, and spiritual self. To use Weberian terminology, the Falun Gong view of self-cultivation is ascetic and this-worldly: practitioners are to remain engaged in their ordinary lives – families, occupations, and other activities – and to view everyday action as the setting for self-cultivation and moral improvement.

Li's teachings indicate that cultivation leads not only to moral improvement, but also to supernatural powers, or what in qigong parlance is called 'extraordinary powers' (*teyi gongneng*). For example, one may experience the opening of a "celestial eye" in a high dimension of one's mind. Such supernatural powers are not, however, the aim of the practice; furthermore, to brag about such powers or display them to others is considered tantamount to abandoning cultivation. The ultimate goal of self-cultivation is termed "consummation" or "fulfillment" (*wanshan, yuanman*).³ Before repression, consummation was considered as an individual-level goal, but the movement's ideological evolution after repression led to it being reconceived as a collective experience (Penny 2012: esp. 183, 218).

Since 1994, Li strongly emphasized the centrality of cultivating one's moral nature and pursuing "consummation" by practicing the exercises and studying Li's writings and lectures on a daily basis. Among these writings, the most important is the 1995 book, *Zhuan Falun*. As an edited compilation of Li's lectures, the book contains a wide range of discourses on such things as how to practice cultivation; qigong and Buddhism; the origins of the cosmos, virtue and evil; spirits, gods, and demons; and practical injunctions for behavior in everyday life. Li exhorts followers to read, re-read, and even memorize the book. A common Falun Gong practice is for practitioners to meet together in person (or even online) to read the book aloud in unison.⁴

Although cultivation is a self-oriented action, Falun Gong has always emphasized social activity and collective identity. Li enjoins members to practice the exercises in groups and to engage in "collective study" of his writings. Collective study, it should be noted, does not include critically discussing the text, but involves group recitation and occasionally testifying about the truth of the text as experienced in one's own life. The social dimensions of Falun Gong encourage a strong sense of collective identity among practitioners. A participant in the movement refers to herself as a "practitioner," "student," "cultivator," or "disciple." These terms all communicate an egalitarian identity among co-religionists that is based upon a shared mission of learning and self-improvement or redemption.

³ Consummation (*wanshan, yuanman*) is a transcendent final state functionally analogous to Buddhist nirvana. For a glossary of many Falun Gong terms, see Wessinger (2003); for an in-depth study, see Penny (2012).
⁴ I participated in several of these meetings in the USA in March 2006 and with Chinese Falun Gong practitioners in Tokyo in July 2007.

In contrast to "practitioners," Falun Gong members also frequently speak of "ordinary people," or *changren*. Semantically speaking, *changren* is to a practitioner what a gentile is to a Jew. Any non-Falun Gong reader of this book shares, along with this author, the identity of *changren*, which means that we are outsiders who may potentially be saved if we "gain the *fa*," but we are currently living in a state of considerable ignorance and are at risk for providential punishment.

Among the human actors described by Li in the Falun Gong cosmos, there is only one other identity beyond practitioner and *changren*: that of Li Hongzhi himself, who is "master" or "teacher" (*shifu*).[5] As Li stated to an audience of practitioners in May 1999 in Toronto:

> You are all people who are cultivating, but I am not. You all must act according to the standards of cultivators. There are no exceptions. [You all] must reach the realm and standards of Consummation. But I am not like you. I have come to teach you this Dharma ("Fa"). The difficulties I accept are the difficulties of each realm of living beings. It is impossible to talk with any person about the things I face. You cannot understand.[6]

Li further emphasizes his extraordinary status by claiming that his teachings are the only true path to salvation and that he alone is the one who has made such teachings publicly available (Penny 2012: 141). "For practitioners," according to Penny, "he is like no other person alive: he is wisdom, compassion, and spiritual power personified" (2012: 78).

Li's success as a salvational charismatic figure recalls both recent and traditional Chinese charismatic movements. Penny's study of Li Hongzhi hagiographies quotes one that describes Li in ways that recall Mao during the Cultural Revolution:

> Falun Dafa founded by Mr Li Hongzhi is like a red sun rising from the east, whose radiance with unlimited vitality will illuminate every corner of the earth, nourish all the living things, warm the whole world and play an unparalleled role in the realization of an ideal and perfect human society on this planet. (Penny 2012: 85)

Although practitioners today are unlikely to see parallels between Li and Mao Zedong, Penny shows that many now see Li as the arrival of the future Buddha associated with the end of days, Maitreya, which Li has neither confirmed or denied (Penny 2012: 108–111). My own field

---

[5] The Chinese term *shifu* contains paternal connotations.

[6] "*Jianada dahui jiangfa, Li Hongzhi, yijiujiujiunian wuyue ershisanri yu Duolunduo*" (Fa Teaching at the Canadian Fa Conference, Li Hongzhi, May 23, 1999 in Toronto), retrieved on July 2, 2010, from www.tiantibooks.org.

work confirms that practitioners often regard Li Hongzhi as divine, although such sentiments are probably much more common among Chinese practitioners than non-Chinese practitioners. For example, in Tokyo, the Japanese and Chinese practitioners I observed met to practice in separate groups. The Japanese practitioners generally treated Falun Gong similar to how Americans frequently treat yoga – as a kind of mystical and cultural enclave or hobby. Mainland Chinese practitioners I met were much more pious in their orientation to Li Hongzhi. On one occasion, a Japanese practitioner remarked on this difference to another Japanese practitioner, saying that the Chinese practitioners treat Li "like a god."[7]

When we consider Li's exceptional status, the egalitarian, but subordinate, status of his followers, and the boundary that separates followers from non-followers, so-called *changren*, we can appreciate how the social solidarity of the Falun Gong community is built on a combination of simple contrasts and unities: there is a vertical relationship of extreme distance between Li and followers; there is an egalitarian bond of fellowship among practitioners, whose worldly differences in class and status are moot before Li's divine superiority; and there is an exclusive boundary separating insider (practitioner) from outsider (*changren*). Naturally, alongside these idealized identities are also hierarchies within formally structured organizations, like *The Epoch Times*, and, at the local level, various informal hierarchies. These may be based on seniority, ability to authoritatively cite Li Hongzhi's teachings, competence in some particular field of activity (e.g., editing or translation), and, at least in New York, personal familiarity with Li and other central leadership (Huang, "*The Social Origin of Falun Gong as a Cult*," unpublished paper).[8]

To anticipate discussion in Chapter 8 concerning the movement's politicization, eventually Falun Gong discourse would characterize its human persecutors, agents of the Chinese state, as pawns manipulated by cosmic forces of evil. In the course of persecuting Falun Gong, the evil forces recruit the naïve public to carry out evil deeds and thus doom those ordinary people, or *changren*, to providential punishment. Through this framework, activists came to understand their political struggle not only as one opposing state persecution, but also as a struggle to counteract the cosmic entrapment of ordinary people into committing crimes of which they are unaware. To "save" ordinary people, then, did not mean

[7] Field notes, Tokyo, July 28, 2007.
[8] In my research, I did not gain access to the guarded inner circle of the community.

converting others to Falun Gong as proselytizing work is typically understood. Instead, it meant to save ordinary people from the divine punishment one faces for even inadvertently supporting the CCP, especially in its
persecution of Falun Gong. In this sense, political activism became
a hybrid religious and political effort for the salvation of *changren* souls
everywhere, with salvation defined as preservation from divine punishment for being on the wrong side of the grand cosmic showdown between
the Falun Gong and the forces of evil.

Falun Gong in China's Religious Context

In the course of its first decade, Falun Gong went from being a qigong
fad to a new religious movement (NRM). Therefore, Falun Gong
belongs both to the "qigong craze" of the 1980s and 1990s and to
the larger trend of religious resurgence that has followed the Mao era.
Yet, care should be taken to note that Falun Gong only represents the
resurgence of one particular genre of Chinese religious activity, which
is a minority form of Chinese religion that is grassroots-based, sectarian, and usually focused on some kind of salvation. The wider field of
Chinese religion, especially before 1949, was long dominated by
a pluralistic mix of religious traditions, including the institutionalized
religions of Buddhism, Taoism, and Confucianism, but also a vast
array of "autonomous groups that formed the social basis of Chinese
religion – households, lineages, territorial communities, professional
guilds, devotional associations, [and] political entities" (Goossaert and
Palmer 2011: 22–23). Unlike the dominant forms of religion in the
West, few of these religious communities demanded exclusivist identification from lay participants. Depending on social context or the
particular needs of the individual, a person might offer food to ances-
tors on a holiday, visit a Taoist priest to heal an illness, and make
a pilgrimage to a Buddhist mountain to gain merit – all without ever
experiencing a sense of contradiction or hypocrisy. Against this dominant religious context, China has also long had a minority religious
tradition of sectarian societies (Ownby 1999), in which participants
"held that they and only they knew the truth, and that it was knowledge of this truth that distinguished them from everybody else"
(Harrell and Perry 1982: 286). Analytically speaking, Falun Gong
belongs to this exclusivist minority tradition, which scholars call "sectarianism" (Harrell and Perry 1982; Overmyer 1981), "Chinese
redemptive societies" (Duara 2003; Ownby 2003a, 2008: 28–42;

Palmer 2007, 2009b), or "salvationist groups" (Goossaert and Palmer 2011).[9]

As a new instance of this older tradition, Falun Gong shares many of the defining features of other Chinese sectarian groups throughout history, including that it is led by a charismatic faith healer, involves health and moral improvement, promotes syncretistic religious beliefs, provides a millenarian interpretation of contemporary history, and exists within a social network of co-believers linked by horizontal and egalitarian ties (Harrell and Perry 1982; Overmyer 1981; Ownby 1999, 2003a, 2008: 28–42). Still, all is not continuity between Falun Gong and the older historical tradition. One of the most intriguing differences between Falun Gong and the prerevolutionary salvationist societies concerns organizational influences born of the socialist era. The post-1980 qigong craze involved a "new, collective form of qigong teaching and practice" in which modern qigong masters provided mass teachings of easy-to-do exercises and "amateur enthusiasts led free collective practice sessions in public spaces" (Palmer 2007: 46, 49). This model of activity contrasts sharply to the imperial-era sectarian traditions, which often involved teaching esoteric methods in secret initiations (Palmer 2007: 46–49). Falun Gong followed this more public, open, and egalitarian – or perhaps "mass" – form of qigong teaching.

Like many sectarian groups in Chinese history (Harrell and Perry 1982; Overmyer 1981), Falun Gong was originally apolitical, but state interference in its activities led the movement to engage in defensive political mobilization. Although the area studies literature on Chinese sectarian groups and the sociological literature on NRMs rarely speak to one another, both literatures converge on the idea that new religious groups are most typically benign relative to the larger society *unless* public authorities attempt to constrain them. Political interference can set a movement on a trajectory of outward hostility, violence, and conflict.

---

[9] Penny criticizes the characterization of Falun Gong as being a continuation of traditional sectarianism on the grounds that such a view obscures the extent to which Li Hongzhi borrowed from New Age discourse from the West and because there is no genealogical link from Falun Gong to the preexisting sectarian groups (Penny 2012: 29, 142). To counter Penny's argument, one might note that syncretism, which is a defining feature of popular sectarianism, is by definition promiscuous relative to sources of cultural content. Recall that the founder of the Taiping Rebellion claimed to be a brother of Jesus, for instance. Further, a direct genealogical link is unnecessary to demonstrate the reproduction of formal and institutional similarities.

In Falun Gong's case, interference set it on a trajectory of nonviolent protest and transnational mobilization.

FALUN GONG AS PROTEST MOVEMENT

In the remainder of this chapter, I make two general observations about Falun Gong's special capacity to marshal collective action in the form of protest. These two observations apply in a global way to the period after the movement was banned in China. Playing off the qigong term *teyi gongneng*, or "extraordinary powers," which are supernatural powers said to be gained by the most highly accomplished qigong masters, I suggest that Falun Gong enjoyed two "extraordinary social movement powers," both of which were tied to its character as a qigong group turned new religion. The first observation concerns how the body, emotion, and healing undergird practitioners' commitment to the moral and ideological beliefs of Falun Gong, including political activism. The second observation concerns the manner by which the group's ethic of activism has harnessed the heterogeneity of the diverse Falun Gong community while simultaneously accomplishing ideological uniformity around shared goals.

Extraordinary (Social Movement) Powers #1: Bodily Healing

At the center of Falun Gong cultivation practice is a set of bodily exercises that are understood to be healing, purifying, and transformative. In my interviews, many practitioners' own accounts of "attaining the Fa" – that is, becoming a self-identified Falun Gong practitioner – are related to a miraculous healing experience brought on through cultivation practice. For example, Ms. Yang, a Chinese female practitioner born in 1946, reported being persecuted in China and eventually made her way to Japan, where I interviewed her.[10] She told me she started practicing Falun Gong in 1996 in Shenyang city. She had had serious health problems, which forced her to retire early. In spite of spending much of her money on medicine and medical treatment, her health problems persisted. Eventually, she could not afford more treatment. In desperation, she tried Falun Gong. She had never practiced qigong before and, having being raised with "an atheist education," she didn't even believe "that kind of

---

[10] Interview, September 2013, Tokyo. All names from confidential interviews are pseudonyms.

stuff." Within two months of practice, however, she claimed to have fully recovered her health. When before people had said that she looked much older than her age, now they remarked that she looked younger than her age. Ms. Yang's story was not unusual among my interviews.

Ms. Yang's health recovery account is instructive also for the way she related it to her disobedience towards the Chinese state. She reported that in 1999 she was pressured to publicly renounce Falun Gong. She consistently refused and, as a result, was arrested twice. "Why did you refuse to publicly renounce Falun Gong?" I asked. In reference to her healing experience, she said to me, "Falun Gong saved my life, so how can I give it up?" Still later, she was detained in a RTL camp and reported severe deprivations and some torture. Under these coercive pressures, she finally agreed to renounce Falun Gong and stopped practicing. As a result of betraying the Dafa, she said, her former health problems quickly returned. When she returned home from the RTL camp, physical pain prevented her from being able to do even household chores. She emphasized to me that her suffering was not only physical, but also psychological. She deeply regretted her betrayal of Falun Gong. One month after being released from RTL, she renounced her statements against Falun Gong and returned to being a practitioner. Shortly thereafter, she said, her health began to improve again.

Ms. Yang's understanding of her own experience suggests how identity and commitment in the Falun Gong community is often rooted in the bodily experience of self-cultivation. For many practitioners like Ms. Yang, entry into Falun Gong came first through a purely bodily approach to health. Some practitioners, however, emphasized instead moral or psychological healing, but these too were sometimes described in bodily terms. A Chinese woman in Kobe, Japan, told me that when she first read *Zhuan Falun*, she immediately felt like she had found what she had been looking for. Here, finally, she felt, was the meaning of life, an explanation of what we should live for. Another Chinese practitioner in Tokyo told me how, when she first read *Zhuan Falun*, she cried incessantly while reading. Similarly, a Chinese man who had started practicing Falun Gong in Japan told me that after he spent a few hours reading *Zhuan Falun* for the first time, he inexplicably found himself weeping.[11] An American practitioner from Boston described to me how years of chronic fatigue syndrome disappeared when he struck a particular pose for the first time in the Falun Gong exercises.[12] In one more example, an American expatriate

[11] Interviews, Tokyo, September, 2009.
[12] Interview, Connecticut, USA, April, 2006.

and retired businessman in Hong Kong met me for an interview in a busy Starbucks. Toward the end of an interview that lasted over two hours, I asked him how he went from "doing exercises, to reading Falun Gong books, to becoming so publicly active as a practitioner." He was overcome with tears as he tried to convey to me his experience. His answer focused on the miraculous healing stories he heard from other practitioners at experience-sharing conferences, and then he related a long list of minor and serious ailments from which Falun Gong had personally delivered him.[13]

Whatever the explanation for the abundance of healing stories, the implication of such stories for mobilization as a social movement is important. Practitioners frequently believe that they have experienced something transcendent, redemptive, profound, healing, and transformative through Falun Gong. That understanding is often, as in the examples cited here, anchored in the first-hand experience of their own bodies. In this way, a practitioner's subjective bodily experience becomes an ultimate signifier for the Falun Gong epistemology, giving extraordinary security to the adopted belief system and to one's commitment to the community that made such a transformational experience possible.

Extraordinary (Social Movement) Powers #2: An Ethic of Activism

Counter to CCP propaganda and common misconceptions, existing research has already demonstrated that Falun Gong is not organized according to a Leninist organizational pyramid in which the street-level activists are mindless drones carrying out the orders of the queen bee charismatic leader (Chan 2004, 2013; Huang, "*The Social Origin of Falun Gong as a Cult*," unpublished paper; Ownby 2008; Palmer 2003; Porter 2003). Instead, to understand how Falun Gong activism has unfolded on a daily basis, we need to look to its community's widely shared and deeply felt ethic of activism. I view this ethic, like the bodily healing experiences described earlier, as a kind of 'extraordinary power,' especially suited to mobilizing broadly diffuse, creative, and tenacious collective action. The community's ethic of activism is, in fact, the reverse of the top–down, obedient drone Leninist model imagined by Falun Gong's detractors. Instead, every follower is enjoined to look within oneself (*kan ziji*) and find what particular gift or opportunity she or he can bring to fruition in the service of the group's broadly shared religious

---

[13] Interview, Hong Kong, July, 2015.

and political mission. Members share the same goal, but each individually feels a duty to realize that goal in its fullest through individual application, creativity, and sacrifice.

I chose the term "ethic" both to mean a kind of moral framework shared by all practitioners and also as an allusion to Max Weber's (2001 [1930]) classic thesis in *The Protestant Ethic and the Spirit of Capitalism*. Falun Gong's activism ethic echoes Weber's argument for how Calvinism fused the notion of calling, as a unique task set by God for each particular individual, with an intensely felt moral injunction to restlessly pursue through one's calling the shared sectarian task of "glorifying God on earth." As in Weber's argument, the particular moral ideology and social dynamics of the religious community shaped a way of life and even new personalities. But, in Falun Gong, the ethic emphasized social movement activism rather than, as in Weber's argument about capitalism, economic activity.

Falun Gong's ethic of activism encouraged creativity and diffusion of successful new tactics. Essentially, everyone in the movement felt an individualized moral obligation not only to act, but also to act according to one's own particular gifts and opportunities. This, in effect, meant that there was much experimentation at the margins of the collective action repertoire. When someone found an activity that worked, they would spread the news. Often information was passed through the Minghui website, which was deliberately set up to encourage overseas practitioners to share their practical experiences of "spreading the Fa." Chapter 3 gave an example of this in the form of Hong Kong practitioners in 2002 learning from Minghui about targeting mainland Chinese tourists for propaganda materials, which has become a standard tactic readily seen in Hong Kong, Taiwan, and Japan today.

Another benefit of this individualistic imperative to identify and carry out protest was that the ethic reconciled the benefits of diversity with the strengths of uniformity. The Falun Gong diaspora community is quite diverse: among just its ethnic Chinese membership one finds different levels of educational attainment, economic class, age, regional identity, citizenship, and language. Non-Chinese membership provides still more diversity. Furthermore, the community is geographically diffused around the globe, meaning that there is plenty of room for that diversity to evolve into regional variations. Nevertheless, I consistently found activists in Japan and Taiwan using the same interpretations to make sense of events, justify forms of activism, and define terms as I encountered in America and online. Cheris Chan's (2013) ethnography of Falun Gong communities in

Chicago and Hong Kong also noted the identical ways that practitioners in both sites interpreted events; Chan even commented that she sometimes had to remind herself which city she was in because comments were so uniform across the two sites.

Pairing uniformly shared goals and interpretations with a restless imperative to individualize one's means to reach those goals had powerful and contagious, self-reinforcing effects within the community. Falun Gong enjoyed ideological uniformity without sacrificing the opportunities that came with heterogeneous membership and a multitude of local settings. Mobilization occurred in a sweet spot between unity and diversity, harnessing the power of both and making its ethic of activism an "extraordinary social movement power."

CONCLUSION

This chapter described Falun Gong's emergence in China, its character as an NRM, and two "extraordinary powers" that strengthened its capacity to mobilize as a social movement. I highlighted the fact that Falun Gong emerged from a milieu that was culturally shaped both by strands of traditional religious culture, which has a long history in China, and by the institutions and discourses that characterized China's socialist era. With only quite minor exceptions – such as Li Hongzhi borrowing in a bricolage way from Western New Age discourse and popular culture – Falun Gong was a thoroughly indigenous Chinese movement. This contrasts to Minyun, which embraced Western and "universal" ideals of democracy, rights, and secularity. How did Falun Gong, an indigenous neo-traditional movement, become a modern-style protest movement? The next chapter begins to tackle that question by narrating Falun Gong's history of politicization.

5

Falun Gong's History of "Stepping Forward"

A CERTIFIED MASTER

Falun Gong began in May 1992, when Li Hongzhi held his first nine-day workshop in Changchun, sponsored by the Changchun City Human Body Research Society. After two successful workshops in Changchun, the government-affiliated, Beijing-based China Qigong Scientific Research Society (CQSRS), or *Zhongguo qigong kexue yanjiuhui*), sponsored two of Li's workshops in Beijing. By September, CQSRS had given Li the official title of Direct-Affiliate Qigong Master (*zhishu qigongshi*) and he had registered his own organization, the Falun Gong Research Society, as a branch of CQSRS (Tong 2002b: 640). Li was quick to exploit his new affiliation and status: between May 1992 and September 1994, he conducted fifty-six workshops. Most of these events, which tallied a total audience of more than 60,000 people, were sponsored either directly by the CQSRS or by local affiliated branch associations, including a 1993 nine-day workshop at the Public Safety College in Beijing. The remaining eleven workshops were sponsored by local qigong schools and various state-owned factories.[1] The military was a frequent official supporter of Falun Gong in the movement's early years (Penny 2012: 97).

Li was also able to gather many other feathers for his cap in this watershed period between 1992 and the spring of 1993. He was

---

[1] "*Li Hongzhi shifu zai shijie gedi hongchuan falundafa dashiji*" (Record of Master Li spreading Falun Dafa everywhere in the world) from www.zhengjian.org, posted on October 4, 2003 by an anonymous Falun Gong practitioner in America. Accessed in May 2006. Although this, like many Falun Gong sources, is written within the context of a polarized political field, the information's accuracy agrees with the summary statements provided by Tong (2002b).

celebrated twice at the Beijing Oriental Health Expos of 1992 and 1993 (Ownby 2003b), he was honored in 1993 by the National Public Security Bureau's director of the China Heroes Foundation, and he was even granted the titles of "honorary citizen" and "goodwill ambassador" by the mayor of Houston, Texas, in August 1993. This last accolade, apparently arranged by Falun Gong enthusiasts in Houston, was the first sign of the movement's transnationalization.

Li's remarkably fast climb to success certainly would not have been possible without the official status he enjoyed from the national agency concerned with regulating qigong. CQSRS gave Li the luster of being officially vetted and scientifically validated. Not only did Li tap the institutional resources and infrastructure of CQSRS, he also used his state-embedded status as part of a discursive strategy to advance his novel claims and authority. For example, in the *Zhuan Falun*, Li Hongzhi cited his official status to authorize his claims and reject competing claims of other qigong teachers.

Now we should ask, how can you tell if a qigong master is real? A lot of qigong masters are self-proclaimed. I've been tested, and I have all the documents from the evaluations that the scientific research institutions did of me. (Li 2003: 231)

Much of the remainder of the chapter from which this quote is taken is a sectarian polemic against other "fake" qigong teachers and counsels people to avoid taking non-Falun Gong qigong classes, using *Book of Changes* astrology, and other such practices.

Another example of Li deploying his official certification comes from a transcription of Li Hongzhi's guest appearance on a 1993 Wuhan radio call-in talk show.[2] In his self-introduction, Li Hongzhi identifies his official status and shows how he found ways to harness state imprimatur to authorize his particular qigong teachings.

I have come here at the invitation of the Wuhan City Qigong Association in order to spread qigong [*chuan gong*]. Since arriving, the Wuhan people, the Qigong Association leaders and comrades have very warmly extended to me great support. I want to express my great appreciation to them for this. What I do is transmit a high-dimensional *gong*. The contents of what I teach are a little extraordinary – many practitioners think they have never heard things like this – because different dimensions have different laws . . . . (Zhu 1994: 2)

---

[2] The author of this article, Zhu Huiguang, is described by Penny as a qigong journalist and possible ghost author of *China Falun Gong* (Penny 2012: 79, 95).

Here, Li used his official credentials to legitimate his unconventional teachings as more profound, of a "higher dimension," than other qigong teachers. In the early period, Li's relationship to authorities and official qigong institutions was positive.

But the official position on qigong became a topic of political contention in the spring of 1994, and continued as such on and off until 1999 (Palmer 2007; Penny 2012; Tong 2002b). Perhaps in response to the changing climate, in September 1994, Li informed the CQSRS that he would stop his nine-day training sessions "to devote his time to the study of Buddhism" (Tong 2002b: 640). Then, in the spring of 1995, Li was invited to Europe by supporters in the Chinese embassies in France and Sweden, where he gave two final nine-day seminars. Between March 1995 and July 1999, Li frequently traveled internationally, teaching Falun Gong in Europe, North America, Australia, New Zealand, Thailand, Singapore, Hong Kong, and Taiwan. In 1998, Li became a legal permanent resident of the USA (Palmer 2007: 249–251; Tong 2009: 45), accompanied by his wife, mother, daughter, and two siblings (Penny 2012: 87).

1996–1999: CONTENTION AND ACCUMULATED BARGAINS

The first state interventions against Falun Gong appear to have been prompted by the success of Li's book, *Zhuan Falun*, which had become a national best seller by the spring of 1996. On June 17, a major newspaper, the *Guangming Daily*, published a scathing criticism of the book as feudal superstition and of Li Hongzhi as a swindler. A wider propaganda campaign targeting the book for criticism followed and then on July 24, the Central Propaganda Department banned the publication of all Falun Gong books.[3] Tensions had also been mounting between the Falun Gong Research Society and its semi-state parent organization, CQSRS. Li withdrew his organization from CQSRS in September and CQSRS formally expelled the Falun Gong organization in November, which, in effect, made Falun Gong, as an organization, illegal.[4] From overseas, Li retained his leadership role for Falun Gong in China through telephone, fax, email, and, later, Internet communication (Palmer 2007: 251). As a result of Li's

---

[3] In practice, the ban was difficult to enforce. Li's books continued to be produced and circulated by publishers in Hong Kong, Taiwan, and smaller mainland Chinese publishing houses (Penny 2012: 55).

[4] CQSRS itself was a casualty of changing political winds and essentially went defunct by the end of 1996 (Palmer 2007).

transnational activities, the leadership of Falun Gong began to shift from China to North America-based diaspora.

The origins of Falun Gong's politicization can be seen in this earliest period of state intervention. After the *Guangming Daily* criticized Li's book in June 1996, and other newspapers followed suit, thousands of practitioners defended Falun Gong's reputation through letter-writing campaigns. The protest activities appear to have been a spontaneous, ad hoc response initiated by ordinary practitioners. Nevertheless, on August 28, 1996, Li issued from overseas a commentary that praised such activism and invested it with religious signification. Li emphasized that defending Falun Gong was "an essential aspect of *Dafa* cultivation." He declared that state interference was "a test" for movement followers: those that rose up to defend Falun Gong would be proven to be the true disciples; those who "feared for their reputation or personal interest," were apathetic, or "spread baseless rumors" would be exposed as the false disciples (Palmer 2007: 249–250).

The letter-writing campaigns of the summer of 1996 were only the beginning of a larger pattern of defensive political mobilization by Falun Gong followers. Between June 1996 and April 1999, Falun Gong practitioners mounted around 300 protest events, many with over 1,000 participants (Ownby 2008: 169; Palmer 2007: 254).[5] Participants were organized locally through "practice sites" and connected transnationally to Li through an Internet-based communication network. Palmer characterized the protest repertoire as follows:

The resistance, anchored in public displays of bodies in movement, was spectacular. Thousands of disciplined adepts appeared at strategic times and places, "clarifying the facts" and demanding apologies, rectifications and the withdrawal of offending newspapers from circulation. Such had never been seen in Communist China: a network of millions of potential militants from all social strata and geographic areas, which did not hesitate to display its power on the public square and confront the media. (Palmer 2007: 252)

That Falun Gong was able to mount with relative impunity these protests between 1996 and 1999 indicates that there existed a space of toleration, or what Charles Tilly called an "accumulated bargain," between Falun Gong supporters and the state:

---

[5] Penny cites the *People's Daily* reporting seventy-eight demonstrations of over 300 people, suggesting a discrepancy that I have not been able to reconcile (2012: 53).

Schematically, every government distinguishes among claim-making performances that it prescribes (e.g., pledges of allegiance), those it tolerates (e.g., petitioning), and those it forbids (e.g., assassinations of officials). The exact contours of the three categories vary from regime to regime as a result of accumulated bargains between rulers and their subject populations. (Tilly 2008b: 149)

Given the vicissitudes of politics in China, the precise lines between tolerated and forbidden claim-making performances is frequently unclear and can arbitrarily shift without any legal rational review or justification. The process of challengers testing limits and state authorities enacting toleration or repression is variable and always ongoing. Nevertheless, there are periods during which, as Tilly puts it, some kind of equilibrium of "accumulated bargains" is achieved relative to what is permissible or not as protest.

The accumulated bargains perspective allows us to see that the Falun Gong had accomplished something quite extraordinary between the summer of 1996 and the spring of 1999. Activists mounted hundreds of tolerated, but confrontational, protests. They did not suffer significant reprisals for their activism. Frequently, the protests appear to have been successful in terms of having their demands met by the media institutions, including Beijing television. At least relative to their own movement's capacity to directly assert legitimacy and speak back to authority, Falun Gong enjoyed an unusual "accumulated bargain" for 1990s China. Palmer (2007) attributed this toleration, in part, to a fissure among the country's top leadership regarding whether to support or discourage qigong.

A consequence of the period of toleration is that it facilitated the emergence of Falun Gong's first set of protest tactics, or "tactical repertoire" (Taylor and Van Dyke 2004; Tilly 1995a, 2008b). As described earlier, these tactics included letter-writing campaigns and sit-ins at offending media institutions. Between 1996 and 1999, practitioners learned how to protest in ways that strengthened Falun Gong's capacity for resistance when the state eventually banned the movement. Not only did domestic Falun Gong protest activism entail the development of networks and communication patterns to coordinate activism, but the successful protest experiences presumably gave participants meaningful emotional, expressive, and social rewards (Jasper 1997). The empowering experience of righteous protest may help account for why during these three years Falun Gong continued to grow even as the wider qigong revival was fading (Palmer 2007: 191–192, 219).

Falun Gong's protest repertoire contained not only scripts for action, but also its own cultural logic. Here we see Falun Gong's ethic of activism first consolidated: Li Hongzhi stated in August 1996 that all practitioners had a moral obligation to publicly defend the movement's reputation. The main rhetorical justifications offered in defense of the movement were substantive rather than based on civil or human rights. The argument simply was that Falun Gong was good for society and defamations of it in the media were based on misunderstandings. The sit-ins and letter campaigns were merely efforts to peacefully correct the misunderstanding. Such cognitive framing of activism is evident in the language used by participants to refer to their protest repertoire. They used such terms as "reflecting the situation" (*fanying qingkuang*), "clarifying Falun Gong's innocence" (*chengqing falungong de qingbai*), or, as it came to be called later and almost universally, "clarifying the truth" (*jiangqing zhenxiang*). A second way to refer to the tactical repertoire drew from Falun Gong's terms for proselytizing, with protest activity described as "spreading dharma" (*hongfa*) or "defending dharma" (*hufa*). As these terms and framing suggest, Falun Gong's tactical repertoire took shape in a creative interaction with its religious ideology and in ways that effaced its political implications.

APRIL 1999: THE TURNING POINT

In April 1999, activists staged protests in Tianjin and, then, more significantly, in Beijing. These protests marked the end of Falun Gong's period of tolerated protest and set it on the path to state persecution. There are many academic and journalist accounts of the April 1999 protest events (Chang 2004; Chao 2001; Ownby 2003a, 2008; Palmer 2007; Penny 2012; Perry 2001; Tong 2009; Zong 2002). I will limit myself to a brief summary.

The spring episode of contention was spurred first by the publication of an essay critical of Falun Gong written by physicist Dr. He Zuoxiu of the Chinese Academy of Sciences, who was a prominent national voice opposing qigong as false science. His essay was printed on April 11 in the magazine *Youth Science and Technology Outlook*, published by Tianjin Normal University (Penny 2012: 56–57). According to a Falun Gong source, between April 18 and 24, several thousand practitioners went to the Tianjin Normal University to "reflect the facts about Falun Gong," which meant enacting the type of protest documented earlier by Palmer.[6]

---

[6] "*Falun Dafa dashiji nianjian*" (A chronicle of major events of Falun Dafa), retrieved on April 26, 2011, from www.zhengjian.org.

We can speculate that participants had no reason to imagine that authorities would react differently on this occasion from earlier protests. Nevertheless, instead of gaining concessions, Tianjin authorities on April 23 and 24 allegedly attacked demonstrators, causing some injuries and leading to the arrest of forty-five practitioners.

The Falun Gong response to the Tianjin arrests involved a major escalation of tactics: over 20,000 practitioners gathered on April 25 in Beijing to peacefully, orderly, and quietly surround from dawn until 10 pm the top leadership compound of the Chinese state, Zhongnanhai.[7] The demonstration was eventually diffused by a meeting between five Falun Gong representatives and some of China's most powerful state leaders, including politburo Standing Committee member and Secretary of the Central Party Political and Legislative Affairs Committee, Luo Gan, and Premier Zhu Rongji (Tong 2009: 5–6). Although most practitioners probably returned home thinking it was a job well done, the April 25 demonstration proved to be the turning point after which the state mobilized its full resources to eliminate Falun Gong.

Why April 1999 unfolded the way it did is complex and debated. Nevertheless, we can see that the events involved a breach of the earlier accumulated bargain between Falun Gong adherents and officials. The first breach appears to have been in Tianjin, when authorities cracked down on demonstrators and arrested forty-five protestors. Repression rather than toleration was a departure from what had become established convention. That breach appears to have stimulated a counter-escalation by the Falun Gong activists. The Falun Gong reaction was simultaneously a continuation and a departure from the prior bargain.

On the one hand, when activists went to Zhongnanhai to petition the national authorities, they were re-enacting the same tactical repertoire they had practiced in other cities and at other times, namely, witnessing to the goodness of Falun Gong and "correcting" the mistakes of institutional authorities who had, in their eyes, misunderstood the movement. On the other hand, the activists departed from earlier conventions by changing the target of protest from (a) media officials to political institutions[8] and from (b) local or regional entities to national leadership. Targeting

---

[7] Zhongnanhai is analogous to the Kremlin or the White House in political significance.

[8] Palmer (2007: 266) documents, however, an exception in which thousands of practitioners in 1998 wrote letters to public security departments and the central government to complain about police surveillance of Falun Gong activities.

political rather than media institutions also meant changing the content of grievances voiced: protesters on April 25 called for political redress in the form of releasing the arrested practitioners and demanding the state once again permit the Falun Gong community to enjoy the rights of association and publication, as they had before the summer of 1996. In this way, we can see the April 25 demonstration as both an organic extension of the kinds of protests that had been tolerated and as a departure from the earlier tacit bargain concerning acceptable protest targets and grievances. The shift in targets and grievance propelled the movement out of the tolerated zone and into the forbidden zone.

REPRESSION AND RESISTANCE IN CHINA

Repression did not occur on April 25. State officials initially defused the Zhongnanhai "mass incident," even though the politburo Standing Committee quickly determined that Falun Gong was a serious political threat and justified repression (Tong 2009: 33–34). In the coming weeks, the politburo secretly organized large-scale preparations for Falun Gong repression, which eventually began on July 21, 1999. During the limbo period between April and July, Falun Gong activists in China and in the diaspora tried to read conflicting state signals relevant to the possibility of repression, including rumors about a warrant for the arrest of Li Hongzhi. On July 19, 1999, the Central Committee of the CCP issued an internal party notice of the ban on Falun Gong. It was distributed in hastily convened meetings throughout the vast hierarchical network of party, military, and mass organizations, reaching an audience of over 60 million party members (Tong 2009: 157). In the following days, security agencies arrested or detained for interrogation 20,000 leading members of Falun Gong (Tong 2009: 102). At 3 pm on July 22, all television programming in China was interrupted to broadcast an official statement banning Falun Gong. A massive media campaign against Falun Gong ensued, along with intensive security operations to dismantle the movement's organizations and coerce followers. Efforts included such measures as making province-wide registries of all Falun Gong practitioners, which were used for monitoring and "de-conversion" (Tong 2009: 60–62).

The repression of Falun Gong was directed by an ad hoc committee called the Central Party Small Leading Group to Deal with Falun Gong, which was run by politburo member Li Lanqing, along with the head ministers for national propaganda and domestic security, Ding Guan'gen and Luo Gan (Tong 2009: 99). As discussed in Chapter 3, the politburo Standing Committee established a new extra-legal agency, referred to colloquially as the 610 Office, exclusively to deal with Falun Gong. The originally ad hoc and extra-legal nature of the 610 Office is emblematic of the overall conduct of the repression. According to Tong, the CCP directed and organized the repression, whereas the State Council and the NPC, which are the executive and legislative branches of the government, largely played secondary roles.

Repression initially involved a massive propaganda campaign against Falun Gong, interrupting and eliminating when possible all Falun Gong organizations, preventing and repressing Falun Gong demonstrations and public displays at local and national sites, and subjecting to coercion individual Falun Gong practitioners. Falun Gong activists in China responded by escalating their protest repertoire of "reflecting the facts about Falun Gong." As early as June 3, 70,000 practitioners arrived in Beijing to protest, but were intercepted, detained, and expelled from the capital (Penny 2012: 62–63). Tong's study shows that, later, nearly 100 Falun Gong protests occurred around the country between July 20 and 22. During the year following the ban, international media reported Falun Gong practitioners arriving practically every day in Beijing, each attempting to go to Tiananmen Square to unfurl banners that said "Falun Gong is Good," distribute pro-Falun Gong literature, publicly carry out Falun Gong exercises, or conduct similar protests. These actions comprised a new and more confrontational version of the protest repertoire that had taken shape between 1996 and 1999. As with the earlier protests, practitioners saw themselves not as making political claims, but as "reflecting the situation" and "clarifying the facts." Unlike the earlier protests, however, the targets and protest stage had become national and the risks of detention and other sanctions much more severe.

Since the ban, Falun Gong followers have been the object of a global, highly coordinated state campaign of repression, defamation, and incitement to hatred (on legal claims of incitement, see Matas and Kilgour 2009; for a detailed account of state repression, see Tong 2009). In the first decade of repression, according to Falun Gong sources such as Minghui (www.minghui.org) and Falun Dafa Information Center (www .faluninfo.net), repression involved tens of thousands of incidents of torture and led to the deaths of more than 3,000 followers (for a discussion of the credibility of Falun Gong sources, see Tong 2009: 122–128). Recent scholarship shows that the repression of Falun Gong

was still a state priority more than fifteen years after the crackdown of
1999 (Noakes and Ford 2015; Tong 2012).

Falun Gong's post-crackdown protest repertoire coalesced around
a disarmingly simple claim: "Falun Dafa Is Good" (*falun dafa hao*).
Although simple, the protest claim was packed with meaning, at least for
practitioners. For those who believed they had directly experienced Falun
Gong's personal benefits of health and spiritual well-being, the claim resonated with deeply held emotions. "Falun Dafa is good" was also a claim to
legitimate public standing as a collective actor. By persistently making the
claim in public venues, activists were performing their collective worthiness,
unity, numbers, and commitment, or what Tilly dubbed WUNC. Finally, the
statement of "Falun Dafa is good," to be refuted, would require the state to
produce credible evidence to the contrary. Given that much of the Chinese
public, at least until January 2001, appears to have found the massive
propaganda blitz against Falun Gong unconvincing (Perry 2002; Tong
2009), the claim put the state on the defensive.[9]

After practitioners were arrested, many Falun Gong practitioners are
said to have continued resistance in various ways, including hunger strikes
and not revealing their identities to prevent authorities from sending them
back to their home authorities and to protect their families from secondary repression. The entire saga of traveling to Beijing, trying to mount
a protest performance, becoming arrested and experiencing detention
came to be viewed as a religious practice of the third of Falun Gong's
cardinal virtues: forbearance (*ren*).[10] In fact, by August 2000 the seeking
out of opportunities to be arrested and punished in order to advance on
the religious path toward consummation became so common that
Minghui editors issued a public instruction against it:

[I]t is a wrong understanding to treat being thrown into prison as the purpose of
stepping forward [ie., protest]. Prisons are evil places used by malicious forces to
suppress Dafa and sabotage the cultivation practice of Dafa disciples. The police
vans are not the Law boat, the prisons are not temples, the labor camps are not the
environment for cultivation, and even less are these the necessary formalities that
Dafa disciples should rely on to make progress.[11]

---

[9] I note that Minghui websites contain many photos of practitioners trying to use
   Tiananmen Square as a stage for the claim "Falun Dafa is good." For example, see media
   .minghui.org/gb/0001/May/26/news_china_052600.html.
[10] Discussions of the role of *ren* in strengthening political resistance are found in Chan
   (2013), Fisher (2003), Hu (2005), and Penny (2012: 73–74).
[11] Retrieved on May 22, 2012, from en.minghui.org/html/articles/2000/8/11/7351.html#
   .T7utHMVv61k.

The party state met these protests by escalating security efforts, inter-dicting traveling Falun Gong practitioners before they reached Beijing, arresting practitioners wherever discovered, and sending them back to their home villages and cities for detention. Protestors typically faced a variety of sanctions, from fines and loss of jobs to multi-year incarceration at RTL camps, psychological hospitals, or prisons. Policy directives and performance targets issued by the central government encouraged local security officials to do whatever they could to stop Falun Gong resistance and especially the protest pilgrimages to Beijing (Johnson 2004; Tong 2009). As a result, torture and other coercion strategies allegedly became common – in fact, so common that the government sought to curb excess violence by making "no unnatural death" a national performance target for penal institutions in their managing the Falun Gong problem (Tong 2009: chapter 5).

The contentious relationship between the CCP and Falun Gong followed a trajectory of escalation between July 1999 and the spring of 2001, after which the relationship appears to have arrived at a kind of homeostasis of ongoing, but routinized, efforts on both sides. As resistance continued after the July crackdown, the state sought ways to bring the movement to heel. In October 1999, Falun Gong was officially branded a "cult" (*xiejiao*), which is the same term used in the imperial era for heterodox sectarian movements that met state repression (Palmer 2008; Perry 2002). Two days after the *People's Daily* editorial calling Falun Gong a cult, the NPC retroactively rushed through legislation justifying the repression (Edelman and Richardson 2003). Contention continued to escalate, with practitioners mounting protests in Beijing and elsewhere, and subsequently facing more and more coercive sanctions.

It is worth pausing the narrative here to consider the scale and the severity of the repression, as it was experienced by practitioners. I have noted already estimates of tens of thousands of instances of torture and abuse and over 3,000 deaths directly or indirectly caused by repression. These numbers are relatively conservative, with some sources (Kilgour, Gutmann, and Matas 2016; Matas and Kilgour 2009; Matas and Trey 2012) arguing for much higher counts and much more heinous atrocities, such as "harvesting" internal organs from living incarcerated practitioners to sell for profit (for an analysis of the organ-harvesting rumors, see Junker 2018). Whatever the precise scope of repression, summary numbers do little to indicate the experiences of the individual lives involved. Each incident must of course be experienced firsthand by the person who is subject to torture or murder and by those who perpetrate the violence. Falun Gong-related organizations, such as the World Organization to Investigate the Persecution of Falun Gong (www .upholdjustice.org) or the Falun Dafa Information Center (www .faluninfo.net) provide extensive information, although the sources are partisan. Two non-Falun Gong-related sources to which a reader might turn are (1) the 2015 Human Rights Watch report on torture in China (Human Rights Watch 2015), which is not explicitly about Falun Gong, but many victims described in it are practitioners; and (2) the series of open letters from the Chinese lawyer Gao Zhisheng to the CCP leadership and his testimony to the US Congress in 2013. Gao was himself subjected to torture, house arrest, and years of solitary confinement for publicizing that information (Biao 2014; Gao 2007; Pils 2009; United States Congress 2013). Forms of torture and death that are alleged in the various sources include beatings by hand, ordinary batons, electric batons, or heavy implements like hammers and iron bars; spraying chili oil or other pain-inducing substances into bodily orifices, including the genitals; sleep deprivation; solitary confinement; being doused naked in cold water and made to stand for long periods in subzero temperatures; and electric baton shots to the mouth, eyes, groin, and anus.

REPERCUSSIONS FOR THE RELIGIOUS MOVEMENT

Having described briefly how Falun Gong and the state's contentious dynamic escalated into militant nonviolent resistance and severe, often violent, repression, I turn now to a different order of complexities: how did repression and resistance become entangled within the internal dynamics of the religious movement? Some of the early reactions among groups of practitioners to repression are captured in ethnographic studies (Chan 2013; Fisher 2003; Palmer 2003) and these generally depict improvised, locally generated activism informed by information and framing distributed through Falun Gong communication networks. From a structural point of view within the community, the early phase of mobilization was shaped by changes in how Li Hongzhi played his role as leader. This issue will be traced more carefully in Chapter 8, but its contours need to be defined here.

Prior to the July ban, Li Hongzhi played an active leadership role communicating, mostly through the Internet from the USA, to his followers throughout the world. In the months between the April Zhongnanhai incident and the July ban, Li's public statements attempted to steer the movement's political confrontation with the Chinese state.

In my view, his statements were inconsistent, sometimes provocative and sometimes conciliatory. When the government fully and openly moved against Falun Gong in July, Li quickly disappeared from public view without warning or public comment. He did not resurface in person until fifteen months later, when he spoke at a Falun Gong conference in San Francisco in October 2000. For the first six months of his disappearance, from July 1999 until late January 2000, even the central Minghui website offered no explanation of his whereabouts or doings. Communication from Li became frequent again in the summer of 2000, although even then he mostly eschewed the role of directing political activism and instead emphasized spiritualizing the conflict as a cosmic struggle between the forces of good and evil.

Li's absence was especially consequential for the way Falun Gong evolved into a protest movement and developed its tactical repertoire. Consider the context: the Chinese state had suddenly launched a full-blown nationwide anti-Falun Gong campaign – the largest of any such campaign against an internal enemy since 1989 – and the movement's only identifiable leader disappeared without explanation. This might have spelled collapse for some groups, but not for Falun Gong. In the main, I attribute such tenacity at this moment to the fact that the community had since 1996 already fashioned a diffuse, self-authorizing protest repertoire and ethic of activism. This repertoire provided to members, without any leadership from above, the skills, networks, know-how, and moral imperatives to "step forward" into the public arena to oppose the state. "Stepping forward," or *zouchulai*, became the term practitioners used to describe becoming activists.

In a broadly diffuse, ad hoc, and creative way, practitioners in China and overseas conceptualized, coordinated, executed, communicated, and revised ways to respond to the repression. As activism took off, new organizations and new leaders emerged in various places. One quite visible example was Mr. Zhang Erping, a PRC national and practitioner who was affiliated at the time with Harvard University. Flawless in English and exceptionally capable as a public speaker, Mr. Zhang became the *de facto* (but never official) spokesperson for Falun Gong to American and international media. But Zhang himself was not the coordinator of grassroots action, nor was any other single individual. The year following July 1999 was for many activists both in China and overseas a creative period of high collective identity, strongly felt shared moral imperative, low central coordination, and a great deal of activity. Reflecting this trend, Ownby noted that activism in the diaspora at this

time consisted of "largely self-directed, self-motivated initiatives" that
were "decentralized, uncoordinated, and dispersed in time and space"
(Ownby 2008: 193). Collective action was coordinated much more by
a spirit of solidarity and common purpose than by formal organizational
management. Grassroots activists innovated "on the ground" and communicated to one another through the Internet, especially Minghui, rather
than by a leadership core publicly guided by Li. Falun Gong discourse
came to refer to all of this new activism as "clarifying truth."

In some important respects, the decentralized, voluntarist dynamic of
"clarifying truth" activism began to change in the summer of 2000. Li
Hongzhi returned at this time to making public statements and strongly
asserting his own master interpretation of events to followers. Although Li
explicitly refrained from directing political activism, due to his charismatic authority, his communications were widely accepted as definitive.
From the summer of 2000 into the early winter of 2001, Li's public
rhetoric emphasized that the repression was a millenarian showdown
between good and evil. In effect, Li did what many charismatic leaders
who have faced repression in other contexts have done: he escalated the
conflict with totalizing polemic that elevated his own role and indispensability (Robbins and Anthony 1995; Robbins and Palmer 1997a, 1997b;
Wallis and Bruce 1986). But unlike Jonestown or Waco, for instance, Li's
rhetoric did not take a violent or isolationist turn. Instead, he strongly
endorsed the tactical protest repertoire invented by practitioners in his
absence. So, the nonviolent protest movement continued, but with its
leader emphasizing a more enchanted and Manichean master interpretation of events.

As loyal practitioners in China continued their protests, state security
intensified efforts to shut down the resistance. Li's rhetoric escalated over
the fall of 2000. Rumors circulated among practitioners that Li himself
would travel to Beijing to protest. He dispelled such rumors through
a statement issued from Minghui on December 1, 2000. A month later,
on January 1, 2001, Li posted a statement to Minghui titled "Beyond the
Limits of Forbearance." Li's posting was ambiguous in meaning, but
appeared to suggest that Falun Gong protesters should depart from their
peaceful tactics and resist in some unspecified more radical way.[12] Two
days later, the anonymous editors of Minghui posted a follow-up commentary to Li's January 1 statement. The official commentary said that
followers must remember that Li's statements are not only intended for

---

[12] Retrieved on January 7, 2009, from www.minghui.org/mh/fenlei/217/zip.html.

human ears, but for celestial beings as well. The ominous, if ambiguous, implications of Li's January 1 posting were intended for that higher-level audience: human activists, by contrast, should not radicalize.[13]

Practitioners were not the only humans reading Li Hongzhi's online statements throughout the fall; Chinese security officials were as well. On September 28, 2000, the Chinese government publicly blasted Li's latest postings to Minghui for being "highly inflammatory" (*feichang you shandongxing*), noting that Li had called for followers to protest at Tiananmen Square on the National Day holiday of October 1.[14] On National Day, hundreds of practitioners converged on Tiananmen Square and were beaten, arrested, and carted away as foreign journalists took photos. The state further escalated repression on October 10, officially declaring that Falun Gong must be eradicated, because it "opposes the Party and the socialist system and subverts the essence of the nation." In effect, this position upgraded Falun Gong from "cult" to "reactionary and hostile organization." Policy changes at this time endorsed more intensive use of coercive tactics, especially RTL, "'close style management' on stubborn Falun Gong members," and isolating mainland Chinese Falun Gong activists from the influence of Li Hongzhi and the overseas Falun Gong community.[15]

After the Falun Gong's protest subverted National Day festivities on October 1, 2000, the crackdown intensified and apparently fewer activists succeeded in making it to Tiananmen Square. In late October, activists again mounted a coordinated effort to protest in Tiananmen Square. On October 26, 200 activists made it to the square and 50 more made it on October 27. Then again on December 31 and January 1, Falun Gong sources reported that several thousand practitioners, including forty from Japan and ten from Taiwan, successfully reached the square to demonstrate.[16]

The start of 2001 became a high point of intensified confrontation and repression. Mainland activists focused on the symbolism of the new

---

[13] See "Read the Scripture(s) with a Calm Mind" retrieved on May 22, 2012, from http://en .minghui.org/html/articles/2001/1/3/5442.html#.T7uxNsVv61k.

[14] Third party media from the time reported that Li had called for followers to go to Tiananmen Square on October 1. At the time of my research, such a statement was not posted on the Minghui site.

[15] "Hong Kong paper on decision to send Falun Gong members to labour camps." *BBC Summary of World Broadcasts.* October 16, 2000. In *Lexis-Nexis: Major U.S. and World Publications.* Also see Human Rights Watch (2002).

[16] See "*Falun Dafa dashiji nianjian*" (A chronicle of major events of Falun Dafa), retrieved on April 26, 2011, from http://zhengjian.org.

millennium by amplifying efforts to reach Tiananmen Square on December 31 and January 1, including trying to fill the square at dawn for the first millennial year's flag-raising ceremony. The response by security throughout the two days was especially ferocious, including multiple reports by international media of practitioners being severely beaten in public, after which street sweepers, who were waiting in preparation, immediately washed the stones of blood (Agence France-Presse 2001; Pringle 2001). I did not find any international media reports from the dawn flag-raising ceremony, although Minghui published a detailed description submitted by a non-practitioner Chinese tourist[17] and one of my interviewees also described being there.[18] Apparently, after the flag went up, many practitioners scattered throughout the vast crowd, called out "Falun Dafa is good," "Clear the name of Li Hongzhi," and other such slogans. Immediately, the square became a melee of police attacking people, punching, kicking, and using batons. The account authored by "a tourist" described a nearby man beaten unconscious, then further kicked and beaten, and then tossed lifelessly into a bus. My interviewee who was present reported being deeply traumatized, repeating several times that the entire square was covered in blood. She too described how quickly and systematically street sweepers were deployed to clean up the blood rather than give first aid to the injured.

From these accounts, it appears that throughout the two days of the New Year holiday there was a huge deployment of police and security, especially those dressed in plain clothes.[19] Much of the square was closed off and tens of vans were frequently used to shuttle protestors to detention.[20] Throughout the day, police would identify people who appeared from their out-of-town accents and style of dress to be Falun Gong practitioners. In order to apprehend potential protestors, police knew to exploit Falun Gong doctrine, which forbids denying one's belief in or defaming Falun Gong. Officers would expose practitioners simply by asking a suspect if she or he was a practitioner, or by demanding that she or he repeat a phrase condemning Falun Gong. Those who refused to

---

[17] See "*Shiji zhi jiao qingen mudu Tiananmen guangchang jingcha de baoli*" (Firsthand witness to the violence on Tiananmen Square at the turn of the century), retrieved on June 9, 2017, from www.minghui.org/mh/articles/2001/1/30/7475p.html.

[18] Interview, July 2015, Hong Kong.

[19] My interviewee reported that a police officer, after she was detained, bragged to her that there were over 10,000 plain-clothed police, in addition to uniformed police and military.

[20] A series of eighteen photos reportedly from this day at Tiananmen can be viewed at www.minghui.org/mh/articles/2001/1/29/7418p.html.

comply or admitted to Falun Gong were sent to detention, which frequently led to brutal treatment and torture if one remained defiant.

Thus, 2001 began with an intensification of state repression and ambiguous, but provocative, rhetoric from Minghui. The Spring Festival holiday, which began three weeks later on January 23, marked a turning point for the movement. On that day, five people reported to be Falun Gong practitioners from Kaifeng, Henan Province, including a twelve-year-old girl and her mother, arrived at Tiananmen, doused themselves in fuel, and self-immolated on the square. The mainland press used this event to sensationally dramatize the depravity and dangers of Falun Gong. Falun Gong diaspora spokespersons denied that these were true Falun Gong followers and accused the state of staging the event. But whatever the facts, which are usefully reviewed by Ownby (2008: 215–220), the Chinese state successfully used the immolation event to finally turn public opinion against Falun Gong. According to *The Washington Post* report in early February:

> Every morning and night, the state-controlled media carry fresh attacks against Falun Gong and its U.S.-based leader, Li Hongzhi. Schools have been ordered to "educate" pupils about the sect. Discussion meetings have been organized in factories, offices and universities. Religious leaders as far away as Tibet have delivered scripted denunciations. In Kaifeng, the post office issued an anti-Falun Gong postmark, and 10,000 people signed a public petition against the group. (Pan 2001)

Still today, I commonly encounter mainland Chinese people whose entire knowledge of Falun Gong appears to be characterized by a narrative of the self-immolation event provided from official media.

After this time, the domestic movement's capacity to mount demonstrations on the square diminished – whether through lack of free and willing activists or due to security agencies better intercepting protesters is unclear. By February 2001, when the CCP held a special "central work conference" on eradicating Falun Gong (as described in the Introduction and Chapter 3), overt resistance through protests carried out in Tiananmen Square had mostly subsided (Human Rights Watch 2002). Some sporadic public displays continued, especially by Western practitioners, who traveled to Beijing to carry out such protests about a half dozen times in the subsequent eighteen months.[21]

In summary, then, late winter 2001 marked a turning point in two ways. First, public opinion in China decisively turned against Falun Gong due to

---

[21] "*Falun Dafa Dashiji Nianjian*" (A chronicle of major events of Falun Dafa), retrieved on April 26, 2011, from http://zhengjian.org.

FIGURE 3 So-called "truth currency" (*zhenxiangbi*). A 10 RMB note (about US$1.50) with a Falun Gong message printed in purple on the right side. The message, which rhymes in Chinese, reads, "Sincerely recite, Falun Dafa is good! Truth, compassion, and tolerance are good! When disaster strikes, your life will be saved" (*Chengnian falundafa hao, zhen shan ren hao, danan lai shi ming neng bao*)

the success of the self-immolation media coverage. Second, Falun Gong's domestic Chinese tactical repertoire changed to underground coordination and activities that carried on the cause while also attempting to evade state repression. Some underground tactics were confrontational and technically spectacular, such as the multiple incidents in which practitioners interrupted provincial television broadcasting to show their own videos, as described in Chapter 3. Most underground activism, however, appears to have been less directly confrontational, but still disobedient. It consisted of making Falun Gong publicly visible, such as handing out literature, posting "Falun Dafa is good" banners, or stamping paper money with pro-Falun Gong statements, as seen in Figure 3 and described by Tong (2012). Falun Gong's underground mode of resistance in China continued as resistance, but not in a form that matches the definition of a modern social movement. Overseas, the situation played out differently.

RESISTANCE IN DIASPORA

As events unfolded in China, Falun Gong activists also mobilized in North America and elsewhere. The creation of communication infrastructure in the form of the Minghui website, established in June 1999, both in Chinese and English, proved to be critical for coordination and diffusion of information and tactics. Although I have argued that the primary initiative and form of Falun Gong activism was self-directed and diffuse, the Minghui website was probably the creation of the leadership group close to Li Hongzhi and included fellow émigré Ye Hao, who had been the coordinator of Falun Dafa Research Society's Foreign Liaison Group. Leadership, thus, played a role, but primarily in the form of providing infrastructure and stating overarching goals. According to its early statement of purpose, Minghui's aim was to help people "properly understand Falun Gong" (*zhengmian liaojie falun gong*) as a response to the worsening political climate.[22] But after repression began, it primarily became a forum for sharing information and experiences within the movement. A day after the CCP Central Committee issued its directive to all CCP branches about Falun Gong on July 19 and conducted massive sweeps to detain Falun Gong leadership, activists in North America mounted demonstrations and lobbying efforts in Washington DC, targeting the Chinese embassy, the US Congress, international organizations, and various embassies.[23] At the same time, on July 22, Minghui editors called for practitioners all over the globe to redouble their efforts to "spread the truth" about Falun Gong. Furthermore, they requested that practitioners write up their activist experiences to share on the Minghui website in order to encourage both mainland and diaspora practitioners to maintain their efforts.[24] Over time, practitioners set-up organizations, sought out the media, created, and distributed literature, then newspapers, and then radio and television media to support their cause. "Clarifying truth" became the most consuming concern in the lives of many practitioners.

One useful measure for observing the mobilization of Falun Gong activists in the diaspora comes from records of regional meetings of practitioners, called either dharma conferences or experience-sharing conferences. Figure 4 shows an increase in overseas Falun Gong collective action after April 1999, based on counts of such meetings. When one recalls that Li Hongzhi disappeared from public view in July 1999, these data also reinforce our picture of Falun Gong activists mobilizing independently of the direction of their charismatic leader. These experience-sharing

---

[22] "'*Minghui*' *bianjibu jinggao duzhe*" (Caution to readers from the editorial department of 'Minghui'), published on June 28, 1999; retrieved on March 10, 2010, from www .minghui.org/mh/download.html.

[23] "*Falun Dafa dashiji nianjian*" (A chronicle of major events of Falun Dafa), retrieved on April 26, 2011, from http://zhengjian.org.

[24] "*Zhenggao tongzhi*" (Call for submissions), retrieved on May 22, 2012, from www .minghui.org/mh/articles/1999/12/22/3083.html. The many thousands of postings that followed from this call have served as the basis for my research on "activism narratives."

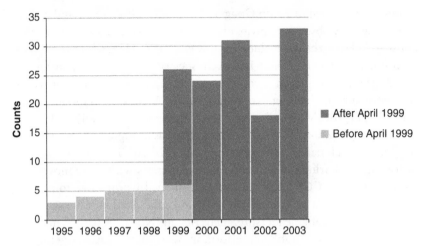

FIGURE 4 Overseas Falun Gong conferences, 1995–2003. Compiled from "*Falun Dafa dashiji nianjian*" (A chronicle of major events of Falun Dafa), retrieved on April 26, 2011, from http://zhengjian.org.

conferences were not congresses of social-movement planning or policy-setting meetings as we saw enacted by Minyun organizations, but are described in Cheris Chan's ethnography from the time as more like spiritual "pilgrimages, or rituals in a broad sense" (Chan 2013: 17). Practitioners emotionally read prepared stories describing their own experiences of being transformed through Falun Dafa practice. After repression, these stories emphasized experiences of "clarifying truth" and horror stories of repression. Chan documented the emotional contagion effect of participating in these conferences. Participation generated feelings of sadness, horror, and indignation regarding the persecution in China, valorized humble efforts to defend Falun Gong despite the odds, and romanticized Li's charisma. All of these micro-sociological processes of interaction, copresence, and collective effervescence served to reinforce ideology and diffuse intensive grassroots activism. Stories and meeting new people also provided opportunities to share ideas and activism know-how.

Over the months, and then years, that followed, activists continued lobbying and other efforts to influence the situation in China. In North America, they set-up organizations, like the Falun Dafa Information Center and the Friends of Falun Gong, which aimed to shape public discourse in ways favorable to Falun Gong. These efforts eventually led to heavy and enduring investments in media companies like *The Epoch*

Times newspaper, New Tang Dynasty Television (NTDTV), Universal Communications Network, Inc., and Shen Yun Performing Arts. Activists created a multitude of other organizations, websites, and campaigns. Some organizations pursued human rights issues, like the World Organization to Investigate the Persecution of Falun Gong, the Falun Dafa Information Center, the Global Mission to Rescue Persecuted Falun Gong Practitioners, and Falun Gong Human Rights Working Group. Activists also have used international law to wage lawsuits against Chinese state actors, including Jiang Zemin, Luo Gan, Bo Xilai, and many less prominent officials. In addition, there have been specialized technical groups led by Falun Gong practitioners, such as the Global Internet Freedom Consortium and the Dynaweb Foundation, to create software that mainland Chinese could use to evade Internet censorship. Dynaweb's software, Freegate (*dongtaiwang*), was distributed covertly in China and was so successful that it was even widely used by Iranian activists during the Green movement in 2009 (Kristof 2009).

In addition to forming organizations, activists also mounted a variety of sustained campaigns. In 2004, *The Epoch Times* released a book called the *Nine Commentaries* (*Jiuping gongchangdang*), which provides a historical polemic detailing alleged ways the CCP has harmed China. Sections from the *Nine Commentaries* are regularly reprinted in the weekly editions of *The Epoch Times*. The *Nine Commentaries* was followed by another book called *Dissolving Communist Party Culture* (*Jieti dangwenhua*). This volume attacked the so-called cultural influences of the CCP. Both books were part of a campaign to encourage Chinese people to renounce their loyalty to any CCP organization. Many other events and campaigns have shaped Falun Gong diaspora activism, including promoting World Falun Gong Day, efforts against alleged "live organ harvesting," protests related to the 2008 Beijing Olympics, and so forth. The Internet, and Minghui especially, allowed practitioners to coordinate and share information, including the latest information on people persecuted in China.

THE DE-POLITICIZING TURN

As "clarifying truth" activism developed in the decade following repression, Falun Gong ideology about political activism went through a process of "spiritualization" (Melton 1985). Spiritualization allows charismatic groups to maintain a positive understanding of collective purpose and to neutralize cognitive dissonance after sustaining a failure in charismatic deliverance. When an event threatens to disconfirm the charismatic authority upon which a movement is based, such as a prophecy that fails to come true, believers reinterpret the event in "such a way that what was supposed to have been a visible, verifiable occurrence is seen to have been in reality an invisible, spiritual occurrence" (Melton 1985: 21). An obvious merit of spiritualizing is that it makes ideology immune to disconfirmation. Spiritualization of ideology is often accompanied by proselytizing efforts to make the wider public understand and embrace the spiritualized interpretation of events. Such efforts to "re-affirm," in Melton's phrase, the charismatic ideology can lead to the counterintuitive outcome of *increased* proselytizing as a response to failed prophesy (Festinger, Riecken, and Schachter 2010 [1956]). Melton argued that increased proselytizing after a failed prophecy turns the gap between ideology and reality into a cause for collective action, staving off disillusionment and maintaining fervor.

Falun Gong leadership began to spiritualize the protest movement through official public statements about six months after repression began (see Chapter 8 for further details). Eventually, doctrine came to explain the CCP repression of Falun Gong as merely this-worldly evidence of a hidden, other-worldly cosmic battle that Falun Gong, through the efforts of Master Li, had in fact already won. Spiritualizing the repression thereby neutralized several sources of cognitive dissonance. When protests began, why had Li Hongzhi disappeared rather than lead the movement? If Li was so omniscient and the Dafa so true, why had neither been able to stop the repression? And, also, why had the wider publics, both in China and the diaspora, failed to recognize what practitioners saw as the injustice and historic significance of Falun Gong's persecution? Along with neutralizing cognitive dissonance, spiritualizing the political conflict led to fusing political activism and religious self-cultivation. Li's interpretation of activism, which will be considered in detail later, canonized "stepping out" and protest as an obligatory means of spiritual self-cultivation on the path to consummation. In this way, protest activism became less adjunct and more central to the community's religious life. Falun Gong effectively used protest activism the way other charismatic groups had used proselytizing when prophecy failed in order to sustain its collective interpretation.

Spiritualization helped to maintain Falun Gong's activism while also, gradually, making it less recognizably political. The emphasis shifted from making public claims in order to force Chinese authorities to "stop the persecution" to using public outreach to "save" the souls of people everywhere from the certain divine punishment that follows from supporting, even passively, the CCP's anti-Falun Gong campaign. A kind of hybridization of political protest and religious proselytizing occurred. Through spiritualization, protest activism became a kind of mopping-up activity by which practitioners saved the innocent souls of people who might otherwise be tricked into supporting the CCP after the cosmic victory against the forces of evil was already accomplished by Li Hongzhi.

Falun Gong's particular form of spiritualization focused on soteriology and a millenarian narrative of the repression. It viewed repression as a final cosmic conflict between good and evil, through which the sinful will be punished and the virtuous rewarded. Eventually, the narrative states, history will culminate in a total triumph of good over evil and Falun Gong practitioners will experience a collective form of consummation (Penny 2012). Anyone who supported the CCP, even passively by accepting the CCP's propaganda about Falun Gong and not recognizing that the Falun Gong is good and the CCP bad, will be punished. As one core practitioner from Taiwan put it to me, the baseline for even being considered for salvation is recognition of the CCP as evil and the Falun Gong as good. The task for practitioners on earth, before final collective consummation, is to save as many ordinary people (*changren*) as possible. The minimum standard for being "saved" is understanding that Falun Gong is good, the CCP is evil, and that the CCP is persecuting Falun Gong.[25] Until history concludes, practitioners are obligated to "save" from divine punishment members of the public everywhere, in and outside of China.

The Falun Gong concept of "saving"[26] is thus a fusion of millenarian missionary work and protest activism. Falun Gong discourse did not define "being saved" as religious conversion, as might a Christian evangelical. Instead, "being saved" only means that one accepts the political movement framing of the CCP–Falun Gong conflict – that Falun Dafa is the hero, the CCP is the villain, and ending the persecution and rule of the

---

[25] Interview with a practitioner in a leadership role, Taipei, September 9, 2013. This individual reported a personal relationship with Li Hongzhi and direct access to Dragon Springs.

[26] The Falun Gong term for "save" in Chinese is *jiudu*. It has a Buddhist connotation and literally means to "be saved by crossing over." It is based on the metaphor of samsara (mundane existence) and nirvana (enlightenment) being separated, as if by a river. The Chinese term does not contain the metaphysical term "soul," but otherwise its Falun Gong usage is similar. My use of "soul" is simply to convey more readily the soteriological meaning of "saving." I discuss saving more in Chapter 8.

CCP are the solution. Salvation depends on accepting this interpretative frame of the political conflict. The task of "clarifying truth" is to give ordinary people the "chance to decide for themselves" and how one's heart interprets the current events of cosmic history will determine if one is saved or damned.[27] Reframing the political conflict as a millenarian cosmological battle has been a source of tenacity and creativity. At the same time, it has led to forms of activism that are less recognizably political, as the following two examples demonstrate.

Since 2004, practitioners have sustained a major campaign called "Quit the CCP" (*tuidang*), which encourages Chinese people to renounce any affiliation with the CCP. Within this campaign, "quitting" the Communist party actually has no legal or institutional consequence. One does not even need to be a member of the CCP to quit the CCP nor does one need to use one's real name when registering as having "quit" in the online registry.[28] Quitting appears to loosely mean renouncing any real or implied loyalty pledged to the CCP ever in one's life. It serves as a kind of marker for mainland Chinese that one has accepted the Falun Gong framing of the repression.

On one hand, this campaign fits well the model of activism described by Melton, Festinger, and others, in that it helps to stave off disillusionment and maintain fervor, without risking objective disconfirmation. There is no objective way to prove whether an activist has "saved" someone, so unlike unsuccessful efforts to stop the persecution, the accomplishment of "saving" others is not falsifiable. Similarly, for those people who might be sympathetic to Falun Gong reasoning, there is a Pascal's wager-like rationale for quitting: if Falun Gong activists are wrong, then no harm will come of quitting but if they are right, there is much to gain. Another benefit of this campaign is that activists can methodically record every instance of a person claiming to agree to quit the CCP, which appears to give activists a self-reinforcing sense of collective accomplishment. In June 2017, *The Epoch Times* claimed that over 275 million people had renounced the CCP.[29] According to the Falun Gong way of understanding things, that means activists were well on their way to saving 300 million people from damnation.

---

[27] Interview with a practitioner in a leadership role, Taipei, September 9, 2013.
[28] See "*Dajiyuan zhengzhong shengming*" (*The Epoch Times* solemnly declares) retrieved on December 5, 2012, from http://tuidang.epochtimes.com.
[29] Retrieved on June 14, 2017, from home page of http://tuidang.epochtimes.com.

The second example of the spiritualized, millenarian framing reshaping activism has been the campaign to revive "5,000 years of Chinese culture" through traveling dance and music performances. Like media activism, which began ad hoc and became professionalized, these variety show performances began ad hoc, local, and mostly amateur as Chinese cultural productions staged for Chinese New Year in various cities. Eventually, they became conglomerated into professional productions staged year-round in hundreds of venues around the world (excluding mainland China) by a single organization, Shen Yun Performing Arts. In 2010, for example, Shen Yun performed in twenty-one countries and ninety-three cities.[30] In each city, local practitioners pay for the venue and promotion costs and sell the tickets. After expenses are covered through ticket sales, proceeds go to Shen Yun. Li Hongzhi is directly involved in Shen Yun activities and teaches that Shen Yun is a more effective means of "saving" people than conventional activism.[31]

Running alongside these campaigns, Falun Gong has also sunk roots in America through the purchase in 2002 of a large property in the rural town of Deerpark, New York. The site is home to Dragon Springs Temple, Shen Yun, and Fei Tian Academy of the Arts, which is a Falun Gong-related college preparatory school (Figure 5). The temple was initially established as a nonprofit organization and reported assets of over $20 million in 2005, after which it ceased public reporting. As of 2013, the 427-acre property contained "a traditional Chinese Tang Dynasty-style temple and numerous other buildings, including residence halls, a library, classrooms, meditation halls, gazebos and gardens" (Brown 2013). Rumors are that it is the residence of Li Hongzhi.

Dragon Springs has been the source of considerable local controversy related to construction practices, zoning, and the closed nature of the community. The temple is absolutely closed to outsiders, including non-Falun Gong practitioners, but also including most ordinary Falun Gong practitioners. Even two core activists in Hong Kong, both of whom dedicated much of their lives to "clarifying truth" and traveling to Falun Gong events, reported to me that they were denied entry when they attempted to visit after traveling all the way to Deerpark in 2010.[32] I tried to visit as a researcher

---

[30] Retrieved on March 16, 2010, from www.shenyunperformingarts.org/calendar.

[31] For instance, see *"Zai xintangren dianshi taolunhui shang de jiangfa"* (Dharma Talk Given at the NTDTV Conference) from August 2009, retrieved on June 12, 2017, from http://minghui.org/mh/articles/2009/8/15/206600.html.

[32] Interview, July 5, 2016, Hong Kong. They emphasized that they were not resentful about the denial, which they understood to be based on a reasonable policy.

FIGURE 5 Dragon Springs, June 2016. On the left is the temple, with a 75-foot pagoda at center, and on the right are the facilities of Fei Tian College and Shen Yun Performing Arts. Building the temple and campus, which includes a large dormitory, performance hall, and large interior and exterior parking garages, and plans for additional construction, have put the community in bitter conflict with many other residents of Deerpark

in June 2016, but was also unsuccessful. In preparation for the trip I contacted a variety of people I had met in my research to try to gain permission, but was denied. Instead, during my two-day visit, I met with local residents, government officials (including the mayor of nearby Middletown), and was given a tour by city officials of property investments made by Falun Gong practitioners in the city. In the end, I was also granted an interview with two practitioners at a country club rather than at the temple compound. One of the interviewees reported having a direct relationship to Li Hongzhi, but neither was willing to officially speak on behalf of Dragon Springs.

The secrecy around Dragon Springs was obvious and was a source of tension within the town. The website of Dragon Springs states that being closed to the public is a security necessity, because it is home to orphans and refugees who "had been tortured in jails and labor camps, lost family members, and continue to receive threats even today."[33] In one telling experience during my visit, I was given a tour of Middletown by a city alderman. Middletown had welcomed the Falun Gong community's

---

[33] Retrieved on June 13, 2017, from www.dragonsprings.org.

investments in the town, including Fei Tian College buying a large section of a defunct hospital and other investors opening a grocery store, a restaurant, and buying commercial buildings. During the tour, we passed an office for *The Epoch Times* newspaper, which publishes a special local edition. There were two staff and an intern. After introducing myself, one of the staff became agitated, saying with hostility, "I know who you are." She drew the alderman into a private conversation in the back of the room and then ejected us from the office. The alderman reported to me that she had said, "He is the enemy." Ironically, in the edition of *The Epoch Times* they were distributing that day, I happened to be quoted making a sympathetic statement toward Falun Gong. The paranoid and secretive dynamics of Dragon Springs were, for me, a somewhat surprising contrast to the more open and forthright treatment (if skeptical at times) that I had generally encountered among Falun Gong practitioners I met in other places.

CONCLUSION

In summary, the history of Falun Gong's politicization, or of activists "stepping out," has an arc that goes from an apolitical spiritual group, to a political protest movement, and finally to some kind of hybrid involving both social movement protest and millenarian religious mission. Within this process, the diaspora Falun Gong community adopted many typical social movement practices, such as forming voluntary associations, performing nonviolent claims through demonstrations and vigils, framing discourses for the media, and using legal strategies to exert pressure on authorities. Most accounts of Falun Gong have taken this protest mobilization as a given, inevitable consequence of state repression and overseas resistance. But such a view obscures the challenges that a protest movement of migrants from authoritarian China face in trying to make public claims on homeland authorities from overseas. These challenges are more obvious when we compare Falun Gong to the democracy movement of Minyun, which had every reason to protest from overseas, but was unsuccessful in sustaining a meaningful level of mobilization. The following chapter explores the history of Minyun in diaspora. The contrast demonstrates that both the scale and the form of the Falun Gong diaspora's protest movement cannot be taken for granted but must be explained.

6

Overseas Minyun: Democracy through Bureaucracy, Factionalism, and Asylum Brokering

This chapter begins by briefly surveying the history of overseas Minyun from its early years, through its only active period of widespread mobilization during the 1989 era, and then into its post-1991 period of "latency" or demobilization. My summary, which is brief and intentionally narrow, seeks to draw out two key contrasts with Falun Gong: that Minyun mobilization was short lived compared to that of Falun Gong and that the qualitative character of its mobilization differed in important ways. In order to specify the most salient differences, I highlight several recurrent patterns that have characterized Minyun's diaspora experience: a quasi-political party organizational form, factionalism, and entanglement with visa and asylum documentation politics. Overseas Minyun's form of activism emphasized hierarchy, bureaucracy, and elite control. At best, these characteristics were ill suited to mobilizing widespread participation across a diffuse diaspora population. Additionally, when contrasted to Falun Gong's mobilization form, which successfully achieved widespread participation and self-authorized, self-reinforcing activism, the overseas Minyun movement does not appear to have achieved the same degree of "social movement-ness." It looks more like an elite tribune, through which counter-elites voice opposition to authorities on behalf of a passive public, as I consider in greater depth in Chapter 7.

From the perspective of comparing Minyun and Falun Gong, an important implication of this chapter is that Falun Gong protest mobilization needs to be explained, rather than assumed as an automatic response to repression. Even though Minyun activists were motivated and determined to create and sustain a protest movement, how they went about doing it undermined their ambitions. The "how" of each movement's efforts to mount protest was shaped by their respective within-movement cultures. This chapter, which focuses on Minyun, shows, ironically, that the democracy movement operated in ways that obstructed rather than facilitated the participation, creativity, and agency that was central to Falun Gong activism.

DIASPORA 1989 VERSUS DIASPORA 1999

Overseas Minyun and Falun Gong both emerged in the context of the post-1978 wave of migration and sojourning from mainland China to democratic countries, especially the USA. Each movement experienced this migration wave at different points in its historical arc. The diaspora-based Chinese democracy movement began shortly after the Chinese government began allowing Chinese students and scholars to travel to Western democracies for study and research. In the 1980s especially, Chinese foreign students and scholars commonly saw themselves as inheriting a tradition of student protest dating from the early twentieth century (Wasserstrom 1990; Wasserstrom and Perry 1994). Given that the USA has been the most attractive destination for Chinese migrants since 1978, including as a destination for foreign study, Chinese foreign students and visiting scholars comprised the majority of Minyun diaspora participants during the 1989 era. Figure 6 shows the growth in the Chinese foreign student population in the USA for four decades starting in the academic year 1977–1978. The line marked "A" indicates the year that the first overseas Minyun organization was founded. "B" indicates the time of the 1989 protests in China, which coincided with the first time that PRC Chinese students outnumbered students from Taiwan.

In comparing Minyun and Falun Gong, one should bear in mind some of the characteristic differences that contrast the 1989 era to the 1999 era, when Falun Gong initially mobilized. Diaspora Minyun activists of the 1980s were expatriates from a socialist China that had only recently reopened universities after the Cultural Revolution. Minyun activists of 1989 and 1990 were, on average, younger, poorer, and less cosmopolitan than Falun Gong activists of the 2000s. For example, the memoir of activist Ding Chu (Ding 2008), who participated in the earliest Minyun organization based out of New York in the latter half of the 1980s, depicts an organization whose management had little knowledge and less experience in building a nonprofit organization, fundraising, or carrying out standard legal practices, such as payroll taxes for staff. As recent migrants

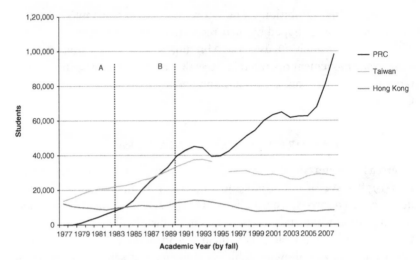

FIGURE 6 Chinese foreign students in the USA by academic year.
Source for 1995–2008 data retrieved on January 5, 2010, from the Institute of
International Education (IEE) at www.iie.org/Research-and-Insights/Open-Doors
/Data; data for other years received through correspondence directly from IEE,
January 2010

and foreign students hailing from a China that was still dismantling the
planned economy, participants had little experience that would have
prepared them for operating professionally in the American nonprofit
sector.

In the decade that separated the Tiananmen protests from the
Zhongnanhai protest, much had changed. Not only had the Cold War
ended and the Internet made global communication cheaper and faster,
but the mainland Chinese diaspora population also had grown richer and
more cosmopolitan. For example, remittances sent home to China from
overseas increased by sixty-seven times between 1995 and 2013 (Hooper
and Batalova 2015). In terms of cosmopolitism, consider the formation by
Falun Gong activists in 2002 of the television broadcasting company,
NTDTV. According to the NTDTV website, the founders were mostly
mainland Chinese immigrants who had extensive experience in business
and media. One founder had "10 years of experience as a vice president of
a leading New York financial services company" and was "the founder,
principal owner, and financier for a Sino–U.S. pharmaceutical joint ven-
ture." Two others had PhDs and had held appointments at Tsinghua
(Beijing), Rutgers, and the University of Pennsylvania. Another had been

"marketing director of Hainan Province Public Television" and had produced "award-winning" documentaries, news programs, commercials, and science programs. Still another had been founder and managing director of a Chinese-language newswire service.[1] These resumes convey a degree of experience and knowledge far exceeding that of Minyun activists in the 1980s and early 1990s.

A BRIEF HISTORY OF OVERSEAS MINYUN

The earliest form overseas Minyun took was the establishment of a Chinese-language journal named *China Spring*, and a social movement organization called the Alliance for Chinese Democracy (*Zhongguo minzhu tuanjie lianmeng*, henceforth "the Alliance"). Both of these were established in December 1982, under the leadership of Dr. Wang Bingzhang. Wang's leadership was especially symbolic because he was the first Chinese foreign student who had been funded by the PRC to earn a PhD from a North American university. Between 1982 and 1989, the Alliance operated with a small staff based in New York City, published its monthly journal, and attempted to be the leading voice of the Chinese democracy movement outside of China. The source of its funding was kept secret until 1988, when a funding crisis and internal politics prompted the organization to openly reveal that it had been receiving financial assistance from the Taiwanese government (Chen and Lu 1993a; Ding 2008). In the seven years leading up to 1989, activities of the Alliance included holding conferences, meetings, and press conferences; publishing a monthly journal in Chinese; staging small protests outside of consulates when Chinese state officials visited; helping dissidents and defectors gain asylum; lobbying non-Chinese governments, especially the US Congress; and coordinating "open letter" campaigns in support of dissidents in China. The Alliance appears to have made a larger symbolic footprint in the political landscape of Chinese diaspora than a count of its actual membership would lead one to expect, which only reached a height of around 600 before 1989 (Ding 2008: 83). Ding Chu's memoir reveals that the Chinese government in the mid-1980s was vigilantly concerned about the threat posed by the Alliance, but the organization itself was weak and perceived with suspicion by the wider diaspora community of PRC Chinese students and scholars.

---

[1] Retrieved on March 17, 2010, from the "About Us" link on http://english.ntdtv.com.

Before 1989, the most active period of diaspora Minyun activism was in 1987 (Ding 2008: 69–70). Overseas students and scholars mobilized in response to events in China, which included student demonstrations for democracy from December 1986 to January 1987 and the subsequent "anti-bourgeois liberalization" state campaign, which targeted the public intellectuals Fang Lizhi, Liu Binyan, and Wang Ruowang. In January 1987, overseas Chinese students and scholars responded to the anti-bourgeois liberalization campaign by publishing an open letter signed by more than 1,000 names, including, according to *China Spring,* over 400 real names rather than pseudonyms (Chen and Lu 1993a, 1993b; Goldman 1994: 214–218). Widespread activism was also stimulated by the arrest in January in Shanghai of Mr. Yang Wei, who was a student at the University of Arizona and member of the Alliance. Yang Wei had been visiting home in December 1986 and became involved in student demonstrations. His connections to the Alliance made him a special target of state repression. Pro-Yang Wei activism among overseas students, scholars, and the Alliance included an open letter campaign and political lobbying in Washington, which led to a Senate resolution calling for Yang's release. According to Goldman, these events mark the first time, at least since 1978, that the overseas Chinese intellectuals mobilized international pressure in support of political dissidents.

After a relatively robust year of activity on behalf of Minyun goals by the Alliance and by overseas Chinese students generally, 1988 was a year of decline. The contentious episode that spurred overseas activism in late 1986 and early 1987 had mostly passed. Furthermore, the Alliance suffered from funding problems and a rocky leadership transition.

The 1989 student-led democracy protests in China began in April in Beijing and seized the attention of all Chinese students studying abroad. Although one can write a history of the Minyun diaspora from 1982 until the present, it was really only from April or perhaps May 1989 and then throughout the following year that there was a widespread, organic mobilization of practically the entire foreign student and scholar diaspora population in support of democracy in China. Outside of those narrow temporal parameters, Minyun activism has almost entirely been carried out by small bands of hardcore activists without widespread support from their potential constituencies. The 1989 era was an exception.

Based on transcripts of Chinese student communications during the spring and summer of 1989,[2] it is clear that virtually anywhere that had a sizeable contingent of Chinese foreign students also became a site for collective action, issuing collective statements, fundraising, and establishing formally independent Chinese student unions. Together, students mounted major demonstrations in Washington DC, Los Angeles, Chicago, Tokyo, Paris, Berlin, and other cities.[3] Part of the mobilization of students and scholars in the summer of 1989 and the following year involved the formation of new Minyun organizations. These included campus chapters of "independent" – meaning independent of the Chinese government – student associations, which were affiliated with national federations, including, most prominently, the Independent Federation of Chinese Students and Scholars (IFCSS) in the US, which held its first convention in Chicago on July 30, 1989.

In addition to associations of diaspora students, the most important new organization to enter the diaspora scene was formed in the fall of 1989, in Paris, by leaders from the Beijing democracy protests who had fled China after the crackdown. These mostly students and intellectuals named their organization the Federation for a Democratic China (henceforth "the Federation"). It was structurally similar to that of the Alliance, including publishing its own journal called *Minzhu Zhongguo*.[4] The Federation attempted to carry the flag of the Tiananmen Square protest movement and be the vanguard organization for Chinese democracy. The Federation, however, suffered for a lack of practical and effective focus beyond publications and conferences. For example, in the year following the June 4 crackdown, the Federation obtained through donations a 1,200-ton ship, which activists named after the Goddess of Democracy statue that occupied Tiananmen in the final days of the student movement. They outfitted the ship to conduct radio broadcasts into China from a location in international waters off the coast of China. From the beginning, the plan looked bold, but not well thought out: broadcasting was to start in May, but no funding had been secured to

---

[2] The source (Ståhle and Uimonen 1989a) and methodology are described in the following chapter.

[3] Table 1 provides a quantitative summary of countries where Minyun and Falun Gong activism took place, as documented in the protest event study.

[4] The English name of the journal is simply a transliteration of the Chinese, which can be read to mean, "Democracy China," "Democratic China," or, literally, "People Rule China."

keep the expensive project afloat past mid-June.[5] After the Goddess of Democracy radio ship sailed with much fanfare from France to Taiwan, authorities in Hong Kong, Taiwan, and Japan all refused to allow the ship to be supplied with transmitting equipment in their harbors; meanwhile, the Chinese government threatened to attack the ship for violating its sovereignty. The effort was abandoned on May 25, just ten days before the first anniversary of June 4.

In addition to activism led by the Federation, overseas student unions also pursued an independent agenda. Throughout 1990, activism primarily consolidated around the project of lobbying the US government. The stated purpose of lobbying was to protect all mainland Chinese students who had been in America during the Tiananmen Square protests from retaliatory punishment in China by persuading Congress to enact a law granting those students permanent residency. This lobbying effort involved extensive coordination led by the IFCSS, based in Washington DC, and successfully culminated in the Chinese Student Protection Act of 1992, which formalized into law President's Bush's earlier executive order to grant protection to Chinese students who were in America during the protests. Ironically, by the time the law took effect, the Chinese government had already implemented a policy of no retaliation against returning foreign students and the "primary beneficiaries of this act were undocumented immigrants from Fujian Province who were not students at all" (Poston and Luo 2007).

After 1990, Minyun experienced demobilization, meaning most people stopped participating in Minyun collective actions, excepting, perhaps, June 4 commemorations. Chen and Lu's history, for instance, describes the June 1991 congress of the Alliance as a low point of mobilization (Chen and Lu 1993c). For the purposes of comparison with Falun Gong, it is significant to note that Minyun's demobilization occurred *before* the Chinese economy took off in the mid-1990s and even before Deng Xiaoping's "southern tour," which was staged to signal to the Chinese public his official endorsement of economic liberalization. I infer from this sequence of events that students and scholars did not choose to exit the movement primarily because the promise of economic opportunities in China undermined their idealism. At the time of demobilization, there was still little reason to expect that China would soon become the land of economic opportunity that it became a decade later. Overseas Minyun did

---

[5] "Radio Free China," *Newsweek*, March 19, 1990. In *Lexis-Nexis Universe: General News Topics.* Online. December 8, 2008.

not end with its wide-scale demobilization after 1990 – there have been many "Minyun" organizations based overseas, including more than a handful of Chinese democracy political parties. But never again since 1990 have Chinese students and scholars living overseas taken up the movement in any significant way.

Given this brief sketch of Minyun's history, I want to elaborate on four points. The first concerns one way that transnational mobilization may have helped directly spur what eventually became the 1989 student movement in Beijing. This instance suggests a pathway by which social movement activism common in the North American context appears to have migrated into the Chinese context of late 1989. The remaining three points describe recurrent patterns in Minyun mobilization that are especially telling in comparison to Falun Gong's mobilization: (1) the organizational form typically pursued by Minyun activists; (2) the disruptive and persistent factionalism within the Minyun community; and (3) the corrupting influence of brokering asylum visas as a means of Minyun mobilization.

A TRANSNATIONAL TRIGGER FOR THE 1989 STUDENT MOVEMENT

Although the story of the student-led democracy protests in China 1989 is well known and studied, rarely is it recognized that an overseas Chinese activist connection played a key role in determining the form and, perhaps, even timing of the earliest phase of the Tiananmen events. This connection also demonstrates the diffusion of a form of protest action, namely the open letter and press conference, from an American cultural source into the contentious repertoire of mainland Chinese national politics.

At the center of the story was physicist Fang Lizhi, whose open letter to Deng Xiaoping in January 1989 helped set into motion events that would lead to the student movement in the spring. In the mid-1980s, Fang had become a popular and influential public voice in China for intellectual, economic, and democratic freedoms. The government moved against Fang, along with two others, through an anti-bourgeois liberalization campaign, eventually ejecting Fang from the Communist party. This crackdown provoked the student demonstrations in support of Fang in the winter of 1986–1987, which were the events in which Yang Wei participated. On January 6, 1989, Fang boldly sent an open letter to Deng Xiaoping calling for amnesty for the political prisoner Wei

Jingsheng. Wei had been jailed since November 1979 for calling for democratic reforms in his famous Democracy Wall essay, "The Fifth Modernization." In hindsight, Fang's January 6 letter appears to have been the opening gambit in the contentious episode that snowballed into the student demonstrations of the spring.

As we saw in 1987, Chinese students and scholars living in North America had adopted and popularized the open letter as a form of collective action. For the Minyun diaspora, an open letter entailed supporters signing a message of protest addressed to authorities and then distributing the letter through press conferences and publication in third-party overseas media. After Fang published his letter in January, on February 16 an additional thirty-three intellectuals from Beijing held a press conference to promote their own open letter supporting Fang and calling for a general amnesty for political prisoners, especially Wei Jingsheng.

The independent press conference, as a form of collective action used by dissidents to reach the public through the media, was by no means a standard protest practice in the winter of 1989 in China. Press conferences and collective open letters depend on an independent media that will broadcast them – in this instance, it was foreign media rather than state-controlled domestic media to which the protest activity was directed. The Alliance spread news of the event to international media and sent news back into China through clandestine networks, in a kind of boomerang strategy of transnational advocacy (Keck and Sikkink 1998). The thirty-three individuals who issued an open letter in support of Fang Lizhi adopted this same open letter and press conference tactic.

The backstage coordination of the February 16 letter suggests that transnational diffusion was an important part of the story due to the central role of a young Chinese man named Chen Jun, who was the final name on the list of thirty-three signatories. Chen had graduated from Fudan University in Shanghai in 1983 and married a British woman, who was a permanent resident of the USA. Through the marriage, Chen had moved to the USA, received permanent residency, and then returned to China (Chen and Lu 1993d; Ståhle and Uimonen 1989b: 21–22, 23–24), where he opened bars in Beijing and in Shanghai. In 1989, Chen's bar in Beijing served as the location for the February 16 press conference and as the headquarters of what activists labeled the "Amnesty '89 Office." Chen later became identified as the organizer of the letter campaign and was forced to leave China in April, after which he returned to the USA and spoke at several speaking engagements for Chinese students studying in the USA. Although Chen Jun was not a member of the

Alliance, the Chinese government blamed the Alliance for coordinating the letter campaign through Chen. The Minyun published history of the period, however, suggests that Chen Jun's connections to the Alliance were indirect. Nevertheless, Chen Jun clearly had played a major role in coordinating the open letter amnesty campaign, including the press conference. The February 16 open letter and transnational campaign not only helped to spark the student mobilization in April, but also were something of a collective action novelty for PRC political contention. Evidence here is not strong enough to reconstruct the full picture of tactical transmission, but it suggests that Chen Jun was a broker (McAdam, Tarrow, and Tilly 2001: 142) who helped transmit standard social movement practices from North America into Beijing on the eve of the Tiananmen protests.

MINYUN ORGANIZATIONAL FORM

One recurrent pattern seen in overseas Minyun activism is the organizational form pursued by activists to coordinate mobilization. The typical pattern, as clearly seen in the founding of the Alliance, the Federation, the IFCSS, and several of the Chinese democracy parties, was for activists to set-up a formal organization with centralized, hierarchical, and bureaucratic control. Typically, each organization created its own written constitution and set-up a bureaucratic division of powers into an executive council, a supervisory council, and a standing executive committee. The central organizations, when possible, consisted of paid staff. Officers for these positions were elected through "representatives," usually at regional or biennial grand congresses (*dahui*) of the associations. At these conferences, participants debated the written constitution, amendments, work programs (*gangling*), and official procedures, all of which were formally drafted, debated, and promulgated.

The Alliance founded by Wang Bingzhang provides the earliest example. It was organized with a written constitution, a central office and branch offices, term limits for top leadership positions, elections based on representation, an executive branch and a supervisory branch, formal procedures for accepting and expelling members, disciplinary procedures, membership cards and membership identification numbers, a centralized comprehensive filing system, and so forth (China Spring 1982; Ding 2008: 81–83). The Alliance held a global conference every other year, numbered consecutively and therefore the title sounds quite similar to the congresses of the NPC (e.g., "The Third Congress of Representatives" [*disanci daibiao dahui*]). Chen and Lu's historical summary of the Alliance depicts these congresses as dominated by disputes over constitutional revisions, formal representation, elections, and structure of the organization (Chen and Lu 1993–1994). Particularly striking in light of historical circumstances is that at the Alliance's Fourth Congress, which took place exactly three weeks after the June 4 repression in China, an entire day of the three-day event was spent debating revisions to the constitution (Chen and Lu 1993e). Making speeches was also a primary activity of Minyun meetings – so much so that Ding Chu's memoir recalls the meeting to elect a new chairman as a speech contest (Ding 2008: 97–98).

The literature on social movement debates the relationship between organization form and mobilization, but one long-standing position is that bureaucratization subverts the efficacy of protest movements (Michels 1966; Piven and Cloward 1977). This analysis seems to aptly fit the Minyun history.

FACTIONALISM

Without doubt, the most disabling social dynamic within the Minyun movement, from its overseas inception until today, has been the movement's recurrent pattern of factionalism. Over and over again, organizations have been established using formal constitutions and officious institutional arrangements, only to break down along some factional division through which different members abandon the movement or align themselves with different organizations. One of the 1989 student leaders who fled to the USA, Shen Tong, described "the problems originating from the dissident groups" as "dirty politics" and worse than any repressive interference from China (He 2014: 104, 106). To illustrate the pattern of factionalism, I summarize what are perhaps the most important organizational – but by no means atypical or uncommon – instances of factional dispute.

In December 1987,[6] at the third congress of the Alliance, founder Wang Bingzhang finished his second and final term as chairman, and a prominent recent arrival to the USA, Mr. Hu Ping, was elected as the new chairman.[7] Hu Ping had gained attention as a dissident in China and

[6] My sources for this account are Chen and Lu, supplemented by Ding Chu's memoir (Chen and Lu 1993a, 1993e, 1993f, 1994; Ding 2008).
[7] Due to Hu's election, he was expelled from the CCP in March 1988 and his passport was revoked by the Consulate. As a result, Hu has been unable to return to China since he left in 1987.

had come to the USA to study for a PhD at Harvard. After Hu became chairman, he discovered over the course of 1988 that the Alliance's financial situation was dire. Furthermore, in spite of Hu's position as chairman, Wang Bingzhang continued to autocratically control from the shadows the Alliance and its secretive, but insufficient, sources of funding. In January 1989, during the same week that Fang Lizhi wrote his open letter to Deng Xiaoping, which in effect set the wheels in motion for the spring democracy movement, Hu Ping called a meeting of the Alliance's three governing bodies in order to discuss expelling founder Wang Bingzhang from the organization. Arguments centered on Wang's allegedly dictatorial style, suspicions about how Alliance funds had been raised and used, and Wang's commercial insurance company, which allegedly swindled people under the name of the Alliance. Wang, for his part, accused another leader in the organization of being a spy for the CCP. On the last day of the meeting, another conflict erupted over three Alliance members who had just been arrested in China for distributing copies of the organization's publication *China Spring*. Hu Ping had forbidden this risky activity, but Wang had secretly orchestrated it, or so says the account later published by *China Spring*. The conflict finally boiled down to a vote in late January 1989 among the standing and supervisory committee members to keep or expel Wang. Initially, it looked like Wang would triumph, but then the person holding the deciding vote chose to withdraw from the Alliance rather than vote. Procedure was stalemated, more chaos ensued, and news of the event was picked up by American, Hong Kong, and Taiwanese media.

In late February, Hu Ping proposed a method for de-escalating the conflict through a new committee composed of himself, Wang Bingzhang, and one other. But constructive efforts were subverted when one of Wang's close associates, Ke Lisi, secretly closed the Alliance's bank account so that the funds could not be used. As a result, the next issue of *China Spring* was published through an emergency fundraising effort. Furthermore, Wang then cancelled the Alliance's phone, which was in his name. By mid-March, Hu Ping had expelled Wang and Ke Lisi from the Alliance and initiated a lawsuit against Wang to return all of the Alliance's funds and to desist from using the *China Spring* name. On March 31, just two weeks before the death of Hu Yaobang and the first student demonstration in Beijing, Wang organized an emergency meeting, called the "Congress to Establish a Chinese Democracy Party," by which a new Minyun organization was founded. Initially, activists joined both Wang's new organization and the Alliance, but this practice was then forbidden at the Fourth Congress of the Alliance in late June 1989, at which point – less than a month after the bloody Beijing repression – people were forced to choose their allegiances between the Alliance and Wang's new Chinese Democracy Party.

All of this internal acrimony unfolded simultaneously with the democracy movement in China. Not surprisingly, when escaped leaders from the Beijing protests gathered in Paris in the fall of 1989, they chose to start yet another organization, which was the Federation, rather than join the Alliance. In October, the Alliance officially decided to permit overlapping membership with the Federation. Eventually, in January 1993, the Alliance and the Federation held a joint three-day congress in Washington DC. The intent of the meeting was to combine the two organizations. However, a variety of problems, ranging from acquisition of visas and funding to procedural debates about how to elect leaders and claims of foul play eventually created pandemonium from which *three* organizations, not one, emerged: the Alliance, the Federation, and the new "Federated Alliance for Democracy" (henceforth "the Federated Alliance"). The new organization claimed to represent both organizations and to be the rightful publisher of *China Spring*. The Alliance entered a lawsuit in order to regain control of *China Spring* from the Federated Alliance, but eventually decided to end the conflict by changing the publication's name to *Beijing Spring* under the editorship of Hu Ping.

These cases of factionalism and organizational dispute were not isolated events, but are important cases of a more general pattern of factionalism and organizational redundancy.

The causes of Minyun factionalism are multifaceted and beyond the scope of the present study, but it should be noted that throughout the Minyun diaspora's history, as well as that of Falun Gong, there have been instances and accusations of subversion and espionage conducted by agents of the CCP. Accusations of people being spies for the CCP or the Kuomintang (KMT)-led government in Taiwan were common. During the Fourth Congress of the Alliance in June 1989, one Alliance member even publicly confessed to being a spy. The ways in which espionage, both real and imagined, has undermined overseas protest activism should not be underestimated.[8] Even in the absence of true "spies," suspicions and

---

[8] I note that some suspect that Ding Chu, whose real name is Fang Zhiyuan, was actually a spy for the CCP, because, after his several years of participation in the Alliance, he was allowed to return to China. If true, this would suggest that his memoir should be read critically. Nevertheless, Hu Ping, who worked with Ding at the Alliance, told me in

accusations of espionage were themselves enough to propel internal divisions into irredeemably polarized conflicts. Although Falun Gong also has had problems with spies, its sectarian culture is considerably more difficult to infiltrate than the open, secular culture of Minyun, which means that the Falun Gong has been less vulnerable to factionalism triggered by real or suspected espionage.

ASYLUM BROKERING

The final point to which I want to bring attention concerns the issue of visa status and mobilization. As already mentioned, the politics of visas and permanent residency in the USA featured heavily in the collective action of Chinese foreign students after the June 4 repression. It may well have been that successful mobilization for visas in the USA contributed to the movement's demobilization. According to one Australian activist I met at a Chinese Democracy Party event, Minyun activism remained vigorous longer in Australia than in the USA, because it took much longer there for a similar law to be passed.[9] But once the law passed, my informant lamented, most participants disappeared from the movement.

The problem of migration and visas is woven in complex ways into the Minyun history. In the mid-1980s, there were several cases of Chinese people attempting, both successfully and unsuccessfully, to defect from China while on visits to the USA. In April 1984, one PRC visitor to the USA tried to defect, broke his leg attempting to evade the consulate staff, and was captured and forced to repatriate. Again in October in New York, a similar event led to the death of a would-be defector in the consulate, the cause of which was said to be suicide (Chen and Lu 1993b). Other forced repatriations of students had occurred in San Francisco and a similar incident led to a death in Japan. These events prompted the Alliance to start assistance work on behalf of asylum cases. In 1986, a key member of the Alliance staff in New York sued the US government for denying his asylum claim due to foreign policy concerns. He won the case, after which he established an organization that went on to help about 300 others (Chen and Lu 1993b).

From this "legitimate" starting point, however, the visa and asylum issue became vulnerable to exploitation as a source of both fundraising

---

a personal communication that Ding's memoir is accurate to Hu's recollection on all of the major issues.

[9] Interview, February 15, 2010, Las Vegas.

and even organizational membership. Ding Chu's memoir extensively describes how the Alliance raised money by providing counseling to Chinese foreign students about how to emigrate to Canada. Although Ding and his accomplices, who were not lawyers, only provided information that was publicly available, they led customers to believe that they were lawyers providing genuine legal services. Corrupt practices related to visas appeared to continue when I was doing my fieldwork.

A common complaint about Minyun organizations in the USA after the 1989 era is that several are involved in the business of securing political asylum status for undocumented economic migrants. I observed this phenomenon in person in two different cities (but among the same organization). The organizational leaders clearly and openly depended on the bartering of asylum documentation in order to support their Minyun activism. Undocumented migrants were recruited into the movement and apparently schooled in activities they could do to build up a convincing asylum claim portfolio. Primarily, these activities appeared to be attending the organization's events, making short speeches or public statements, and participating in the organization's protest demonstrations. At all of these events, photographs would be taken and short news summaries published, which then were put in the participants' asylum documentation files. I observed one such "protest demonstration" in Los Angeles. The event was brief and hardly more than a photo opportunity for the participants. About a dozen participants arrived at the consulate in two cars. They formed a line holding protest signs at the corner of the intersection and took several photos. The protestors carried no literature or information to hand out to people on the street or to those who were coming and going from the consulate. As soon as the photos were taken and a few interviews were accomplished with two sympathetic Chinese media sources, which had been contacted in advance, everyone packed up and left. I would be surprised if anyone in the Chinese consulate was ever aware that a demonstration had occurred.

In my discussions with several leaders from the organization, and with two Chinese immigration lawyers who regularly worked with the group, people openly discussed how the asylum brokerage process was a symbiotic relationship: the Minyun leaders needed followers to look like a movement and the undocumented workers needed residency papers for security and survival. Although everyone recognized that the arrangement was not ideal, and everyone emphasized that few, if any, of the asylum seekers ever returned to the Minyun organization after they were granted asylum, it was generally acknowledged that the relationship served both sides well enough. At least for the organization, I observed the purpose of activism had not devolved solely into a commercial business for brokering asylum visa documentation, but was still embedded in genuine, if ineffective, efforts to work for Chinese democracy. By contrast, I am unaware of any instance of Falun Gong activists manipulating asylum law in order to foster the appearance of greater mobilization than they can muster on the basis of their own strength. The one immigration lawyer with whom I discussed the topic said he had encountered a false claim of Falun Gong belief by someone trying to gain asylum, but such claims are difficult to substantiate because an applicant's competent knowledge of the Falun Gong literature can be readily challenged.

COMPARATIVE IMPLICATIONS

What implications can one draw from Minyun's overseas history when compared to that of Falun Gong? The most obvious point is that Minyun was not able to sustain much grassroots mobilization over time. The fact that the movement largely dissipated before Deng Xiaoping's Southern Tour indicates that the causes for that decline cannot be attributed to China's economic takeoff undermining idealism, but need to be explained by other factors. My analysis has identified three recurrent patterns that compare starkly to Falun Gong's sustained mobilization.

First, the Minyun's organizational form was consistently bureaucratic, emphasizing formal organizations, written constitutions, rules, and elected, term-limited leadership. The form appears to have aspired to that of a political opposition party, complete with the bureaucratic infrastructure that goes with that dream. Why the Minyun pursued this organizational model cannot be answered based on my research, but at least two relevant templates were culturally available to activists. The first, of course, was the CCP itself. The CCP's prerevolutionary activities in France may have provided historical resonances for diaspora activists, and certainly the CCP provided the most deeply experienced and taken-for-granted model for what wielding political authority looked like for aspiring elites coming from the mainland. The second template that perhaps influenced Minyun came from Taiwan. From the 1970s until 1987, when martial law ended, the democratic opposition movement to the KMT took the form of the *dangwai* movement, or "movement of the opposition party." The emphasis on opposition through institutional politics was an effect of Taiwanese political reforms in the 1970s, which permitted relatively free and fair elections for the national parliament

(Chiou 1995) within the context of martial law. Although it was illegal until 1987 to organize an opposition political party, political elites and democracy activists from outside of the KMT ran for public office under the unofficial banner of *dangwai* (which literally means "outside the Party"). Throughout the 1970s and most of the 1980s, *dangwai* activists organized campaigns for elections, published dissident magazines (which were frequently shut down), and led public protest movements. Eventually, *dangwai* activists in 1986 overtly rejected the ban on independent political parties and publicly announced the formation of the Democratic Progressive Party (DPP). As a political party in name and not just deed, the DDP achieved legal recognition the following year. Other democratic reforms followed quickly (Chiou 1995; Roy 2003).

There are several reasons to infer that the democracy movement in Taiwan, including its emphasis on political party formation, influenced overseas Minyun. The first is simply that the *dangwai* movement was unfolding with intensity and momentum throughout the entire emergence of overseas Minyun, culminating in success in 1987. Second, the Alliance, the Federation, and the Federated Alliance all did what many *dangwai* groups in Taiwan did: they published a dissident magazine. Elites across different global Chinese settings, including Taiwan, America, and France, shared expectations for what democracy activism looked like. Third, articles on democracy activism in Taiwan frequently appeared in the Minyun flagship publication, *China Spring*, indicating interest and knowledge by overseas Chinese intellectuals and activists concerning the *dangwai* movement. Because the Taiwan movement focused on establishing an opposition party, it makes sense that Taiwanese activism provided a model to overseas Minyun that encouraged seeing the achievement of an opposition party as an ultimate, if still distant, goal.

The organizational template of a quasi-political party, however, was poorly suited to mobilization in diaspora. Simply maintaining and running a formal institution, according to highly bureaucratic rules, which were themselves frequently debated, absorbed too much time and too many resources. Furthermore, the bureaucratic model emphasized hierarchy and impeded decentralized, grassroots, voluntarist, creative initiative by participants. In this respect, Minyun's organizational template was the exact opposite of Falun Gong's ethic of activism, which imbued each individual with a sense of personal duty to "step forward," but did not dictate the means or attempt to coordinate in any high degree the specifics of protest. The Falun Gong organizational form avoided paralyzing battles over leadership while maximizing the resources and creative capacities of a heterogeneous community. The new religious movement had higher levels of grassroots participation and found more rewarding and meaningful ways to engage members. Ironically, the democracy movement emphasized hierarchy and centralized control, whereas the indigenous Chinese new religious movement encouraged self-authorized, direct participation and autonomy. The latter model was not only more participatory, it was also better suited to diaspora, where the activist community was thinly spread across many cities and contexts. Any bureaucracy would struggle under such conditions to coordinate effective action; one that aspires to be a stateless political party or exile government faces even higher challenges.

The bureaucratic, political party model also contributed to Minyun's persistent factionalism. In contrast, Falun Gong's egalitarianism among practitioners coupled with its high moral imperative for individual initiative and activism was especially successful at minimizing factionalism and sectarian splits. Tensions and some factionalism has occurred (Fisher 2003), and certainly more has occurred than an external researcher can observe, but these have not undermined Falun Gong's general unity. The community's transcendent basis for solidarity helps buffer the divisive forces of factionalism. For example, at his dharma talks, Li Hongzhi has directly admonished followers against internal disputes by reminding practitioners that they are all equal before the Fa. To struggle over power, he emphasized, is to pursue vain attachments that one must overcome through moral cultivation. If conflicts arise, one is enjoined to "look within" (*kan ziji*) and "exchange experiences" (*jiaoliu*) with fellow practitioners until unity is restored.

Finally, asylum brokering, when compared to Falun Gong activism, also presents a stark contrast. Simply the existence of such a corrupt practice demonstrates the degree to which the Minyun failed to motivate a genuine diasporic constituency. That is, in order to appear like a social movement, some Minyun activists appear to have resorted to an instrumental and dishonest use of selective incentives (asylum visas) in order to motivate participation. There is irony here as well. The Minyun aspired to be, and always claimed to be, a "social movement." Asylum brokering suggests how far some were willing to go to keep up this image. The Falun Gong, by contrast, never intended to be a social movement and its members vigorously rejected the label whenever I raised it. Nevertheless, from the sociological perspective, the new religious movement realized what the democracy movement aspired to and eventually could only pretend to be.

PART III

MAKING SOCIAL MOVEMENTS IN DIASPORA

7

Publics, Proselytizing, and Protest: Tactical Repertoires Compared

This chapter uses the familiar aphorism "actions speak louder than words" to compare the kinds of actions, or "tactical repertoires," undertaken by the Minyun and Falun Gong diaspora. Regardless of the ideologies, self-definitions, and goals these two movements professed, how did activists actually carry out protest? What were the real things they did? How much did these activities, these protest repertoires, correspond to the contentious repertoires that Charles Tilly identified as signature to the 'modern social movement'? What does the way each movement protested tell us about its degree of 'social movement-ness'?

To answer these questions, I collected data using software designed for quantitative narrative analysis to count protest tactics mentioned in reports by activists from both movements over two comparable periods of time. This method allows one to view all of the protest actions of each movement as a set, or what social movement scholars call a tactical repertoire. From the tactical repertoire data, I drew inferences about how well each movement adopted the ideal-typical social movement technology – that is, I assessed each movement's degree of 'social movement-ness.' In preparation for the analysis, the chapter describes my data collection and analytical methodology. I include this information here, rather than in the Appendix, because it is necessary in order to make sense of the tactical repertoire data. Nevertheless, some readers may want to skip the methodological discussion and move on to my substantive conclusions.

The conclusions from the tactical repertoire study are as follows. First, there are important differences in how both movements protested; those differences are apparent when the total inventory, or repertoire, of each movement is compared. I have referred to these differences elsewhere as "tactical dispositions" (Junker 2014b); in this context, however, the key point is that the two movements protested differently in relation to the publics to whom and for whom they tried to speak. The Falun Gong emphasized outreach to every possible public as a source of leverage for their cause. The Falun Gong regarded publics as a source of power. The Minyun's tactical repertoire emphasized large gatherings and speaking as a united voice of "Chinese students and scholars" in opposition to the homeland state. Minyun activism positioned publics (American, diasporic, and in China) as an audience, but not as a direct source of power. This is the key contrast I seek to demonstrate. The difference in how each movement oriented itself in relation to publics, I argue, has important implications for how each movement instantiated, or not, the modern social movement as an ideal type.

Next, I draw on secondary literature and my other research to explain why the tactical repertoires of these movements differed in how they regarded publics. I argue that the difference was culturally specific to their respective traditions of collective action in China. Ways of doing things in China were initially replicated in the diaspora of both the Minyun and Falun Gong, even though many more forms of protest were conceivable in democratic societies, especially in the USA with its history of social movements. Although activists in both movements took advantage of the freedoms and many new practices available in the democratic polities, the *overall pattern* of tactical repertoires of both movements in North America, Japan, Europe, Australia, and elsewhere still reproduced cultural expectations about collective action that took shape in China. In the case of Minyun, the political context of China in the 1980s, especially the absence of civil society and a social movement sector, selected for and reinforced a traditional, elitist, and in some ways authoritarian tactical disposition. This means that the Minyun's repertoire was, ironically, more bound by traditional culture than the Falun Gong's, for reasons that will be explained. By contrast, the Falun Gong's repertoire was shaped by its character as a proselytizing religious movement. Proselytizing undergirded its ethic of activism, thereby shaping how activists oriented themselves to the general public. When the Falun Gong became politicized, practitioners redeployed these already familiar *hongfa* proselytizing scripts toward social movement aims – in other words, making public claims against authorities. The Falun Gong's *hongfa* proselytizing ethic, know-how, networks, and collective identities evolved into what activists came to call "clarifying truth" (*jiang zhenxiang*). Proselytizing became protesting, and that is why the Falun Gong's tactical repertoire keenly emphasized reaching the public, a feature that Tilly identified as historically specific to the modern social movement.

This analysis also has a take-away conclusion for social movement theory, which has argued that the "modularity" of the social movement repertoire allows it to spread and universalize. Modularity, in these two cases, was clearly mediated by each movement's distinct within-group culture. That mediation influenced how well its members adopted the social movement form of protest. The Minyun had the ideological beliefs suited to take up social movement activism, but not the collective cultural disposition that would orient activism toward publics in the classic formulation. The Falun Gong, by contrast, had the opposite profile of strengths and weaknesses: it had a progressive dispositional orientation toward publics that formally matched the social movement ideal type, but its ideological beliefs were traditionalist and eventually undermined the proto-democratic potential latent to that progressive tactical disposition. I further consider this final implication in the book's final chapter. For social movement theory, however, it is important that we recognize that modularity is mediated not only by environments, but also by within-movement culture.

STUDYING TACTICAL REPERTOIRES: RESEARCH DESIGN AND SOURCES

I used a protest event study to document and compare the two movements' tactical repertoires over a set time period. One of the cornerstone ideas emerging from the post-1970 wave of scholarship on social movements is the idea that *how* people engage in protest is socially learned and historically specific. A tactical repertoire, as I use the term here, means a set of protest tactics that is specific to a particular movement or challenger (Taylor and Van Dyke 2004). We can speak of Falun Gong having its repertoire and Minyun having a related, but potentially different one. This concept is a derivative of a more general theoretical claim advanced by Charles Tilly, who argued that historically specific struggles between the state and popular challengers shape the "contentious repertoire" or "contentious performances" of any given regime context. In his view, collective contention is:

[A] product of learned and historically grounded performances. In a given time and place, people learn a limited number of claim-making performances, then mostly stick with those performances when the time to make claims arrives. Contentious performances change incrementally as a result of accumulating experience and external constraints. But in the short run they strongly limit the choices available to the would-be makers of claims. (Tilly 2008b: 4)

The central idea is that collective protest is historically and culturally conditioned. This means, on the one hand, that repertoires are "clustered, learned, yet improvisational" (2008b: 15) – they both constrain and enable tactical action. And, on the other hand, repertoires have histories and are culturally constituted. As Sidney Tarrow states in reference to the cultural implication of this theory, "The repertoire is therefore not only what people do when they make claims; it is what they know how to do and what society has come to expect them to choose to do from within a culturally sanctioned and empirically limited set of options" (Tarrow 1995: 90–91). A repertoire is a generalized model for protest that is shared, in a taken-for-granted way, within a community of actors. So, by comparing the tactical repertoires of different movements, we not only see what they actually did, but also gain insight into the cultural models of protest that are shared within that group.

Although the concept of repertoire has received attention for decades, how to research tactical repertoires still presents some challenges. An individual tactic can be traced historically from its first appearance, such as how the petition that was invented by abolitionists later became a generalized form of protest (Hochschild 2004; Tarrow 1998). But how does one examine a set of tactics, which is what the concept of repertoire conveys? My solution was to do a protest event analysis and record every form of protest action ("tactic") mentioned by both movements in their own reports for a two-year period of time. The total inventory of tactics I recorded is a measurement of the tactical repertoire. To record and code data, I used the software developed by Roberto Franzosi for quantitative narrative analysis (Franzosi 2004, 2009, 2012). Although conceptually straightforward, implementing the method entailed several complexities.

First, researchers of protest events have typically collected data from major newspapers. Newspaper accounts are reliable for studying events of general public consequence (Davenport, Soule, and Armstrong 2011; Earl et al. 2004; Koopmans 1998), but not sufficient for inventorying a movement's full tactical repertoire. Newspapers will only report a small, newsworthy subset of activities. Much of the activity of a social movement never reaches the attention of the general media (Taylor and Van Dyke 2004: 268). For this reason, I gathered data from what I call "activism narratives," meaning reports about protest activities written by the participants and circulated through movement publications. These reports include a broader range of happenings and thus are better suited to document a movement's repertoire. The merits of using activism narratives are relative, since such narratives will also be incomplete and reflect particular biases within the movement community. As further discussed later, for instance, Falun Gong narratives almost never mention fundraising, whereas fundraising is commonly mentioned in one Minyun source. This difference partly reflects what activists actually did, since Falun Gong doctrine strongly discourages asking for donations, but also reflects what activists consider acceptable to narrate.

A second complexity in comparing the movements according to activism narratives was finding analogous sources. Collecting activism narratives for the Falun Gong diaspora movement was relatively easy. The primary Falun Gong website, Minghui, aimed from its beginning to collect and disseminate participants' accounts of their own public activism. The website keeps an archive, sorted by topic, of all its postings. The "diaspora news" section of the website includes thousands of activist-authored, Chinese-language narratives about protest activities done in diaspora. The two-year period examined here includes 8,796 such postings. Since coding all of these articles would have been too labor intensive, a random sample of 535 articles (~6 percent) was selected for coding.[1] Of these coded articles, 367 contained information about diaspora collective action events that met coding requirements.

Collecting analogous data on Minyun was, by contrast, challenging, one reason being that the 1989 democracy movement occurred before the Internet revolution. Ideally, one should compare sets of activism narratives that use the same form of media, and thereby control for the effect of media form on content. Although this was not possible, I was fortunate that one source was available that bears some resemblance to the Falun Gong data. During the 1989 era, Chinese foreign students used an international network of computers available at research universities to communicate and coordinate collective action through two electronic forums. These digital forums allowed overseas Minyun participants to share news quickly without the expense of the telephone or delay of the mail (Yang 2003, 2009:28–29, 159). During the Tiananmen protest period, at least

---

[1] All 8,796 article titles were entered into a spreadsheet, then SPSS was used to randomly select a sample of 6 percent. That percent was based on estimates of how long it would take to code each article, resources available, and what number would be large enough to allow for valid inferences.

one of the two China-focused electronic newsgroups in existence, Social Culture China, briefly became the most heavily trafficked of all digital forums (Ståhle and Uimonen 1989b: xxxv). Transcripts of these electronic communications were later published in two volumes as *Electronic Mail on China* (Ståhle and Uimonen 1989a) and covered six months of Minyun activism. The transcripts have the merit of being similar to the Falun Gong web-based communications. The Minyun electronic communications were user generated, cost and editing were minimal, and reach was instantaneous and global. Unfortunately, the transcripts of electronic Minyun communication only cover six months and were edited for publication in ways that may distort the picture of events collected from the data. Worse still, original source materials appear to have been lost.[2] In order to take advantage of the transcripts, but also correct for shortcomings in the source, I also used two Minyun print journals as sources of data covering the entire time period. The Minyun data is therefore a composite of different sources. Although this is not ideal, it still offers the best view we have on what the 1989-era Minyun tactical repertoire actually was.

The Minyun journals I used as sources were both published in diaspora (New York and Paris) and covered the dates February 1989 to January 1991. The journals were *China Spring* (1989–1991) and *Minzhu zhongguo* (1990–1991). The print journals contained monthly summaries of movement events as well as feature articles that referred to specific events. The Minyun print journals do not have the merit of approximating the form of the Falun Gong source, but they cover the full two-year period, are also in Chinese, and have not been edited by third-party publishers. Because of structural differences in the electronic versus print sources, the data sets were not combined and are treated separately. All three types of sources are further discussed in the Appendix. For clarity, I will refer to the data from the Minyun print journals as "In-print Minyun" and the electronic communication transcripts as "Online Minyun."

The final complexity I note concerns the time periods I compared. I collected data from two years of each movement's respective diaspora mobilization, starting in February 1989 for the Minyun and in October 2000 for the Falun Gong. In making this selection, I aimed to cover the entire arc of the 1989-era Minyun movement overseas, from emergence to dissipation. For the Falun Gong, I also aimed to cover the

---

[2] According to personal communications with the original publisher.

movement's early phase, but data from the earliest months were not available. I instead chose a window of time overlapping with the consequential events of January 2001, including the escalation of protest in China, the self-immolation incident, and the post-immolation turn towards lower-risk activism within China.

CODING REPERTOIRES

Working with a small team of research assistants, I read and coded the sources for information on diaspora protest events, defined as protest actions involving more than one participant and occurring outside of mainland China, but including Hong Kong, Macau, and Taiwan. Because all sources were published in the USA, Canada, or France, the data present a view of Minyun and Falun Gong mobilization from Chinese media in the global West. For each event, we coded time, place, and tactics. In order to maximize observations on the means of collective action, every protest practice mentioned in each event narrative was coded separately. One activist narrative might describe several forms of action, such as marching, gathering signatures for a petition, and fundraising. In that case, the event was coded containing three forms of action. If that same event narrative mentioned marching in several places, "marching" was only counted once for that event. Each form of action was counted only once per event, but any event could contain several forms of action. When the same data source included multiple accounts of a single event, the various narratives were cross-checked and combined so that the event and its related tactics only appeared once in the data. Codes were created inductively according to terms used in the articles. The system was flexible in that if any new collective action type was attempted and not already on the list of possible codes, it was simply added. We used the software called Program for Computer-Assisted Coding of Events (PC-ACE) to record and verify data (Franzosi 2009: 89–96).[3]

To help the reader appreciate the sources and coding, I provide example activism narratives from each of three sources, Online Minyun, Inprint Minyun, and Minghui. At the end of each example, I indicate which codes were given to each narrative. In selecting these examples, I picked texts to represent at least one style of text in the source from which it was drawn, recognizing that each source has a variety of genres of texts that met the criteria for coding. For the Falun Gong source, I chose an example that does not explicitly emphasize political activism (although examples

---

[3] Including both input–output and semantic coherence verification (Franzosi 2009: 89–96).

of explicit political activism are common in the data). Instead, I chose an example that demonstrates coding collective actions that appeared in the data, but focused on religious themes more than political ones.

Online Minyun Example: (source language: English)

Subject: Chinese People's Relief Trust established in South Florida!!!!!!!!!!!!!!!!!!

Date: 11 Jun 1989 16:49:15 GMT

We, Chinese students in South Florida community, including students from University of Miami, Florida International University and Florida Atlantic University have initiated and materialized the establishment of "Chinese People's Relief Trust" through legal procedures. The sole purpose of this Trust is to provide humanitarian assistance to those common people in China as consequence of recent and ongoing violence.

Hereby, we ask for your aids to extend this effort by spreading the news, coordinating the donations in your areas to this Trust, and so on. As Trustees, we have legal responsibilities for achieving the goal of the Trust by providing the money to the right hands. Although we are fully aware of the difficulties ahead, we are determined to achieve our goal. We already have connections with people in China, and any information on the reliable channels are deeply appreciated.

Please feel free to contact the Trustees listed below, or direct your messages to me on this bulletin board, as soon as possible.

Posted below are the press release of the Trust and a letter from Governor Bob Martinez of Florida.[4] (Ståhle and Uimonen 1989c: 153)

Codes for this activism narrative were: Date: 6/11/1989; Place: unspecified, Florida, USA; Action Repertoire: Public collective statement, Create organization, and Fundraising.

The next example comes from the June 1989 issue of *China Spring* (pp. 31–32). This excerpt is from a larger article about collective actions by overseas Chinese students in support of the student protests in China. The events described in the article all took place on April 29, 1989.

In-print Minyun Example: (source language: Chinese, translated by author)

(Chicago) Three hundred foreign students from mainland China, coming from more than ten schools in the American midwest, on the afternoon of the same day [April 29], demonstrated in front of the Chinese consulate of

---

[4] I have not reproduced these contents for the sample.

Chicago. They called out their support for the democracy movement of mainland students, and also called for the CCP to respect basic rights as stipulated in the constitution, to officially recognize the legality of the Student Solidarity Union, and to not use violence to repress the student movement.

Overseas students held placards with slogans like, "Human Rights are Not a Crime," "Support the Student Movement," and "The Only Future for China is in Democratic Reform of the Political System." Students formed an orderly circle along Chicago's busy Michigan Avenue and loudly chanted "Democracy" and "Freedom." It was a moving scene.

The demonstrating students had printed many fliers, which they distributed to those watching along the streets; they also set up a donations box for collecting funds to send to China to help the Student Solidarity Union to publish a journal that can be an independent voice. In order to insure the orderliness of the demonstrating students, the organizers of this action, Wang Shenglin and Li Sanyuan, carried walkie-talkies and a megaphone, so the entire demonstration process was quite well organized.

Four students representing the demonstrators – Wang Shenglin (Northwestern University), Liu Xiucai (University of Wisconsin), Lu Jianping (University of Chicago), and Wang Songlin (University of Kentucky) – received permission to enter the consulate and deliver to the CCP an open letter from the Chinese Student Solidarity Union North America Chapter and declarations from students of each school. At the same time, they talked with Consulate General Counselor Zhang Nian for almost an hour.

At 5 o'clock, overseas Chinese students who participated in the demonstration promised to return to the University of Chicago campus to discuss detailed problems in the founding of the Chinese Student Solidarity Union North America Chapter.

Codes for this activism narrative were: Date: 4/29/1989; Place: Chicago, Illinois, USA; Action Repertoire: march/rally/demonstration, open letter/petition, leafleting, public collective statement, fundraising, and public meeting.

Falun Gong (Minghui) Example (source language: Chinese, translated by author)[5]

Record of Our Spreading the Dharma in Shiprock City, New Mexico

Author: A Practitioner in America

I heard from a Spanish-speaking practitioner that every year in early October in the city of Shiprock, New Mexico, there is a large-scale parade and gathering put on by Native Americans. A huge number of

[5] "*Xinmoxige Jianshicheng hongfa jishi*" (An account of *hongfa* in Shiprock, New Mexico), published on October 11, 2001 and retrieved on May 7, 2012, from www.minghui.org.

people attend. This year's event was to be on October 6. This kind of large gathering is a perfect opportunity to spread the Dharma [*hongfa*] and clarify the truth [*jiangqing zhenxiang*]. Shiprock is about seven or eight hours' drive from Denver. Although it is a bit far, we thought of how the Master has said, "Everything in the world came for this Dafa" (from "Teaching the Fa at the Washington, D.C. International Fa Conference"). We realized, isn't this the perfect chance to bring the Dafa to Native Americans? Is this not a chance that has been arranged for us to make merit? Therefore, we absolutely had to go. So, we practitioners in Denver started preparing right away. We quickly printed 10,000 flyers. By using every connection we could, we succeeded in registering a float in the parade.

The number of practitioners who could actually go were not many, so all together we only had eight. These eight included one four-year-old, a six-year-old, and one senior who was over 60. The day before leaving, we asked again for help from Colorado practitioners. One female disciple from Phoenix, after helping with *hongfa* in Roswell, New Mexico, heard that we needed help, so she drove by herself six or seven hours to come help us.

When we finally arrived [in Shiprock] after 10 o'clock at night, all of the hotels were completely full, so we had to spend the night in the car. The early morning was very cold. The children woke up freezing. The disciple from Phoenix didn't even have a sleeping bag, so she spent the whole night freezing in the car. Then there were four disciples who only arrived in town at four a.m. and just had a few hours to sleep. We all felt miserable, but thought of the Master's words, "Difficulty leads to merit; difficulty, this is a good chance to accumulate merit" (from the Dharma Talk at the 2001 Experience Sharing Conference in Canada). Everyone determined to overcome their suffering and "help the Master's world mission," to not waste the opportunity provided to us by the Master, and live up to our predetermined vows.

The parade was the biggest regional parade we had ever seen. The line of floats was so long, it stretched farther than we could see. There were so many Native Americans on both sides of the road, visible for three or four miles. We entered our car into the parade convoy and the remaining six Dafa disciples, who were arduously toting thousands of Dafa flyers, distributed the flyers to people in the crowds. Each disciple was very earnest, striving to give a flyer to every single person. One disciple would call out to people, "This is the most valuable thing you will get in your life. Please take this flyer and don't miss this great opportunity." One after another, people would look over curiously while spontaneously reaching out their hands to take a flyer. Our float car was the only car in the parade that had no connection to Native American culture, so many people carefully read the Falun Dafa banner and also frequently came and took one of the fliers we distributed from the car.

After more than four hours, none of us had had a drop of water or bite of food. Each disciple was very exhausted. One woman had not eaten anything for 24 hours. But everyone was feeling very happy because we had distributed more than 7,000 fliers, which would bring the Dafa to many people and cause many people be saved.

After the parade, we also went to the local library and left two copies of the book *Falun Gong* and some fliers. Then, finally, we set out on the road home to Colorado.

Codes for this activism narrative were: Date: 10/6/2001; Place: Shiprock, New Mexico, USA; Action Repertoire: march/rally/demonstration and leafleting.

One limitation in this coding method was that the action repertoire codes do not tell us about the scale of the protests described. Many (but not all) of the Falun Gong actions, as in the example text, involved a small number of Falun Gong participants exploiting (relatively) local opportunities for collective action. By contrast, many of the Minyun activism narratives recount larger events with more people. The Chicago demonstration in the In-print Minyun example mentions 300 participants, which is much more than the eight – including two children! – described in the Falun Gong narrative. The Online Minyun example does not quantify the number of students involved, which is a reason that we did not code the tactical repertoire data according to the number of participants. Such data is frequently omitted. As a consequence, findings presented here only depict differences in how activists protested, not differences in the scale of participation.

FINDINGS

The first question I address with this data is, where were the movements most active in diaspora? These sources indicate that both movements were busiest in North America and Western Europe, as seen in Table 1. In total, the Minyun literature reported events in twenty-six different countries, whereas the Falun Gong sample reported events in forty-one countries. Since the Falun Gong data is a small sample of the total number of sources, the true Falun Gong geographic diffusion of events in this period was greater still. Nevertheless, the center of gravity for both movements was the USA and Canada. Tables 2 and 3 show the most common tactics we counted in the Minyun data for the in-print sources and online sources, respectively. The percentage shown is percent of all the recorded actions in each source (absolute counts are in in brackets).[6] In total, roughly 60 percent of the action

---

[6] Since the narrative of a single event can mention more than one form of action, counts are not mutually exclusive relative to events. On average, Falun Gong narratives mention more forms of action per event than Minyun accounts. The ratio of action form to event, defined by

TABLE I *Geographic distribution of protest actions as a percentage of source data*

Region	Falun Gong: % (number)	In-print Minyun: % (number)	Online Minyun: % (number)
North America	44 (207)	45 (196)	75 (291)
Western Europe	25 (117)	38 (165)	15 (59)
Hong Kong, Macao, and Taiwan	12 (58)	6 (27)	3 (10)
Australia and New Zealand	8 (37)	3 (13)	2 (9)
Other Asian Pacific countries	5 (24)	2 (7)	2 (7)
Eastern Europe and Russia	3 (16)	2 (9)	0 (0)
Other	1 (7)	0 (0)	0 (0)
Unspecified	1 (6)	4 (19)	3 (12)
Total	100 (472)	100 (436)	100 (388)

Note: Events in this table are defined by unique time and place. Because a single protest event can contain multiple forms of actions, total counts in Table 1 do not agree with those in Tables 2, 3, and 4.

TABLE 2 *Most common In-print Minyun collective actions*

Rank	Action Form	Percentage (number) n=531
1	Conference or roundtable	19.4 (103)
2	March, rally, or demonstration	13.4 (71)
3	Public collective statement	13.4 (71)
4	Petition or open letter	8.3 (44)
5	Formal lecture	7.5 (40)
	Total listed	62 (329)

forms mentioned by In-print Minyun and Online Minyun are constituted by only six activities. These are: (1) formal conferences or roundtable discussions, usually held on university campuses; (2) marches, rallies, or protest demonstrations; (3) making public collective statements, which were issued to

distinct time and place, are as follows: Falun Gong = 1.97; Online Minyun = 1.24; and In-print Minyun = 1.19. The higher ratio for Falun Gong means that Falun Gong narrative conditions encouraged more detail and/or that more forms of action occurred at events.

TABLE 3 *Most common Online Minyun collective actions*

Rank	Action Form	Percentage (number) n=518
1	Petition or open letter	21 (106)
2	March, rally, or demonstration	16 (81)
3	Public collective statement	13 (69)
4	Public meeting	12 (60)
5	Fundraising	11 (57)
	Total listed	73 (373)

the press; (4) distribution of petitions or open letters among movement constituents; (5) formal lectures, which involved publicly advertised events in which a public figure spoke to an audience; and (6) public meetings, in which (usually) students and scholars met on campuses to discuss events, form organizations, draft and issue public statements, and/or organize marches and demonstrations. In addition to these six actions that account for 60 percent of all actions mentioned in both sources, the Online Minyun table also includes "fundraising," which accounts for an additional 11 percent of the total tactical repertoire. In fundraising, participants sought money from friends, colleagues, institutions and Chinatown businesses. Money was collected to send to protestors in China, either as cash or as equipment such as fax machines.

The two Minyun sources display quantitative and qualitative differences. Figure 7 shows event counts over time for the Minyun movement, differentiated by source.

The six months of digital Online Minyun data, which unfolded in real time, captured many more events than the In-print Minyun data for that period. Because the electronic communications were not edited publications but were the actual communications between activists, they are more inclusive than the print journal sources. The arcs of both counts are similar for the six months of overlap.

One difference between the two sources, as seen in Figure 8, is that the online source portrays a more confrontational movement than the print media. In-print Minyun sources emphasized actions like formal conferences, whereas Online Minyun emphasized disruptive forms of action, like marches and petitions, but also activist meetings and fundraising.

TABLE 4 *Most common Falun Gong collective actions*

Rank	Action Form	Percentage (number) n=941
1	Public display of Falun Gong exercises	13.8 (130)
2	Leafleting and street canvassing	13.5 (127)
3	Petition or open letter	9.1 (86)
4	March, rally, or demonstration	7.5 (71)
5	Dressing uniformly	6.0 (56)
6	Collective prayer	4.9 (46)
7	Public outreach event	4.6 (43)
	Total listed	59.4 (559)

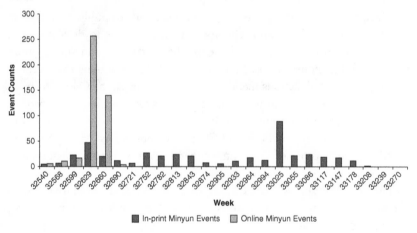

FIGURE 7 Minyun event counts
Sources: *China Spring, Minzhu Zhongguo*, and Ståhle and Uimonen (1989c)

The latter two are the kinds of backstage events that would not be mentioned in journal publications, so the differences between the sources are easily reconciled in reference to the media forms: activists used the electronic bulletin boards to coordinate actions, not to report as public media. In spite of the differences, it should be noted that the repertoires described by each set of data are not that far apart and each contribute to a more complete picture of the overall Minyun diaspora repertoire.

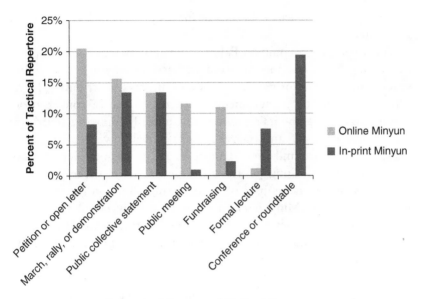

FIGURE 8 In-print Minyun and Online Minyun compared

Table 4 displays the dominant forms of Falun Gong collective action reported in the website postings.

The list contains most of the actions listed in the Minyun data as well as several additional ones. The most frequent Falun Gong "tactic" – doing the Falun Gong self-cultivation exercises as a public performance – does not immediately look political at all. This activity was coded as "public display of Falun Gong exercises" whenever it was intended by activists to be observed by the public. The tactic was typically combined with making political claims about the persecution of the Falun Gong through signs posted nearby and/or through a division of labor in which some activists did the exercises and others handed out fliers and tried to engage the bystander public in conversations. For example, I observed practitioners in 2015 doing "public display of Falun Gong exercises" in front of the iconic Taipei 101 tower in Taiwan, a common destination for tourists from mainland China. When I observed the event, they divided labor so that some did the ritual exercises while others canvassed the public, especially targeting Chinese tourists.[7] In the data source, completely non-political religious gatherings to do the self-cultivation exercises were also sometimes mentioned. These were coded

---

[7] Observation and interviews, Taipei, Taiwan, September 2013 and May 2015.

as a separate form of action, accounting for 2.9 percent (27 instances) of the repertoire.

The second most common Falun Gong activity was "leafleting and canvassing." This action involved activists occupying some public space, setting up information tables and displays, distributing literature, and trying to engage members of the public in conversations about Falun Gong and its repression in China. The next two entries in the table, petitions and marches, respectively, were also in the Minyun repertoire and their definitions are the same. Nevertheless, I note that Falun Gong petitions entailed activists gathering signatures from strangers, as part of a canvassing effort on the street, for instance, whereas Minyun petitions were usually circulated among student and scholar networks. Minyun petitions dominate the Online Minyun data because electronic mail was an important means by which petitions were distributed.

Three more Falun Gong activities in Table 3 need to be defined. "Dressing uniformly" refers to movement participants wearing coordinated clothes, like matching shirts bearing Falun Gong emblems. "Collective prayer" is, in these data, a specific Falun Gong form of coordinated prayer that began, at the behest of the religious leader, in May 2001. In collective prayer, referred to as "sending forth righteous thoughts" (*fa zhengnian*), all Falun Gong believers are supposed to engage in concentrated prayer four times a day. The appointed times vary by time zone so that the action is conducted in complete global simultaneity. Li Hongzhi preached that the prayers are a powerful tool in a cosmic battle between good and evil, with real-world consequences for the CCP.[8] Due to the politicized interpretation of the prayer ritual, I consider it part of the tactical repertoire. Finally, the last action falling within the 60 percent cutoff was "public outreach event." These are counts of instances when activists presented about Falun Gong to a formal audience, like at a college or in a municipal library. These were similar to leafleting and canvassing in that they also involved direct outreach to the bystander public and involved making political claims as well as religious proselytizing.

---

[8] Penny provides an especially vivid description of "sending forth righteous thoughts" (Penny 2008: 142–50).

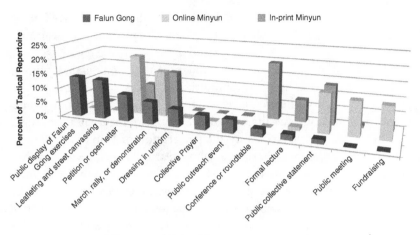

FIGURE 9 Minyun and Falun Gong protest repertoire compared

COMPARING THE MINYUN AND FALUN GONG TACTICAL REPERTOIRES

Figure 9 compares all of the action forms discussed earlier for each of the three sources, sorted by rank within the Falun Gong repertoire. The two movements shared some forms of action, but also differed in important ways. Both the Falun Gong diaspora and Minyun activists carried out marches and demonstrations, gathered signatures, submitted petitions, and made collective public statements. Following Tilly's notion of contentious repertoires being shared across populations, these commonalities fit our expectations since both emerged and operated in a wider shared context.

The two sets of repertoire also contain differences. First, I analyze routine Minyun practices that were absent in Falun Gong, and then do the same for routine Falun Gong practices that were absent in Minyun. Online Minyun commonly reported public, deliberative meetings, which were virtually absent from the Falun Gong repertoire. In practice, Minyun meetings involved PRC students and scholars on university campuses deliberating over what to do, drafting and issuing collective public statements, planning demonstrations, creating formal organizations, and coordinating fundraising to support student protestors in China. The Falun Gong data does not contain open and deliberative meetings. Falun Gong organizing usually involved local cells of activists creating and executing protest actions according to campaigns disseminated through the Minghui websites and Falun Gong social networks (Ownby 2008). In these smaller settings, practitioners reported to me deliberating with one another through an informal consensus that they referred to as "exchanging" (*jiaoliu*). Deliberation among practitioners certainly occurred, but not in ways that appeared in the repertoire data.[9]

Another difference between Minyun and Falun Gong is that Minyun participants engaged in much fundraising, whereas Falun Gong participants did not. This difference is related to the particular tactical dynamics between Falun Gong and the Chinese state. One of the accusations made by Chinese authorities to justify the persecution of Falun Gong is that Falun Gong leaders are charlatans who cheat followers of their money. Falun Gong activists deny the accusations. James Tong found little independent evidence supporting the government's claims (Tong 2002b). Nevertheless, a tactical consequence of the interactional dynamic is that Falun Gong participants have explicitly eschewed direct fundraising, since it would appear to give credence to the state's accusations. This is not to say that the Falun Gong fundraising and income generation have not occurred. Instead, whatever fundraising occurred did not surface in the website activism narratives.

Except for public meetings and fundraising, however, the Falun Gong repertoire contained all of the remaining major actions present in the Minyun repertoire, even if only as minor forms of action. In addition, the two most common Falun Gong collective action forms – public displays of Falun Gong exercises and leafleting, and street canvassing – were absent or barely present in the Minyun repertoire.[10]

As a nonreligious, political movement, Minyun of course did not contain distinctive religious or ritual content that could be publicly performed as part of a campaign to resist Chinese state propaganda. This first entry in the Falun Gong repertoire, along with other entries such as "collective prayer," is a politicization of sectarian religious practices. The deployment of religious activity in the service of making political claims represents a kind of action that is categorically different from any present in the Minyun repertoire.

The second most common Falun Gong activity, "leafleting and canvassing," also represents a categorically different form of action than any found in the Minyun repertoire. Falun Gong participants spent much

---

[9] Interviews, Taipei, Taiwan, September, 2015.
[10] Leafleting and canvassing appeared once in the Online Minyun data and five times in the In-print Minyun data, which is less than 1 percent of either data set. Public collective statements appeared thirteen times in the Falun Gong data, accounting for 1.4 percent of the data set.

more time and energy than Minyun activists in personal, face-to-face efforts to persuade members of the wider public of the merits of their cause. Although it is not surprising that only the Falun Gong repertoire contained a religious category of action, it is less clear why Minyun activists did not engage in one-to-one efforts to persuade and seek support from publics. Instead of canvassing efforts, much of the Minyun tactical repertoire was dominated by *en masse* activities – petitions, marches, conferences, lectures, issuing collective statements, and public meetings. This means that typical Minyun protest performances were organized public events like conferences and lectures, to which the public might be invited, or were large collective actions (marches, rallies, or meetings). Minyun activists commonly made public claims *en masse* ("public collective statements") and those claims were usually intended for the generic public audience rather than for individuals. Minyun activists spent virtually no time trying to personally enlist support through persuasive outreach to individual strangers, with the exception of fundraising. By contrast, Falun Gong activists spent much of their time trying to persuade whatever public was at hand to hear their claims.

What significance do these differences have for understanding how the two movements differently took up the technology of the modern social movement, that is, for their comparative degrees of "social movement-ness"? How do we account for these different mobilizing patterns? Where do they come from and what are the implications of comparing the "social movement-ness" of each case?

REPERTOIRES, PUBLICS, AND THE SOCIAL MOVEMENT

In my preliminary discussion of the concept of tactical repertoire, I stated that a repertoire is not just what people do, but what they know how and expect to do; it is a generalized cultural model for protest shared within a community of actors. In these two tactical repertoires, we can discern two quite different models, each of which reflects different expectations about the role of the public relative to the protestors. Falun Gong practitioners emphatically sought the attention and support of publics wherever they undertook "clarifying truth." Often, this was carried out in personal, one-to-one efforts at persuasion. True, due to their cultural marginality as a new religious movement, these efforts have not been widely successful. Yet, the efforts still reveal a particular orientation toward the general public operating within the movement. By contrast, democracy activists enacted performances of protest that emphasized collectively voicing opposition to homeland authorities. Publics, in this cultural model, mattered to activists as audience for their demonstrations and their media images, but activists did not call upon publics to become directly involved.

How challengers orient themselves to the public is not universal, but historically contingent. Modern social movements, as discussed in Chapter 1, are sustained campaigns involving an interactive field of players. In Tilly's description, a "campaign always links at least three parties," the protesters who challenge authorities, the authorities who are targeted, and "a public of some kind." Publics, he noted, include "potential participants in future campaigns, citizens whose interests the campaign's outcome will affect, and spectators who learn something about the politics of their regime from the struggle, even if they do not participate" (Tilly 2008b: 120). We can also note that publics are the source of resources that challengers need to mobilize and, when elections can be shaped by the issue at stake, an important direct source of leverage against authorities.[11]

Seen in the long view of history, social movements were the result, in part, of vast historical changes, rooted in the emergence of parliaments, print capital, and democratization, that occurred between the eighteenth and twentieth centuries, led by North America, Britain, and Western Europe. Through these processes, publics gained increased representation and influence over the decisions of authorities (Tarrow 1998). As publics became more important to those in charge, public opinion became a source of leverage for those who wanted to challenge what authorities were doing. If one can get the public emphatically on one's side, one can shape election outcomes and other sources of influence. The increased importance of public opinion is a key reason that drama and performance, rather than instrumental battles of force, are central to modern protest (Alexander 2006, 2017). Challengers do not try to meet their goals by threatening authorities with damage or death or by directly seizing what they want, whether it is grain, gasoline, or territory (except symbolically, as in Occupy Wall Street). Challengers leverage public opinion against authorities by dramatizing social issues and thereby shaping public debate. The aim is to transform the indifferent public into indignant audiences who are willing to join activists in demanding change from authorities. Transforming public sympathy into action (e.g., getting donations of money or signatures on a petition, making phone calls to congress,

---

[11] The dilemma diaspora activists face regarding bystander publics who are not citizens of China will be discussed separately later.

or joining a march) is an essential step in the social movement process, a process that depends upon challengers orienting themselves to the public as a source of power and moral authority.

The Falun Gong's tactical repertoire was intensively oriented toward influencing and garnering the support of publics in every context in which activists operated. Canvassing, which dominated the tactical repertoires, were efforts to persuade and gain support in one-to-one outreach to publics both Chinese and non-Chinese. Practitioners sought very hard to transform the bystander public into indignant audiences who would sign petitions, write to authorities, denounce the CCP, publicly support Falun Gong, and so forth. The formal social relations linking activists, publics, and authorities accorded with the classic social movement model of protest.

In Minyun, participants aspired to make a social movement, but the social relations they enacted through their tactical repertoire did not emphasize transforming public opinion into political pressure through active support. Instead, Minyun protestors emphasized themselves as counter elites – students and scholars – in dyadic opposition to authorities. Publics were the audience for these protest performances, but activists did not target publics for persuasion, recruitment, and resources. The core social relations within the Minyun cultural model of protests only weakly conformed to the classic model. In regard to each movement's formal orientation towards publics, we can say that the Falun Gong had more "social movement-ness" than the Minyun.

MINYUN'S COLLECTIVE ACTION IN CHINA

Why did Minyun activism cast the bystander public into a passive role? There are a variety of potential answers, all with reasonable claim to part of the explanation. Let us first consider the question from the perspective of strategic rationality. One might conclude that, generally speaking, Chinese diaspora activists should not bother much with bystander publics. Such publics – like Americans walking past a Minyun demonstration in Chicago – have no standing or real stake relative to domestic Chinese politics. So, to invest efforts in garnering support from bystander publics in diaspora is a bad investment of precious resources. Although this reasoning makes sense, there are several reasons that it does not stand well as a historical explanation for the formation of the Minyun's tactical repertoire.

First, the question of how to engage the bystander publics in protest does not appear to have been central to debate among Minyun participants. Rather, the key debates were if and when to found an official opposition political party and whether or not violence was acceptable. To engage bystander publics or not was not the debate. Instead, orientation to the bystander public appears to have belonged to the habitual, "instinctual," or dispositional kind of culture that shapes social movements (Junker 2014b; Zhao 2010). Another problem with the strategic rationality explanation is that the Falun Gong faced the same dilemma relative to bystander publics as the Minyun, but made the opposite "choice": their tactical repertoire cast the bystander public into an active, participatory role. Like the Minyun, this outcome was not the result of strategic calculation but emerged in an organic way from preexisting scripts and taken-for-granted orientations.

Finally, the strategic rationality explanation suffers the weakness that it is probably wrong. Engaging the support of "overseas" publics can, in some cases, be used to pressure homeland regimes, usually through pressure on the politicians of the democracies where those diaspora publics reside (Keck and Sikkink 1998). Moreover, bystander publics are a potential conscience constituency (McCarthy and Zald 1977) who can provide resources like time, money, skills, and networks. In addition, the Falun Gong example suggests that efforts to enlist support from bystander publics may itself reinforce mobilization by giving participants concrete and meaningful tasks even when they are thinly spread out across many cities and countries.

Minyun's orientation on the public is probably better explained as a consequence of the model for protest that diaspora activists inherited from the protest context in China. There is wide agreement among scholars that the student movement of 1989 was deeply shaped by traditional Chinese culture (Esherick and Wasserstrom 1990; Pye 1990; Wasserstrom 1990; Yang 2009; Zhao 2001, 2010). Provocatively, Zhao Dingxin (Zhao 2000) has even argued that the 1989 movement was more traditional than its earlier pro-democracy predecessors of 1919 and 1935. How might the strong influence of traditional culture on Minyun help account for overseas Minyun's orientation to the public?

According to traditional status hierarchies, the relationship of Chinese intellectual elites to the wider public was far more elitist and hierarchical than the relations found in the social movement model. Many scholars during the 1989 era and since have criticized student protestors and Minyun leaders for elitism. Esherick and Wasserstrom, commenting on student discourse, stated that "the students seem to have read the *min* in *minzhu* [the *demo* in *democracy*] in a limited sense to refer not to the populace at large but mainly or exclusively to the educated elite of which they are part" (1990: 837). Chan and Unger (1990) criticized students for keeping "at arm's length" the workers who wanted to unite with students, criticized the liberal intelligentsia for actually favoring "new authoritarianism," and criticized exile leaders for neglecting the inclusion of social justice in the movement program. Zhao (2001, 2010) similarly critiqued the student leaders for operating in a "highly authoritarian manner" and abusing resources to enjoy privileges like good cigarettes and liquor.

Why was a movement for democracy carried out in a way so counter to its own ideals? One possible explanation is long-standing cultural tradition. Yang Guobin, for example, argued that Minyun's 1989-era cultural orientation on power and authority derived from Chinese "emperor-worship mentality" (Yang 2009: 85). He noted how, in imperial China, Confucian officials were supposed to act as the moral conscience of power and reprimand the imperial administration when justified. According to Yang, this tribune-like normative script for protest still pervaded Minyun activism of 1989. A different cultural explanation can be drawn from the 1989 movement's immediate context of patriarchal, authoritarian models of exercising power. As Zhao Dingxin notes, "Movements acting in an authoritarian regime are also likely to copy the culture of authoritarianism even though the movement is fighting for democracy or other lofty goals" (Zhao 2010: 45). Chapter 6 likewise noted the similarity between overseas Minyun organizational forms and the CCP. For one more example of Beijing students mimicking the CCP, note how student activists organized control of Tiananmen Square using a militaristic control structure. Chai Ling, leader of the hunger strikers, had the title of "Commander-in-chief of the Defend Tiananmen Headquarters" (*Baowei Tiananmen guang-chang zhihuibu zongzhihui*). Similarly, a leading diaspora figure of the 1989 Minyun movement[12] described to me how Minyun leaders were like "generals" who commanded "troops," that is, the protesting crowds. This particular Minyun leader lamented that in diaspora there were plenty of exiled "generals," but no "troops" to mobilize. Ironically, his lament unreflexively took for granted the authoritarian leadership structure implicit in his analysis. When we immerse ourselves in the logic of Minyun activism, we find ourselves a long way from the Falun Gong's

---

[12] Interview, New York, December 2, 2009.

ethic of activism, which called upon each person to find her or his own best way to "step forward."

Reducing Minyun's tactical repertoire to a reproduction of the traditional or authoritarian Chinese mind-set, however, is overly deterministic. After all, Falun Gong also grew out of Chinese culture, so why was it not also traditionalistic and authoritarian in its collective action form? Why did these particular elitist cultural patterns, and not some other aspects of the vast cosmos of Chinese experience and culture, become so influential at this juncture? Zhao, Esherick, and Wasserstrom have made separate, but mutually reinforcing arguments on this point. Zhao (2000, 2010) tackled this issue by arguing that traditional culture played such a formative role in 1989 precisely because China lacked a developed social movement sector and civil society. Zhao reasons that in societies lacking a social movement sector, protests will be spontaneous and poorly organized; as a result, how people protest will be more influenced by "habits and taken-for-granted routines" (2010: 41) than by strategic reasoning. Without social movement organizations planning, designing, and disciplining movements, protestors instead uncritically and haphazardly enact well-known cultural scripts, such as those disseminated through fiction and other media. Zhao cites the famous example of three students kneeling in supplication as remonstration of authorities during Hu Yaobang's state funeral. This act was not planned in advance, but protestors, officials, and publics all shared a common "schemata of interpretation" that allowed everyone to read the action as one of feudal-era remonstration. In Zhao's view, traditional, elitist culture dominated in Minyun because it was the moral script that most resonated with the wider publics. If a civil society had been established or mass media culture been more pluralistic, publics and protestors might have availed themselves of different shared "schemata" leading to different ways of protesting. In fact, Zhao argued that this was the case for the democracy protests of the Republican era, which is why the 1989 protests were more traditional than those in 1919.

Esherick and Wasserstrom's analysis of the 1989 protests was, on this point, similar to Zhao's, but also directly dealt with the question of relations between protestors and bystander publics. Like Zhao, they argue that because China lacked a civil society, the only way that people could protest was by spontaneously usurping public rituals as ad hoc political street theater. In these unruly performances, the bystander public became the performance's audience. Moreover, the boundaries between audience and performer were permeable. The audience often, and unpredictably, joined in the performance; students sometimes resisted such participation in order to maintain discipline and defend their movement's status as a student movement. Esherick and Wasserstrom's dramaturgical analysis suggests a richer interpretation of publics than I offered previously. Nevertheless, the way publics joined into political theater was quite different than the role of publics in the social movement model. Social movements intend bystander sympathy to be translated into resources and participation in campaigns that continue until the cause is won or lost. There was no mechanism in 1989 China to transform public sympathy either into sustained movement campaigns or into votes that could hold politicians accountable to public opinion. Publics mattered for the pro-democracy movement, but not in the same way that they do in a society that has a developed social movement sector where campaigns are possible.

A conclusion from all of this is that the absence of civil society and China's repressive context of 1989 helped produce Minyun's traditional, elitist repertoire. Without strong organizations to plan and execute strategic action, protesters improvised symbolism and tactics within the bounds of a widely shared culture, most of which was known through officially mediated filters. Widely shared culture included traditional motifs like scholars remonstrating emperors, Republican-era democracy protests, and authoritarian, patriarchal, or socialist models of authority.[13] Less visible, but still a part of the available culture, were shared expectations for the relationship between protestors and publics. These expectations did not include seeing the public as the source of resources and participation for sustained campaigns simply because such campaigns remained impossible.

This explanation for the elitist character of the Minyun tactical repertoire has an important implication for the comparison at the heart of this book. Not only does this explanation account for the strong influence of elitist, traditional culture in Minyun at that juncture in history, but the explanation also suggests that *any explicitly political movement* coming out of China during this era should have been poorly disposed in the diaspora to view bystander publics as a source of power and legitimacy. Politics in China simply did not, and

---

[13] The hunger strike, which had little Chinese precedent (Esherick and Wasserstrom 1990), somehow slipped into the mix, perhaps through Gandhi in India or media coverage about other anti-imperialist and anti-capitalist movements.

largely still does not, have a place for publics in a way analogous to the
ideal typical social movement. The institutional infrastructure of opposition campaigns and the accountability possible through electoral politics did not exist. For protestors, publics were audiences to perform to,
to make indignant, to bring to tears, to inspire to join in the performance, but not – and this is key – to mobilize as fellow campaigners,
fellow citizens, and fellow voters. If that is the case for protests coming
out of China in the late twentieth century, why did the Falun Gong see
the public so differently?

FALUN GONG'S COLLECTIVE ACTION IN CHINA

Falun Gong's religious movement culture provided a variety of possibilities for collective action that were unavailable to the Minyun. Falun Gong
participants knew and shared the common cultural forms from which the
1989 democracy movement fashioned its repertoire, but Falun Gong
practitioners also shared a subculture of qigong and of Falun Dafa in
particular. The previously mentioned tactical repertoire data showed that
Falun Gong protests contained two types of tactics that were absent from
Minyun. First were those tactics that were religious but deployed as part
of the protest repertoire. The most important of these was public performance of the Falun Gong self-cultivation exercises. The second type of
tactic mostly absent in the Minyun repertoire was efforts to persuade and
gain support from bystander publics and fellow Chinese in diaspora.
These efforts included canvassing, leafleting, and getting signatures for
petitions. More generally, the community's vast investments in creating
public media, like NTDTV and *The Epoch Times*, are also outgrowths of
this dimension of the movement's tactical repertoire.

Both these types of tactics evolved out of religious forms of collective
action that were central to Falun Gong from its earliest period. First,
publicly performing self-cultivation rituals was a convention of the qigong
craze throughout 1980s and 1990s China. Not only the Falun Gong, but
most qigong groups of the qigong craze era spread through people meeting in public parks to do the exercises together (Chen 1995, 2003; Palmer
2007). Those collective activities also functioned to display that particular
form of qigong to the public and attract recruits. The banning of Falun
Gong in China invested those conventional actions with new meanings.
To continue to do the exercises in public in China was a provocative
challenge to authority, which was met with immediate repression. Thus,
as described in Chapter 5, mainland Chinese protests continued to

emphasize being seen publicly as Falun Gong believers, but those displays primarily took the form of unfurling banners at Tiananmen Square and other locations. Overseas, public performances of self-cultivation exercises in the conventional form were stepped up. Listed here as the most common element in the tactical repertoire, Falun Gong activists used the self-cultivation rituals to demonstrate their moral standing and to gain attention from the public in an eye-catching way. Is it not a dramatic display to stand together with fellow meditators, arms raised and in still concentration, while the busy city jumbles on all around you? Practitioners made qigong into WUNC – what Tilly called displays of worthiness, unity, numbers and commitment.

Reaching out to canvas and persuade nearby publics has a similar history. As described in Chapter 5, during the Falun Gong's surge to popularity between 1992 and 1999, followers in China adopted a proselytizing-like practice called *hongfa*, or "spreading Dharma." *Hongfa* involved collectively entering public spaces, like city parks, to recruit new members through one-on-one conversations about the benefits of Falun Gong.[14] When Minghui editors called for activism on July 22, 1999, they did it by calling for increased *hongfa*. In the earlier sample activism narrative from Minghui, the narrator describes their activities at the Shiprock parade as *hongfa*. The canvassing documented in the Falun Gong repertoire data evolved as a result of politicizing *hongfa*, which eventually activists separately termed "clarifying truth." Activists had redeployed their familiar habits of proselytizing into defending the movement from persecution. From the Falun Gong's proselytizing tradition, activists simply shifted from religious to political persuasion. When Falun Gong was banned and activists in China mobilized defensively, both forms of action – publicly doing Falun Gong self-cultivation rituals and *hongfa* proselytizing – continued but picked up new urgency and new significations, first in China and then in diaspora.[15] What had been

---

[14] For a rich description of *hongfa*, see Ownby (2003b: 316–317). Ownby also makes the point that, technically speaking, Falun Gong practitioners do not believe in proselytizing: "[M]ost Falun Dafa practitioners believe that people are 'destined' (*you yuanfen*) either to be saved or not, and thus usually do not actively attempt to convert nonpractitioners – although they are always happy to welcome a newcomer into the fold"(2008: 140). For my discussion, I do not split these particular hairs. *Hongfa* aims to recruit new members to a religious community, so I regard it as a form of proselytizing.

[15] To be more precise, *hufa* (defending dharma) political defense of Falun Gong began in 1996 when the movement first became the object of repressive state interference; post-1999 *hufa* was initially an amplification of the earlier *hongfa* practices.

religious activity became civil disobedience in China and became routine protest activism overseas.

Cheris Chan's fieldwork captured early moments in Hong Kong when practitioners were wrestling with the new reality of the ban against Falun Gong and Li Hongzhi's disappearance (Chan 2013). Her description of a meeting on July 22, when practitioners first struggled to form a common reaction to the ban, shows that practitioners were not given instructions from any central offices in New York or elsewhere about how to respond. Furthermore, expectations were low that protest in Hong Kong could influence events in China. But there was also recognition that symbolic protest was worthwhile and even a moral imperative of being a practitioner. A male practitioner in his fifties argued against activism, saying, "It's useless to petition. They [the Chinese authorities] won't change their attitude." But a female practitioner in her forties responded that the instrumental effect of protest was not the only purpose of protest. "We have to show the public that we are still FLG [Falun Gong] learners! Show them our strong belief and faith!" Notice how the female practitioner emphasized the moral virtues of defending Falun Gong (*hufa*), particularly through displays to the public. Her logic expressed a model of relations between Falun Gong, the public, and authorities that had evolved through routinely doing self-cultivation exercises at public locations, *hongfa* proselytizing, and post-1996 *hufa* activism in China. After much debate and brainstorming, meeting participants concluded to stage a protest at the office representing Beijing in Hong Kong. Similar processes of grassroots debates, brainstorming, and activism planning also were taking place in North America (Chan 2004; Palmer 2003) and probably anywhere that Falun Gong was active.

I conclude from this analysis that the Falun Gong's tactical repertoire differed from that of the Minyun largely due to its preexisting cultural repertoire as a new religious movement. Most importantly, perhaps, was the way practitioners were already oriented towards persuading the public through proselytizing and public qigong displays. The scripts, habits, sensibilities, and expectations of proselytizing prefigured how Falun Gong reacted to state interference and persecution. Thus, religious movement culture shaped how Falun Gong oriented itself to the public in a way that, once political mobilization began overseas, activism overseas quickly embodied the triadic relations between challengers, authorities, and publics that are signature to the form of the modern social movement. Falun Gong had a way around the constraining limits of traditional and elite culture that had shaped the Minyun repertoire.

The comparison between the Minyun and Falun Gong tactical reper-toires exposes another ironic way that our social science expectations are defied by a close look at these cases together. The progressive democracy movement was in fact *more* constrained by traditional culture, including elitist, authoritarian, and patriarchal norms, than the new religious move-ment that has roots in Chinese tradition. Minyun activists aspired to realize a liberal and progressive Chinese modernity, but the materials from which they fashioned their efforts led them to reproduce forms of organization, authority, and relations to the wider public that were ill suited not just to protest mobilization in diaspora, but also to their own ideological purposes. By contrast, Falun Gong was a self-consciously "traditional" movement, aspiring to save "5,000 years of Chinese civili-zation" from the moral pollution of both modernity and the CCP. Nevertheless, Falun Gong more adroitly adapted its protest to the condi-tions of social movement activism because its proselytizing religious foundations predisposed practitioners to orient themselves to the public and to authorities in ways that were structurally congenial to the social movement model. The neo-traditional salvational society, and not the democracy movement, contained in its cultural makeup a kind of DNA for treating the public as a source of legitimacy, power, and resources for sustained campaigns.

8

Clarifying Truth and Saving Souls

Throughout this book, I have been exploring the question of what the relationship is between Falun Gong as a religious movement and its mobilization as a protest movement. Chapter 7 argued that the community's background in *hongfa* proselytizing facilitated practitioners to readily adopt the social movement model of protest. But the relationship between Falun Gong as a religious movement and its politicization is not limited to this one dimension. The full story, which I attempt to sketch in this chapter, is more complex. It was not only that religious culture, i.e., proselytizing, influenced how Falun Gong became politicized. Politicization also changed the religious culture of Falun Gong. Moreover, a dynamic interaction unfolded between the religious and the political. Much of that interaction can be observed through the ideological work that took place to reconcile politicization, the Falun Gong belief system, and the charismatic authority of Li Hongzhi.

The arc of the history goes like this: Falun Gong originally was not political. Conflict with the state as early as 1996 prompted proselytizing routines to become protest mobilization, eventually leading to full-blown transnational protest campaigns starting in 1999. In the arena of religious ideology, practitioners needed to make sense of how their experiences of "stepping out," or public activism, related to the Falun Gong belief system. Ideological innovation occurred to justify activism and, in effect, made "clarifying truth" central to the ultimate religious purposes of the community. In order to reach spiritual "consummation" one had to become a political activist. This was a development unimaginable in 1994, for instance.

Yet, this change was not the end of the interactive dynamic between religion and politicization. A second, somewhat de-politicizing social process also occurred subsequent to the first. As described in Chapter 5, over the first decade of protest campaigning, Falun Gong became increasingly focused on saving the souls of the public in the style of a millenarian religious movement. Activism changed from primarily making claims on homeland authorities and stopping the persecution to instead focus on saving ordinary people before they were "weeded out" in the struggle between the cosmic forces of good and evil. This new ideological development in the movement preserved the community's emphasis on "stepping out" and public activism, which had come out of Falun Gong's protest mobilization. At the same time, it also made such activism less directly political. Activism gradually became less intent on changing the homeland authorities in Beijing and more focused on saving souls. A process of de-politicization had begun.

The millenarian turn in Falun Gong was highly consequential, and useful, for sustaining mobilization and preserving Li Hongzhi's personal authority. Spiritualizing the protest movement as soteriological drama symbolically refocused the movement on Li and thus buttressed his authority. Recall that Li had disappeared during the entire year when activists forged the transnational protest movement. Li appears to have played no direct role in the huge mobilization that took over so many practitioners' lives. Even when he was absent, many followers expressed hopes during the first months of protest that Li would appear in Beijing to save practitioners in China (Chan 2013). But he did not play that or any other direct role. His standing as a leader was, at best, ambiguous at that time. Li's irrelevance to his own movement posed a legitimacy problem that millenarianism helped to solve. In the spiritualized framing of millenarianism, even when Li was absent, he remained the movement's main hero, because he was actually active in the cosmic arena battling the forces of evil. As a millenarian interpretation came to dominate Falun Gong activism, "clarifying truth" came to be understood as less about politics and more about supporting the great soteriological mission of Master Li.

Spiritualizing contention also had the consequence of justifying, in effect, endless mobilization. Activism that failed to change the authorities in Beijing could still be interpreted as rational and satisfying because it succeeded in the invisible theater of salvation. Moreover, the millenarian turn allowed for more feel-good mobilization, like promoting Chinese music, rather than the grim work of publicizing torture and alleged organ harvesting. In fact, Li explicitly linked Shen Yun Performing Arts to millenarianism by claiming the artistic performances were more effective at saving the public than conventional political activism. Thus, as Shen Yun emerged to be the focus of diaspora activism, the movement became less political even as it preserved the orientation to the public that was forged during the period of politicization. To summarize the historical trajectory in total, I conclude that even though religion, especially prose-lytizing, helped propel Falun Gong into its progressive form of protest activism and transnational politicization, it was also religion, here in the form of charismatic authority and millenarianism, that undid the progressive possibilities in such activism.

WHAT IS "POLITICAL" ANYWAY?

Many scholars have recognized that Falun Gong was a religious movement that became political (Bell and Boas 2003; Chan 2004; Chen, Abbasi, and Chen 2010; McDonald 2006; Ownby 2008; Penny 2012; Thornton 2002). Scholarship that is primarily focused on religion has noted how politicization led to greater romanticization of Li's charisma, amplified apocalyptic rhetoric, and encouraged millenarian fervor within the global Falun Gong community (Burgdoff 2003; Chan 2004, 2013; Ownby 2003b, 2008; Palmer 2003; Penny 2012). Scholarship (and journalism) that has focused on protest and human rights (Johnson 2004; Perry 2001; Tong 2002b, 2009) has either ignored the religious contents of the movement or has examined how the religious structure and contents of the movement contributed to effective mobilization (Chen, Abbasi, and Chen 2010; Fisher 2003; Lowe 2003; McDonald 2006). This chapter aims to bring these two different perspectives together and parse out the interactive dynamics between religion and politics for Falun Gong over time. To do so, however, requires that I clarify how the word "political" pertains to this case.

In general, Falun Gong practitioners, and Li Hongzhi in particular, have rejected the notion that Falun Gong is in any way political (or is even a "social movement"). So when I speak of "politicization," my terminology belongs to the viewpoint of the observer (etic) rather than to that of those observed (emic). The word "politics," according to the Falun Gong perspective, connotes power-hungry people scheming and jockeying for influence, status, resources, and control. Politics are sordid, dangerous, and morally corrupting. This view on politics, like Falun Gong's view on "religion" (see Chapter 4), makes sense in the mainland Chinese context, where being political is commonly regarded with both cynicism and fear.

As Falun Gong practitioners started "defending the Fa" (*hufa*), they needed to reconcile their belief system with their emergent protest repertoire of "clarifying truth." In this process, activists had to reckon with the specter of whether the movement was becoming "political." From our etic point of view as social science observers, protesting authorities is a politically consequential act, so the movement was becoming politicized. But from the emic point of view of participants, it was not political because Falun Gong was not aiming to gain worldly power or engage in the sordid, Machiavellian struggles of ordinary people. This distinction will be important in the later analysis, because Li Hongzhi directly discussed the question of being political. Thus, for clarity, I will refer to "clarifying truth" not as political, but as "public activism." In that way, we can speak of Falun Gong as reconciling its public activism with its religious ideology. Also, we can observe how its public activism, over time, shifted emphasis from making claims that bore on authorities in China to activism that emphasized the soteriological project of saving souls.

FROM REDEMPTION TO PUBLIC ACTIVISM

The purpose of being a practitioner in the early days of Falun Gong was never to resist repression, the state, or to commit one's life to "clarifying truth." The original purposes of Falun Gong practice were fundamentally personal and individualistic in nature. These included such aims as physical and spiritual health, healing from disease and trauma, freedom from pain and anxiety, moral improvement, inner peace, belief in a meaningful orientation on daily life and the world, and having more peaceful and fulfilling personal relations with one's family and friends. After a decade of repression, the purposes of being a practitioner had changed. Top among the moral imperatives for any practitioner became saving everyone everywhere from providential punishment by "clarifying truth." This change in the goal-orientation of the movement is entwined with Falun Gong's turn towards public activism. It evolved from a movement focused on an individual-level object of change, i.e., personal redemption through cultivation, to a movement focused on a supra-individual object of change, i.e., saving members of the public through "clarifying truth." This transformation in the ultimate concern of the community neatly fits a morphology of social movements developed by anthropologist David Aberle (1982 [1966]), so I will rely upon his framework to conceptualize the changes that Falun Gong underwent.

Aberle's typology of social movements classifies them by two dimensions. First, how much change does a movement promise or seek? Some movements seek total, revolutionary change, whereas others seek partial, reformist change. New religious movements like Falun Gong frequently are oriented towards a totalistic change, like total change of the self through salvation or total change of the social community through a utopian communal project. The second question asked by Aberle's typology is, what is the movement's object of change? Does it seek to change the individual participant or does it seek to change some kind of supra-individual entity, like society as a whole? Aberle labels the individualist type "redemptive," because the object of change is some kind of redemption of the personal self. Redemptive movements promote such goals as nirvana, salvation, or a good rebirth. Falun Gong's version of this was consummation. A second type of movement is, according to Aberle, socially "transformative," because such movements seek to transform a supra-individual object, like society. Transformative movements promote such goals as missionary conversion, communalistic seclusion, creating heaven on earth through good works, or communist utopia. In response to repression, Falun Gong created the supra-individual goal of stopping the persecution. This goal, however, was reformist rather than revolutionary. Later, Falun Gong's supra-individual goal became saving souls everywhere, which was transcendental and revolutionary.

Aberle further theorized that these categorizations of "reformist/revolutionary" and "redemptive/transformative" are dynamic: historical circumstances can prompt a popular movement to evolve from one form to another. A redemptive movement, like Falun Gong, when confronted with political interference or some other environmental challenge, can become a transformative movement. Aberle's typology is useful for seeing connections between the politicization of Falun Gong and how leadership reconciled ideology with public activism. Central to this relationship is the shift in ultimate concerns from redemptive to supra-individual and transformative. Nevertheless, I hasten to add a critical disclaimer: Aberle's taxonomy is "ideal typical" in Weber's sense, meaning that the reality is more complex and messy than the intellectually constructed types. In fact, Falun Gong never abandoned the individual person as an object of change, but instead subsumed the goal of personal redemption within the larger supra-individual mission of saving others.

To trace how personal redemption and public activism intersected, I divide the history of politicization into four periods and track the evolution of ideology relative to public activism. My sources on ideology are public statements made by Li Hongzhi and the Minghui website editors, who were anonymous, but sanctioned by Li as authoritative. Although activists led the movement in terms of inventing its protest repertoire, Li Hongzhi and Minghui editors were the authorities who ultimately navigated how to reconcile the tension between the competing values of personal redemption and public activism. The Appendix explains my use of sources under the section heading "Minghui Website."

1996–1999: Competing Values Emerge

To begin, let us return to Falun Gong's initial contentious encounter with the state, as described in Chapter 5. The first state interventions against Falun Gong occurred in the summer of 1996, when the *Guangming Daily* criticized Li Hongzhi's book in June and other newspapers followed suit. In response, thousands of Falun Gong practitioners defended Falun Gong's reputation through letter-writing campaigns. The letter-writing campaigns appear to have been a spontaneous, ad hoc response initiated by ordinary practitioners. Shortly thereafter, on August 28, 1996, Li posted Internet commentary that praised such activism and invested it with religious signification. Li's commentary emphasized that "activism to defend Falungong" was "an essential aspect of *Dafa* cultivation." He declared that state interference was "a test" for movement followers: those that rose up to defend Falun Gong would be proven to be the true disciples; those who "feared for their reputation or personal interest," were apathetic, or "spread baseless rumors" would be exposed as the false disciples (Palmer 2007: 249–250).

David Palmer attributes Falun Gong's militant political activism to this period and especially to Li's equation of religious "cultivation" with public activism (Palmer 2007: 252). Ownby, by contrast, argues that Palmer overemphasizes the importance of Li's comments and that cultivation and political action were still considered to be quite different by practitioners (Ownby 2008: 169). What we can be confident about, however, is that the endorsement of activism by Li raised the specter of competing values between cultivation, which aimed at personal redemption, and public activism, which aimed at a social change mission. That this doctrinal conflict immediately mattered to the community can be inferred by the next statement issued by Li, which followed a week later. Titled "Cultivation is Not Political," this statement stressed that "cultivators" should keep away from worldly affairs. Li said, "other than doing a good job with his work, a cultivator will not be interested in politics or political power of any sort; failing this, he absolutely isn't my disciple" (Li 2001: 32). Li did not address how practitioners were to adjudicate between the competing values of personal redemption and public activism.

Falun Gong activists in China engaged in about 300 protest events between 1996 and April 1999 (see Chapter 5). During this period, Li repeatedly emphasized the public defense of Falun Gong, while simultaneously stressing the importance of "cultivation" as a non-political act. For example, in June 1998, activists conducted an especially provocative demonstration, which was an eight-day sit-in at the Beijing television (BTV) station. Ownby points out that BTV ought to "be considered the rough equivalent of the *People's Daily* as a mouthpiece for state policy" (Ownby 2008: 169). Shortly after this event, Li issued a related commentary in which he tried, on the one hand, to affirm the activism of the Beijing protestors, but, on the other hand, to emphasize that that others should not follow suit. Furthermore, he stressed that "Dafa should not get involved in politics ... Dafa is not taught for these purposes, but rather for cultivation practice" (Li 2001: 48–49). In summary, between 1996 and 1999, the supra-individual goal of defending Falun Gong through public activism emerged as a new duty of practitioners, but its precise relationship to personal redemption was not clarified.

April–July 1999: Self-Cultivation as Paramount Goal

The Falun Gong protests in Tianjin and Beijing in April 1999 marked the start of the next period. In the three months between the April protests near Zhongnanhai and the July 21 ban on Falun Gong, the CCP investigated, planned, and positioned resources in preparation for repression. From the perspective of Falun Gong, these months were an opaque limbo period. State agencies sent mixed signals, such as conducting arrests of leaders in some places while officially denying state preparations for repression (Tong 2009: 32–51). By mid-June at the latest, Falun Gong activists in China and overseas were already aware of the ominous direction of state activity, but were unsure about what was coming (Tong 2009: 41). In diaspora, there were three Falun Gong convocations of practitioners between April and July at which Li Hongzhi made speeches and took questions from practitioners. Li also conducted several interviews with international media and issued several public statements that were distributed through the Minghui website. During this time, the official, if anonymous, editors of the Minghui website also posted several statements in regard to the escalating conflict with the state.

From these public statements, I synthesize two points: First, Li's position on public activism during this period was consistent with the ambiguous position described during the 1996–1999 period. He endorsed some kind of public activism while also emphasizing that Falun Gong is ultimately about personal cultivation and, thus, his disciples should not engage in the political issues of "ordinary people" (*changren*). Second, during this time, Li and the Minghui editors consistently diagnosed the conflict with the government in reformist, rather than revolutionary, terms. The problem, they stated, was caused only by the typical factional struggles of Chinese politics, into which Falun Gong had been unfairly dragged, and, in particular, there were only a few bad individuals in the government who were deliberately misleading leaders about Falun Gong in order to gain power and influence.

Both of these points were made by Li on various occasions, but for illustration I cite Li's June 13, 1999 public statement posted on Minghui to his global community of followers, which reads (in full):

> The things that have transpired in recent times have already done serious harm to the many Falun Dafa students. At the same time, they have also tarnished the nation's image severely. With regard to the information the students have on how the relevant regions or the relevant departments have directly or covertly interfered with and disrupted Falun Gong students' practicing, and with regard to the situation in which some people used their power to stir up a Falun Gong "incident," to put a broad segment of the people and government in opposition to one another, and to thereby gain politically, the students can report these cases through the normal channels to different levels of the government or to the country's leaders.
>
> But we are cultivators [*xiulian de ren*]. Don't get involved in politics and don't let the events that occurred a little while ago disrupt you. Calm your minds, resume your normal practice [*zhengchang liangong*] and Fa-study, be diligent and cultivate solidly, and continually improve yourselves. (Li 2005: 8)

Notice how Li, at least here, both endorsed activism, but also sought to tone it down. Practitioners should only "report" matters "through normal channels" to recognized authorities. Then they should get back to their primary work of personal cultivation and "improving" themselves. The statement indicated that the community's ultimate religious concern was to remain focused on the individualist goal of self-cultivation. The words, "but we are cultivators," emphasize that self-redemption still defined Falun Gong's collective identity and purpose. Such a statement, of which there are several other equally clear examples from the speeches Li made in May and June, nicely exemplifies the "redemptive" orientation of ultimate Falun Gong concerns on the eve of repression.

Second, this statement also diagnostically framed the conflict with the government by saying it was merely "political," in the cynical sense that the Chinese term (*zhengzhi*) more strongly connotes. Li used the term to connote selfish struggle over power by individuals who aimed to "gain politically" by using "their power to stir up a Falun Gong 'incident,' to put a broad segment of the people and government in opposition to one another." In the period between April 25 and July 22, this reformist interpretation of Falun Gong's conflict with the government was the standard framing offered by Li and Minghui editors. In interviews in May, Li blamed the conflict entirely on the Public Security Bureau and, within that bureau, "only one or two individuals" who "were doing bad deeds using their power" (WOIPFG 1999). In a June 16 interview with the Japanese media, Li specifically blamed Luo Gan (Penny 2012: 65), who was one of the politburo members that met with Falun Gong representatives on April 25. Similarly, on July 15, the Minghui website posted an editorial (only in Chinese) for its Falun Gong readership. The editorial diagnosed the conflict this way:

Some high level leaders in the Chinese government have uncritically believed the deliberately damaging rumors created by an extremely small group of plotters. Alas, this has made state propaganda agencies foment [anti-Falun Gong] public opinion and every level of government engage in severe repression, [making] for a swift and violent momentum to vigorously destroy the practice environment of mainland practitioners throughout China. This extremely small group of people has plotted to turn black into white, to fabricate lies out of thin air, to deliberately confuse one thing with another in order to trick those party, government and military leaders and the broad masses who do not yet understand the truth of Falun Gong.[1]

As these examples demonstrate, when diagnosing conflict, Falun Gong authorities on the eve of repression framed the contention within the context of sordid worldly politics. There were, however, alternative interpretations that also appeared, which framed the conflict most broadly in terms of cosmological tests of the devout. Such framing can be seen, for example, in one of Li's last public statements before he disappeared from view at the end of July. On that occasion, he claimed that Falun Gong was

---

[1] Retrieved on July 11, 2010, from www.minghui.org/mh/articles/1999/7/15/10656.html; my translation.

humanity's "last hope" and that one wrong thought might lead a person to being "weeded out" by cosmic history (Li 2005: 11). Such cosmological claims were in keeping with Li's overall theology, which had deployed such millenarian logic since the early years of the movement. Nevertheless, it is significant that in July 1999, his millenarian claims were still quite general, and he had not yet clearly specified the cosmological dimensions of Falun Gong's conflict with the Chinese government. Later statements, after June 2000, make stronger and much more specific claims about how the contention was a result of a larger cosmological battle.

July 1999–June 2000: From the Self to the "Environment"

After July 1999, Li Hongzhi disappeared from public view and issued no statements until June 2000.[2] The Minghui website, however, issued at least seventeen authoritative editorial statements (all but one in Chinese only) between its inception and when Li once again took up the public podium.[3] In these statements, we can trace the beginnings of the shift in ultimate concerns and in the framing of contention.

On July 19, the Central Committee of the CCP nationally distributed an internal party notice of the ban on Falun Gong. On July 20, public security agencies began mass arrests and the ban was officially publicized on July 21. The CCP internal notice was leaked before the official ban was publicized and Falun Gong activists in China immediately launched dozens of protests around the country (Tong 2009: 52–53). In North America, the Minghui editorial board issued a public statement on July 19, titled "Awaken!"[4] The statement pled for Chinese state leadership to not repress Falun Gong. "Awaken!" reiterated the reformist, this-worldly diagnosis of the conflict between Falun Gong and the state. It asserted that the conflict was caused only by an extremely small group of corrupt and power-hungry politicians. The statement's rhetorical thrust was that leaders should "awaken" to reason and desist from the plans to repress Falun Gong, which would bring harm to China. The argument included both pragmatic and vaguely cosmological justifications.

---

[2] Li posted a photo of himself in meditation on the Minghui website on January 19, 2000. In May, he released a short poem for distribution through Minghui. His first substantial public statement appeared on Minghui on June 16, 2000.
[3] Li may have also been involved in writing the editorial postings or directing their content.
[4] Retrieved on July 11, 2010, from www.minghui.org/mh/articles/1999/7/19/8621.html.

On July 21, the day that the CCP officially interrupted all television broadcasting in China to announce the ban on Falun Gong (Tong 2009: 52), the Minghui editors posted a "call to action"-style manifesto for the Chinese Falun Gong readership.[5] The statement's title, "The Environment," portended the shift in ultimate concerns from changing the private self to changing the social world, or "environment," in which the self resides. The gist of the editorial was that personal cultivation occurs in an "environment," which inevitably produces "tribulations, frustrations, and setbacks." Such difficulties, it stated, are not external to the cultivation process, but are in fact the objects on which cultivation practice occurs; therefore, given that Falun Gong is under attack in this world, the correct route to cultivation success is in taking action in the world to defend Falun Gong. The editorial read, in part:

How do [we] defend, protect, and harmonize with the Fa [Dharma]? How do [we] step out this way? This is the road which cultivators must take. This is crucial for us.

The essay ends as follows:

Every disciple must quickly and bravely stand up to protect the Fa. Disciples in China and overseas must mobilize to protect the Fa. Urban and rural disciples all must rise up to protect the Fa. [It will] make us bravely advance our spiritual cultivation and, in the midst of disaster, make us keep our steady pace, thoroughly steeled, into consummation.

Personal cultivation is linked in these passages to public activism through the notion of the "environment" as the source of trial and an object upon which cultivation is exercised. Whereas the June 13, 1999 statement by Li displayed a more restrained endorsement of public activism, such as reporting incidents to officials "through the normal channels," the Minghui editorial far more vigorously endorsed general mobilization. The shifting of rhetorical emphasis from personal cultivation to the world within which cultivation occurs signaled how movement discourse was shifting away from the personal self and toward the supra-individual public world, defined here in the abstract language of "the environment." This transition fits Aberle's typology.

The next Minghui editorials related to the framing of contention were published in late August. The first was in English and the second in Chinese.[6] Both texts were statements issued for the general public and

---

[5] Retrieved on July 11, 2010, from www.minghui.org/mh/articles/1999/7/21/3087.html.
[6] See "*Heping shangfang heli hefa; qiangshi zuiming tian qian ren yuan*" (Heaven and Man will decry when peaceful petitions, legitimate and lawful, are made into criminal offenses),

both criticized the "show trials" that were conducted against Falun Gong members who had been arrested in July. The emphasis of the English text is on human rights and rule of law. The Chinese text also emphasizes human rights and rule of law, but additionally provides a substantive defense of Falun Gong, saying that the movement is beneficial for society. The Chinese text contains a few phrases indicating millenarian notions, but the overall text is a this-worldly argument decrying the repression. Later, on December 26, the Minghui editorial board again spoke out against the criminal prosecution of Falun Gong leaders in China.[7] As in the August statements, the text emphasized rule of law.

On January 19, 2000, Minghui editors posted a photo of Li Hongzhi alone in sun-drenched meditation, sitting perched on an austere cliff face overlooking an unnamed rocky canyon.[8] The photo reassured followers about Li's safety and continued leadership, but it was enigmatic about where he was and what he was doing. The posting of the photo also confirmed to the general Falun Gong audience that Minghui editors were in some kind of direct communication with Li. After the posting of the photo, the authoritative discourse from Minghui editors took a strongly other-worldly turn, and on February 23, Minghui editors posted a sort of cosmological manifesto.[9] The statement compared the persecution of Falun Gong to the persecution of Christianity in the fourth century and to the persecution of Buddhism after Shakyamuni's lifetime, embedding all of these persecutions into a cosmology of good and evil facing off in history:

In history, with the appearance of any great faith has followed huge tribulations for humanity. How much more true this must be for the Falun Buddha Dharma! Falun Buddha Dharma is the principle of the entire universe; it is the true Dharma, which has never before been told. It is impossible for such a great and orthodox Dharma teaching to enter the world without corresponding tribulations. To cultivate in the grand orthodox Dharma not only requires a special practice

retrieved on July 11, 2010, from www.minghui.org/mh/articles/1999/8/27/5230.html and "*Huyu guoji shehui bangzhu zhongguo heping jiejue falun gong wenti [yingwen]*" (Call for International Society to Help China Peacefully Resolve the Falun Gong Problem [English]), retrieved on July 11, 2010, from www.minghui.org/mh/articles/1999/8/25/4956.html.
[7] Retrieved on July 11, 2010, from www.minghui.org/mh/articles/1999/12/26/4545.html.
[8] As of this writing (2017), the photo is on the homepage of Mingui.org.
[9] "*Bianji bu: zai jie zai li, yongmeng jingjin*" (Editorial Office: Persistent efforts, bravely advance). Retrieved on July 11, 2010, from www.minghui.org/mh/articles/2000/2/23/2043.html; my translation.

environment, but inevitably also demands that [cultivators] endure the sufferings and difficulties of the purifying battle between good and evil.

The editorial then described the protest efforts and sufferings that Falun Gong followers had experienced since the movement was banned. The summary concluded by saying that the persecution was a rich cultivation "environment" through which "true practitioners" advance quickly:

> In the nearly ten months since April of last year, the Great Dharma has created a rich cultivation environment for all true cultivators of the different conditions and different levels. This has allowed all committed and true cultivators to quickly soar and fleetly progress towards consummation in a brief span of time. At the same time, the cultivation experiences and continued progress of many practitioners within this extraordinary environment have further demonstrated the greatness and completeness of the Falun Buddha Dharma.

Notice, again, the term "environment," which is the concept linking the self-oriented language of "cultivation" to political mobilization. In the essay's final paragraph, the authors use the term "cultivation" in a way that breaks from its constraints as an individual-level activity. The term "cultivation" is de-individualized and portrayed as a supra-individual force, like an "army" that advances through history:

> At this extraordinary historical juncture, when the East will dawn in the darkest hour, when tribulations are still present, when the test is still ongoing, when cultivation progress not seen for ten thousand years is still unfolding, the mighty cultivation army is firmly advancing.

Equally as important as what this text says is what it does not say. The framing of movement activism is entirely cosmological, if not millenarian; there is no mention of human rights or rule of law, and no references to a small band of corrupt plotters influencing the state. From February 2000 onward, official framing from Minghui editors and Li Hongzhi himself consistently emphasized cosmological and millenarian interpretations. Rule of law and human rights framings disappeared.[10]

---

[10] There are, however, several Falun Gong-oriented formal organizations, like the Falun Dafa Information Center, dedicated to resisting the repression by advancing criticisms based on human rights and rule of law. However, the materials produced by these organizations are oriented primarily for non-Falun Gong audiences.

After June 2000: Social Movement as Millenarian Mission

On June 16, 2000, Li Hongzhi issued through Minghui his first substantive statement since returning to public life, titled "Towards Consummation."[11] The statement began to revise the meaning of "consummation" from a personal, individual-level goal to a supra-individual, transformative goal, as theorized by Aberle. Li's statement claimed that the persecution was a test organized by cosmic forces and that its severity was proportional to the purity of the "Great Dharma," or Dafa, taught by Li. In the next excerpt, Li claimed that the current period in history is characterized by an extraordinary cosmological process called *zhengfa*, which is translated alternatively as either to "validate" or "rectify" the Dharma, or as "Fa-rectification:"

What is unfolding at present was arranged long ago in history. Those disciples who have stepped forward to validate the Fa [Dharma] in the face of pressure are magnificent. ... Those disciples who have come through the comprehensive and most rigorous tests have laid a rock-solid foundation for Dafa in this world, have displayed in the human world the true manifestation of Dafa, and at the same time have consummated their own most magnificent positions. The evil will soon be completely eliminated, the vile ones in the human world will receive due retribution, and sins can no longer be allowed.

The statement claims that during the "period of validating Fa" (*zhengfa shiqi*), the end of history is near: those practitioners who are being tested might still reach consummation if they hang on, whereas those who fail will be damned. Li's interpretive framing of events is entirely cosmological. The statement foments salvational anxiety and coaches followers to continue resistance.

In July, Minghui editors issued a statement[12] that followed Li's spiritualizing lead. The statement claimed that the CCP and the Chinese state were only the pawns of evil cosmological forces:

Since July, 1999, the evil beings in the universe ... have been controlling those lives within the Three Realms that are about to be eliminated, and especially the dregs of humanity, to bring damage to Dafa and to Dafa disciples. Looking at its manifestation on a human level, it is the Chinese Communist Party that is inflicting damage on the Dafa with government action by mobilizing police,

[11] *"Zouxiang yuanman"* (Towards consummation), retrieved on January 7, 2009, from www.minghui.org/mh/fenlei/217/zip.html; my translation.
[12] "Our Compassionate and Venerable Master," retrieved on July 11, 2010, from www.clearwisdom.net/html/articles/2000/7/19/7647.html; Minghui translation.

military troops, radio broadcast stations, television stations, diplomacy, and secret agents to spread their destruction far and wide.

The Minghui editors went on to claim that the cosmological forces had been in direct battle with Li Hongzhi during his absence and that the struggle, which Li won, caused his hair to whiten and his person to suffer in other untold ways:

In the face of this kind of vicious and dangerous situation, Master gathered together all of this karma and the huge physical elements composed of evil. Master used his own body to bear them, and, at the same time, to destroy these huge evil elements. Because these evil beings had gathered such an enormous amount of karma and venomous elements, it took Master nine months to destroy it using his powerful energy potency. However, because the evil elements and the karma were so immense, they also caused serious damage to Master's body. Master's hair has turned gray ... Such a compassionate and venerable Master – in the course of rectification of the Fa [*zhengfa*], Master has exhausted everything for sentient beings.

This editorial accomplished several tasks: it explained why Li was absent for nine months when Falun Gong was under attack, why he remained central to the movement even though he had disappeared, and, finally, why his health visibly degraded during that time. All these claims depended on the cosmological battle interpretation of repression, on spiritualizing the contentious politics. Furthermore, this statement says that the invisible, unseen, but more real battle had been won already and that events here on earth are only the mopping-up processes that unfold before Dafa's eventual complete triumph.

In August and September, two more Minghui statements were issued which pushed further, in Aberle's terminology, the shift in ultimate concern from personal redemption to supra-individual transformation. The first editorial, titled "The Purpose of Stepping Forward is to Validate Dafa," is a commentary about the ultimate aims of Falun Gong participation in public politics. Published on August 8 in both Chinese and English,[13] it begins by quoting the June 16, 2000 Li Hongzhi passage cited earlier. Then it argues that "personal cultivation," which Li Hongzhi only a year earlier had clearly emphasized was the ultimate concern of practitioners, was not as important during "these times" of cosmological culmination. Instead, the most important activity, argued the text, was

---

[13] "Editorial: The Purpose of Stepping Forward is to Validate Dafa," retrieved on July 11, 2010, from www.clearwisdom.net/html/articles/2000/8/11/7351.html; Minghui translation.

"validating the Great Dharma" (*zhengshi dafa*), which, in practice, meant sharing the "truth" about Falun Gong with more and more people:

> Under such cosmic changes, and at this historical moment when "the wicked and evil will soon be eliminated," *whether one can go beyond the boundary of individual cultivation* [*chaoyue geren de xiulian*], whether one can truly adopt the standpoint of the Fa, and whether one can give the highest priority to validating Dafa and letting more people know the truth about Falun Gong, and thus fulfill one's historic duties in the process of promoting and safeguarding the Fa, have become of utmost importance for every practitioner in China and overseas ... *In a very broad sense, our safeguarding and promoting the Fa is an act of selflessness and being compassionate to all sentient lives.* (Italics added for emphasis)

In directly comparing this text to the pre-repression June 13, 1999 statement by Li, we can see that what Li referred to as "ordinary" or "standard" cultivation (*zhengchang liangong*) is redefined in this text as "individual cultivation" and is labeled as something mundane and limited, to be surpassed ("go beyond" *chaoyue*). Furthermore, the statement extols acting on behalf of "all sentient lives," which is an orientation of action toward supra-individual aims, rather than only for one's individual redemption. Thus, the reorientation of ultimate religious concerns from the self to the social, as Aberle theorized, appears to be a major discursive task of the text.

In late September, a second Minghui editorial goes further still in articulating the idea that current times call for a greater, supra-individual form of "cultivation" than that practiced before persecution. The editorial goes so far as to forge a new term for this kind of cultivation, calling it "Dharma rectification cultivation" (*zhengfa xiulian*):

> Fa [Dharma] rectification cultivation practice [*zhengfa xiulian*] is not the same as regular cultivation practice. The process of Fa rectification cultivation practice is to melt together with the Fa rectification, and thus, only because of this can one become a true particle of the universal Dafa after one completes cultivation. Regular cultivation practice [*putong xiulian*], on the other hand, is cultivation practice of human beings and has nothing to do with Fa rectification (i.e. the Fa rectifying the heavens and the earth) .... only by participating in this process of Fa rectification can one cultivate to become joined together with the Fa, otherwise one will have nothing to do with this occurrence of Fa rectification cultivation and then it simply cannot be considered a consummation attained through Fa rectification cultivation.[14]

---

[14] "Advance towards Consummation through Cultivation within Fa Rectification," retrieved on July 11, 2010, from www.clearwisdom.net/html/articles/2000/9/26/8138 .html; Minghui translation.

In spite of the idiosyncratic terminology, the major discursive point here is clear: the non-political, self-oriented "cultivation," which Li emphasized in June 1999, is redefined as merely "regular self-cultivation" (*putong xiulian*), appropriate only to cosmologically mundane times. The greater shared mission of the Falun Gong community, and the only "true" goal of Falun Gong during these extraordinary times when history is nearing its conclusion, is to carry out "Dharma rectification cultivation." The new form of "cultivation" aimed to "melt" the individual practitioner into the supra-individual "universal Dafa." Dharma rectification cultivation still included the standard Falun Gong exercises and studying Li's teachings, but now also included a mandate to "validate Fa" in the public world. Under the new thinking, the theological contradiction between "cultivation" and public activism, which had caused Li's ambivalence between 1996 and 1999, was erased. Protest movement activism became fully embraced as a core activity of Falun Gong faith.

The redefinition of "cultivation" within Falun Gong discourse marks the shift in ultimate concerns from the personal to the supra-individual. The means of "cultivation" expanded beyond studying teachings and doing exercises to also include the Falun Gong protest repertoire, which was referred by such terms as "stepping out," "clarifying truth," and "validating Fa." The shift occurred, as we saw, along with an evolution of the movement's interpretation of the conflict. Instead of Falun Gong being viewed as a pawn in a back room political struggle, the new framing portrayed the Falun Gong in an "end of days" battle of good versus evil and one in which Li Hongzhi played the central, but hidden, role.

Reframing repression and protest as only the visible manifestation of a hidden cosmic battle was instrumental for Li to immunize himself against at least three logical challenges to his charismatic leadership. First, cosmological framing accounted for the existence of the repression within a framework that gave Li a messianic role, thus reinforcing his authority; second, his hidden battle against the forces of evil provided an account for why he was absent during the first year of protest mobilization; and, third, the framing also provided, as we will see later, an account for why he did not play any role in the invention of Falun Gong's protest repertoire. Was Li truly at risk of having his charismatic authority undermined by these three sources of cognitive dissonance? Although I cannot answer this question, we know that his disappearance just when contention intensified mattered to practitioners. Cheris Chan's fieldwork in 1999 (Chan 2013) shows that Li's disappearance was a source of intense cognitive dissonance for core followers. She documented how practitioners neutralized that dissonance through romanticizing Li's charisma much in the same way Li did for himself when he reappeared and advanced a cosmological interpretation of events.

Spiritualizing Falun Gong's protest efforts also helped Li account for his lack of leadership in the formation of Falun Gong's tactical repertoire of "clarifying truth." On December 9, 2000, in Ann Arbor, Michigan, Li dealt directly with the problem of followers spontaneously launching a protest movement without his being in charge. Li claimed that since political persecution was a cosmological "test" leading to salvation or punishment, he had to assure the test's validity by withdrawing himself from directing his followers. To quote from Li himself:

During this [Fa rectification] process, the students encountered numerous specific problems and many difficulties. At first they didn't know how to deal with them. Later on, they gradually came to understand, and through trial and error they figured out what to do. I didn't say anything, especially during that time period, because the test wouldn't count if I were to speak (...)

I also wanted to see how my disciples – those magnificent gods who will reach consummation in the future – would act in the midst of this catastrophic tribulation ... But every step you've taken amidst the tribulation has been done on your own. I didn't say a word. Overall, you were able to take a really righteous path. Although not everyone's thoughts have been one hundred percent correct, what's displayed in all that you've ultimately done is magnificent, for Master wasn't around then. Those beings who have caused this tribulation for us – those old beings – are in admiration, speechless, when it comes to this. Whether it's what was supposed to be done or what was supposed to be endured, you have come through nobly, righteously, and remarkably (...)

During this one year, in your clarifying the truth, in the process of your cultivation, and in the process of your safeguarding the Fa, there have been all kinds of tribulations and you've encountered all kinds of difficulties. Relying on your own thinking and decisions, you've made it through. Master hasn't done all this in vain. Whatever Master has done for you was worth it![15]

Read critically, the statements can be seen as an effort by Li to neutralize any disconfirmation of his charisma resulting from his not taking the helm when the political contention went into high gear. But in Li's effort to reconsolidate authority for himself, he also powerfully amplified the existing moral imperative incumbent on practitioners to individually take initiative and act in public politics. Following Li's logic, a practitioner must not wait for instructions from the leader, but instead must independently "step out" into the public and take action. Failing to

---

[15] See "Teaching the Fa at the Great Lakes Fa Conference in North America" retrieved on June 18, 2018, from http://en.minghui.org/html/articles/2000/12/23/9114.html.

act on one's own independent initiative means failing the cosmic test and thereby missing the opportunity for salvation.

By finding a way to take credit for the political activism generated by his followers when he was out of public view, Li ironically reinforced the proto-democratic potentiality of Falun Gong activism. According to his doctrine, every individual must exercise her or his own moral authority to decide when and how to act in the public world on matters of political conse-quence. Rather than brainwashing the obedient drones of a charismatic leader, as anti-Falun Gong propaganda suggest, Li's ideology went in the opposite direction when it came to public activism. Herein lies perhaps the most subtle proto-democratic potential of the Falun Gong movement, even though millenarianism eventually undermined its fulfillment. As a movement, Falun Gong provided the cultural ideals, social context, and incentives for members to forge a new kind of political subjecthood, a new kind of activist personality that elevated the sovereignty of the individual conscience relative to state authority. To be a practitioner, one had to make personal choices and action in the public sphere to defend divine truth and sectarian community life against the corrupt, profane state. The way that this religious movement amplified the autonomy of individual moral sovereignty echoes how Max Weber and others argued that Protestantism forged the subjective conscience of the modern democratic citizen. I will return to this interesting theme in the final chapter.

SAVING SOULS

These innovations in doctrine all pointed toward a new goal orientation for the religious movement, which Li called "saving" people's souls (*jiudu, jiuren*). The particular way in which Li formulated the notion of saving others from 2000 onwards was not only emblematic of the shift in the movement's ultimate goals, but was also shaped by and reinforced the public activism that followers had innovated on their own. Although it is tempting to see "saving" as a purely soteriological and non-political endeavor, unrelated to social movement activism, that would be incorrect. After Li returned to public, he defined "saving" in a way that directly implied making claims on public authorities and communicating social movement framing to the non-Falun Gong public, both of which are central to the definition of a social movement.

To appreciate this meaning of "saving," it is helpful to contrast how Li discussed "saving others" before repression and after his year-long silence. Li had been referring to his saving others since at least 1995

(Penny 2012). Before July 1999, Li had frequently spoken of his own ability to "save" people and also taught that when followers proselytized for Falun Gong, they were helping Li save people. "Saving" in this sense was roughly consistent with the evangelical Christian notion of saving souls; it referred to religious recruitment and conversion. Li emphasized during this period that when ordinary practitioners helped him to "save others," it was a *secondary* task to their own "cultivation." In May 1999, in New Zealand, for instance, a practitioner asked Li about balance between proselytizing and individual cultivation. Li's answer:

Elevating your own cultivation is still the most important thing. If you have extra time and you can help others gain the way [convert to Falun Gong], then this is also one of the best things you can do.[16]

By contrast, consider how Li emphasized the activity of saving others in his first post-seclusion public appearance, which was to an audience of about 800 in October 2000 in San Francisco.[17] In this new formulation, he equated the activity of "saving others" not with religious proselytizing, as it had been before, but with the protest repertoire that had been improvised by ordinary followers when Li was absent. Li also began at this time to emphasize saving others as a paramount religious goal. In particular, Li said that "clarifying truth" "saves" non-Falun Gong practitioners from doom by helping them understand the truth about Falun Gong:

Do you all understand? During the time when the evil enveloped the earth, many people were fooled by the venomous fabrications and deceitful lies, and they had hatred toward Dafa and my disciples. Those people have been doomed to be weeded out in the future. Yet even so, by having clarified the truth, we've allowed them to know the facts and get rid of their previous views and evil thoughts. It's very likely they will be saved. (*Applause*) Our clarifying the truth to the world isn't any sort of political struggle, nor is it doing things to address certain matters. I'm telling you that this is your mercy, and you are truly saving future people! (*Applause*) If those people's thoughts don't turn around, think about it, they're done for. I think you should, as a student, a cultivator, do these things from the perspective of mercy, too. Inform people of the truth, tell them about it – this is also rescuing people.[18]

---

[16] Retrieved from http://gb.falundafa.org/chigb/newzland.htm on October 2, 2018. Another example of Li's discounting the centrality of the role of practitioners in "saving" others can be seen in the May 21, 1996 posting called "Don't Make Wild Statements" (Li 2001: 23).

[17] The audience estimate comes from *"Falun Dafa dashiji nianjian"* (A chronicle of major events of Falun Dafa), retrieved on April 26, 2011, from http://zhengjian.org.

[18] I edited the Falun Gong translation for clarity and fidelity. Retrieved on July 11, 2010, from http://en.minghui.org/html/articles/2000/11/5/9115.html and www.minghui.org/mh/articles/2000/11/3/106.html.

Despite Li's insistence that "clarifying truth" was not a political activity, the consequence of this redefinition of "saving others" was to equate "saving" with the core social movement activities of making public claims that bear on the interests of authorities and communicating movement framing to the wider public.[19] According to Li, when "ordinary" people understand Falun Gong's contentious situation in terms favorable to the movement, they will be protected from the providential punishment that inevitably follows even passive alignment with the "forces of evil." Therefore, "saving" activism, as in the Shiprock activism narrative translated in Chapter 7, was religious, but strongly overlapped with conventional social movement activism. It emphasized ordinary people reaching out to members of the public to persuade them about a matter of public concern (i.e., the persecution of Falun Gong). Apocalyptic rhetoric, religious mission, and political repression interacted to facilitate and strengthen the community's adoption of public activism.

In my field research, which started well after this period, I repeatedly heard from Falun Gong practitioners about the importance of "saving" others. For instance, in July 2007, in Tokyo, an older female Chinese activist told me how she made phone calls every day to China trying to convince people to formally renounce any affiliation with the CCP. She asked me if I knew why she spent her time this way. Still a novice to Falun Gong subculture, I answered naively that the campaign aimed to undermine the influence of the Communist party. She emphatically declared that I did not understand the movement. The reason for the campaign was to "save" people: "We want to save people. God is going to destroy the CCP and we are trying to get as many people out as we can before that happens."[20] Similarly, in August 2010, I interviewed a participant in a Falun Gong vigil in front of a Chinese consulate in Los Angeles. The daily vigil, I was told, had occurred every day on which the consulate had been open since the year 2000. Like the informant in Tokyo, the interviewee explicitly emphasized to me that her primary motivation for activism was to "save people" (*jiuren*).[21] Similar comments were made to me during an interview with a representative of the Falun Gong newspaper, *The Epoch Times*.[22] All of these respondents

---

[19] These are two standard aspects of social movements as defined by the political process and contentious politics perspectives (Benford and Snow 2000; McAdam, Tarrow, and Tilly 2001; Tarrow 2011; Tilly 2008a).

[20] Interview, Tokyo, July 29, 2007.

[21] Interview, Los Angeles, August 24, 2010.

[22] Interview, Los Angeles, August 28, 2010.

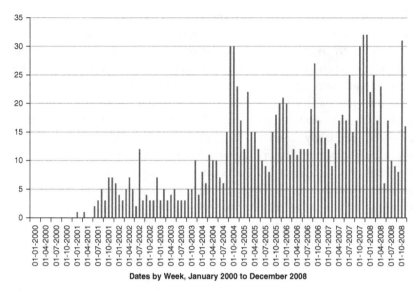

Dates by Week, January 2000 to December 2008

FIGURE 10 Counts by week of Minghui activist postings that include *jiudu* (救度) in the title.
Article titles retrieved May 8, 2009 (www.minghui.org/mh/download.html)

were adult immigrants to either the USA or Japan from mainland China and were what Chan (2004) termed "core" practitioners in the diaspora.

We can also see the diffusion over time of the term "saving" (*jiudu*) within in the Falun Gong community at large by looking at articles posted to the Minghui website by ordinary practitioners. Figure 10 shows counts of articles in which the article title included the term *jiudu*, with data collected from nine years of postings. No articles using the term *jiudu* appeared in any title before February 2001. The term gains wider use in 2001 and appears to become more significant after spring 2004.

POLITICS AND SOTERIOLOGY IN ACTIVISM

What came out of the dynamic evolution of religious doctrine and public activism were three different types of Falun Gong diaspora public activism, all of which coexisted during my period of research. There was, first, activism that was conventionally political, in that it aimed to stop the persecution and used discourses and strategies common to human rights groups and other protests organizations. Some examples of this type are the Falun Dafa Information Center, the Friends of Falun Gong, and the World Organization to Investigate the Persecution of Falun Gong. These organizations relatively closely conformed to social science expectations for social movement organizations. A second type of activism thoroughly fused recognizably political activism (in our etic use of the term) with millenarian, soteriological activism. What marks this type is that motivations for activism and even some strategic decision making appears to have been oriented primarily towards "saving," yet, at the same time, the immediate practical effects appear, from an etic point of view, to be political. Such activism worked simultaneously on two registers, political and soteriological. The Quit the CCP campaign (*tuidang*) is an example of this kind of activism. Practitioners primarily understood their activism as soteriological, but its activities involved claims and actions that bore on the interests of Chinese authorities.

One of the major activities of the Quit the CCP campaign, as mentioned by the aforementioned Chinese immigrant in Tokyo, was "truth calling" (*zhenxiang dianhua*). "Truth calling" entailed practitioners outside of China making phone calls to people in China to try to convince whoever picked up the phone to quit the CCP, in the sense described in Chapter 5. There have been hundreds of thousands, if not millions, of such phone calls. When I researched "truth calling" in 2015, I found the organizational infrastructure to be complex and highly developed. There was specialized software created for truth calling, banks of callers who shared information, trained one another, collected phone number lists, and coordinated across time zones, languages, and countries. Some calling involved automated messages played by computer, but personal firsthand calls were considered most effective. In truth calling, when practitioners succeeded in having a conversation (in most cases, recipients hung up), the practitioner tried to persuade the recipient to abandon the CCP. Their arguments were political, as in claiming the CCP was corrupt or violated internationally recognized human rights, and soteriological, as in warning the recipient that, without exception, "good and evil receive just deserts" (*shan e you bao*).

A subsection of "truth calling" only targeted local officials and bureaucrats directly involved in specific incidents of repression against practitioners in China. These calls were referred to as "anti-persecution" or "rescue" calls. In this tactic, practitioners in China, using censorship-evading software, would send information to Falun Gong activists in North America about local repression incidents, such as practitioners being involuntarily sent to "legal education centers" or "black jails."[23] North American activists would compile and distribute that information to Chinese-speaking Falun Gong activists outside of China, primarily in Taiwan, Southeast Asia, Australia, and North America. Those practitioners then would place as many calls as possible to the specific people involved in the repression, such as at police stations and detention facilities, the Domestic Security Brigade, and RTL centers. Whenever possible, practitioners used personal phone numbers and even called family members of police officers to add additional pressure.

For example, in one case from 2011, a practitioner and primary school teacher, Ms. Zeng, was allegedly abducted by authorities from her work and forcibly sent to a black jail in Anlu City, Hubei.[24] Supporters in China compiled information about the case and the phone numbers of relevant people to target for "truth calling." The information, as posted to Minghui, included contact information for the Anlu City Police Chief, the director and deputy director of the Anlu 610 Office (including his home number), assistant directors in the Anlu Police, and several members of the Anlu Domestic Security Brigade. Also listed were names and contact numbers for family members of officials. For instance, after the name of the deputy director of the 610 Office, one finds the full names, cell phone numbers, and/or place of employment of his wife, his younger sister, his younger sister-in-law, and that woman's husband. Practitioners would be expected to make calls to these family members to shame the official by describing torture used in such facilities, international standards regarding human rights, and – perhaps most effectively – how news of their family member's activities has been exposed overseas. Along with all of these shaming tactics, they would also try to persuade the call recipient to quit the CCP and avoid eternal punishment. The calls, then, were simultaneously political and millenarian.

---

[23] Legal education centers were rumored to be the most excessive and brutal of anti-Falun Gong de-conversion institutions. According to human rights lawyer Teng Biao, "On a scale of worse to the worst, torture occurs far more frequently and cruelly in detention centers than in jails, and labor camps were still worse, but the so-called legal education centers are the worst of all. The number of innocent citizens tortured to death in these centers across China is in four figures." See http://chinachange.org/2014/04/03/what-is-a-legal-education-center-in-china/, retrieved on May 24, 2015; also see Amnesty International (2015).

[24] See "*Hubei Anlushi '6–10' you ban xinaoban pohai Falungong xueyuan*" (Anlu City 6–10 Office in Hubei Province holds another brainwashing session to persecute practitioners), published online September 20, 2011 and retrieved on June 26, 2014, from www .clearwisdom.net/html/articles/2011/10/6/128558.html.

The number of "rescue calls" made by diaspora practitioners appears to be great. In a 2010 report on only the first four months of one particular "rescue" operation, the coordinator reported that they had made calls related to 453 persecution cases, including a total of 10,473 calls to unique numbers. In that time, the report claims, 615 people from the agencies agreed to quit the CCP and forty-eight practitioners from thirty-five cases were saved.[25] The low success rate for quitting implied here (e.g., roughly 6 percent) corroborates the common complaints by activists, who reported that most of time the call recipient either hung up right away or spewed curses and berated the caller. But the overall pattern suggests a sustained and vigorous campaign. Synthesizing politics and soteriological mission, then, has, in some cases, reinforced activism without fully undermining its political significance. For this hybrid form of protest activism, Falun Gong's millenarian turn was a source of both tenacity and creativity.

A third type of Falun Gong public activism has focused on revitalizing traditional Chinese culture. These activities have included music and dance performances; international competitions for classical Chinese dance, cooking, and costume; and a New York State-accredited secondary school and college focused on arts. Within this area of activism, Shen Yun Performing Arts has become the major organization (see Chapter 5). Li Hongzhi has been directly involved in the production of Shen Yun shows, but the promotion and management of shows in nearly 200 cities around the world depends on local practitioners' volunteer work and pocketbooks.

These cultural activities are not explicitly political. Activists understand them within the context of the millenarian soteriology and the persecution of Falun Gong, but the primary emphasis has been on revitalizing Chinese culture, as defined by Falun Gong. Shen Yun performances have not been advertised as political or affiliated with Falun Gong. Nevertheless, the shows are saturated in the Falun Gong worldview. The shows I attended opened and closed with scenes depicting a cosmological, religious narrative of history.[26] The opening scenes showed divinities descending to Earth to initiate human culture, which was depicted as Tang Dynasty-like China. The final act in the last two

---

[25] "*Zai dadianhua yingjiu pingtai shang gongtong duixian shengsheng shiyue*" (Fulfilling Sacred Vows Together on the Rescue Calling Platform), retrieved June 30, 2014 from www.minghui.org/mh/articles/2010/9/8/229351p.html.

[26] I attended performances in 2011, 2013, 2014, and 2015 in either Hartford or Chicago.

shows I attended were fully millenarian: in each case, the show enacted a modern Chinese city suffering cataclysmic destruction by natural forces (earthquake or tidal wave, for example), all of which was then suddenly reversed by a Buddha-like figure descending to earth and initiating an era of utopian, post-millenarian bliss. Between the dramatic bookends of gods founding human culture and a millenarian reckoning was a variety show of dance and musical performances in the style of the annual China Central Television (CCTV) New Year's Gala. Some of the performances were completely nonreligious and non-political; some were didactic political sketches dramatizing the repression of Falun Gong; and some were operatic songs praising the Dafa. During the last two years of performances I attended, I did not see or receive literature about the persecution of Falun Gong, and most of the production's content was non-political.

Even though Li Hongzhi defined "saving" in 2000 in ways that reinforced social movement activism, in Shen Yun we see the logic of saving leading the movement in a much less political direction. According to Li, the real purpose of Shen Yun is to save members of the public more quickly and efficiently than prior forms of activism. Consider this statement at a conference in 2009:

Now the effects of Shen Yun Performing Arts shows today [are obvious]. Everyone knows, everyone has seen them fulfill an [important] role. If a thousand people enter the theatre, when they leave [they are] already changed. When compared to other clarifying work endeavors you all do, under most conditions, it is impossible to have this kind of immediate and visible effect. Until now it has been impossible to reach this degree or reach this many people. The performing arts shows can fulfill this function.[27]

Shen Yun is superior to political activism, such as the canvassing we documented in the movement's post-1999 tactical repertoire, as a form of saving. Furthermore, Li also emphasized the indispensability of seeing the show in person. Even watching the show online or by DVD is insufficient. As Li stated, "When people are there in person, the matter of their salvation is taken care of right then and there, and they are saved."[28] The ticket prices for shows are relatively expensive, as are the venues that activists rent. Promoting the show and filling the halls, necessary in part to

---

[27] "*Zai Xintangren dianshi taolunhui shang de jiangfa*" (Fa teaching at the NTDTV conference), Li Hongzhi, June 6, 2009, retrieved on August 24, 2009, from http://minghui .org/mh/articles/2009/8/15/206600.html.

[28] "Fa Teaching Given at the 2015 New York Fa Conference," retrieved on July 2, 2015, from http://en.minghui.org/html/articles/2015/5/31/150850.html.

keep local practitioners from footing the bill, puts intense pressure on practitioners when Shen Yun comes to their area. Li's elevation of Shen Yun over other forms of more political public activism has probably contributed to Shen Yun's success. The organization's total assets increased from 3 million dollars in 2008 to over 61 million dollars seven years later in 2015.[29]

In summary, this third type of public activism remains focused on reaching the wider public, but only weakly resembles political protest. Its ideological justification, however, followed the same millenarian logic of saving that Li used to explain his absence and his centrality to the protest campaigns. Moreover, the Shen Yun project has become a major focus of activists everywhere outside of China and Hong Kong (where it cannot perform). The shift away from politicized forms of saving to cultural projects like Shen Yun thus marks a de-politicizing turn in the movement.

CONCLUSION

During the decade of the 2000s, Falun Gong diaspora protest activism changed from being explicitly political and largely based on human rights framing to a millenarian movement aimed at "saving souls" before the end of history. This switch marks a transition from a protest movement that was recognizably political and proto-democratic to one that was both politically and culturally marginal. The switch was motivated primarily by within-movement exigencies related to the legitimacy of the leader's charismatic authority. Initially, and somewhat counterintuitively, spiritualizing the movement contributed to maintaining mobilization and reinforcing the ethic of voluntarism and creativity that led to the invention of Falun Gong's tactical repertoire and various campaigns. But, eventually, the effect of millenarianism was to squander whatever progressive, democratic cultural potential was inherent to the social movement form of mobilization. In conclusion, the relationship between Falun Gong as a religious movement and its mobilization using social movement technology boils down to this: religion was both part of Falun Gong's making and undoing as a protest movement.

---

[29] Information retrieved from Guidestar.org and based on Shen Yun Performing Arts EIN# 20–8812402. There are also additional related organizations. Shen Yun Foundation Inc., for example, reported total assets of over 6 million dollars in 2014.

9

Conclusion

MORE MOMENTS IN DIASPORA PROTEST

In August 2010, I went to the Chinese consulate in Los Angeles to observe a protest demonstration planned by a Minyun group calling itself the Chinese Democracy Party (CDP).[1] This event was briefly described earlier in my analysis of asylum brokering. I depicted the Minyun protest as, in part, a photo opportunity for building portfolios of evidence for asylum-seeking undocumented immigrants. But, since Falun Gong activists had regularly held vigils and "clarifying truth" work outside of Chinese consulates in the USA, I expected this protest event would also give me an opportunity to compare both movements in "real time" and observe interactions between them. Having spent the previous day interviewing members of the CDP, I went to the consulate ahead of the appointed protest time in order to meet and speak with Falun Gong practitioners.

Arriving before the CDP activists, I found a handful of practitioners spread between two different entrances for the consulate. In front of the main entrance, practitioners had draped banners on the bushes near the building's entryway. Both banners were in Chinese only, one reading "Falun Dafa Is Good" and the other "Dissolve the CCP, Stop the Persecution of Falun Gong." Two older practitioners, a man and a woman, were quietly studying the *Zhuan Falun*. They paid no heed to me as I walked by. Their job in this case was to maintain the banners.

As I approached the consulate's second entrance, which is where the visa office is and most transactions happen, I saw three or four female practitioners "clarifying truth" on the sidewalk. One woman approached

---

[1] The following description is from field notes taken on August 24–25, 2010.

me and, speaking practiced, but not fluent, English, offered me materials
to read. In accepting the materials, I opened a conversation in Chinese.
Our conversation was typical of many I have had with practitioners who
are "clarifying truth." She told me how Falun Gong is good, good for
one's health, and how the CCP is evil. "Why would you repress a good
thing?" she asked me. Another practitioner interrupted our conversation
to tell me that the daughter of the woman with whom I was speaking had
been jailed for practicing Falun Gong. So I asked the mother about her
daughter and learned that she had just been released after several years in
a Guangzhou prison. "She is a good person," the mother insisted. In the
course of this conversation, the leader of the CDP arrived and, seeing me,
summarily interrupted us. The Falun Gong activists tried to give him
literature too, but he waved it away saying that he had already seen it.

   CDP activists showed up together in two cars. Their protests consisted
of staging a photo of eight or so demonstrators holding signs on the
sidewalk by the entrance to the consulate. All, I was told, would eventually seek asylum status. The demonstration was part of a national
campaign in support of the Chinese dissident Liu Xianbin, who had
been arrested about two months earlier for his publications and speech
on foreign websites.[2] After CDP leaders spoke with the two invited
reporters, one from Radio Free Asia and one from the *World Journal*,
a Chinese-language North American newspaper, the activists moved to
leave. I found, in this less scripted moment, a chance to ask two of the CDP
leaders about Falun Gong. In a way that indirectly acknowledged Falun
Gong's greater capacity to mobilize its community, one jokingly remarked
that their cause also "needs a master [*shifu*]."

   I returned the following day to spend more time with the Falun Gong
activists. One had migrated to the USA two decades earlier, had worked in
the field of medicine, and converted to Falun Gong due to healing experiences. She told me that when she started practicing Falun Gong in 1996,
she suffered from high blood pressure and a gastric ulcer. Falun Gong
cured these and she had since been healthy and vigorous without ever
taking medicine. Another practitioner reported that she and her husband
were both practitioners in China when Falun Gong was banned. Her
husband was killed in the repression. Eventually, she fled China through
Thailand and received asylum in the USA about two and half years before

---

[2] Liu Xianbin was sentenced to ten years in prison for "inciting subversion of state power."
   Since 1989, he has spent thirteen years in prison for his democracy and human rights
   activism. See "Who Is Liu Xianbin?" retrieved on May 31, 2012, from http://laogai.org.

my field visit. The literature distributed by the women contained information in both English and Chinese. I received materials claiming that the self-immolation incident of 2001 was staged by the Chinese government, a special handout published by *The Epoch Times*, and a DVD about Jiang Zemin. I learned from practitioners that they traveled by public transportation three hours each way, for a total of six hours per day, to get to the consulate. They were not paid, but some practitioners donated money to support their efforts. They also reported that Falun Gong activists had been coming to this Chinese consulate every day that it had been open for business since sometime in 2000. When they were not doing "clarifying truth" here, they frequently did "truth calling" to China over the Internet.

I asked the one who said her husband had been killed in the persecution about her perception of the CDP demonstration the previous day. She gave me this analysis: the democracy activists were good people standing on the side of justice. Falun Gong shares some things in common with them, but Falun Gong is also different. "Because we, we are cultivating. Cultivating our hearts. Truth, compassion, forbearance." She emphasized that practitioners take a moral position on accepting suffering and that practitioners don't calculate strategically about costs and benefits like other people (*women bu jijiao*). They want to save others and, saving others, she remarked, "makes one very happy and satisfied."

These additional moments in diaspora protest return us to the governing question of my study: why did Falun Gong, especially in contrast to Minyun, succeed in adopting and implementing the social movement form of activism? Is it, as the CDP participant suggested, because Falun Gong has a leader to whom all pledge loyalty? Such an answer seems especially apt from a Minyun activist, given how the movement has been faction-riven since the mid-1980s, with each faction consolidated behind its own, separate leader. Or is the Falun Gong's mobilization success, as my Falun Gong informant said to me, due to the fact that Falun Gong practitioners wage protest as a moral and religious end in itself? Regardless of success or failure in changing authorities, the rewards of Falun Gong participation are intrinsic to the act of protest itself.

This explanation, too, is apt when compared to Minyun. Falun Gong created a solution for Mancur Olson's (1971) free rider dilemma and Minyun did not. Olson's logic says that, when people are struggling to realize a public good, it is more rational for an individual to avoid participation and let others make the necessary sacrifices. Since, in the end, public goods are shared by everyone, the individual's most rational choice is to get a "free ride." For example, enjoy free speech in a democratic China without personally sacrificing to make democracy a reality. In addition to the promise of salvation, Falun Gong activists frequently experienced participation as its own reward. Social movement scholars have called such selective incentives for protest as "solidary incentives" (McAdam 1982) or "emotional in-process benefits" (Wood 2001). Falun Gong's "in-process benefits" of participation included participating in a world-purifying moral mission, being in solidarity with co-believers, all the emotional and health benefits that followed from faith in Falun Gong cultivation, and the promise of ultimate salvation. These were immensely strong buffers against the atomizing forces of Olson-like self-interest; these in-process benefits also propelled mobilization forward in a reinforcing cycle.

Minyun, of course, did not have a religious worldview in which to embed and motivate activism. But it did have a shared set of ideals that were capable of motivating huge personal sacrifice and deeply felt social solidarity, as vividly seen in the spring of 1989 in China. The emotional and solidary benefits of participation, however, were hard to realize in diaspora given the patriarchal factional competition within the community and the bureaucratic model of mobilization that prevailed. When I conducted field research, aside from already exiled dissidents and the very occasional idealist or ideologue, the only people I found mobilized for the Minyun cause were those seeking the selective incentive of legal immigrant documentation: hardly a recipe for mobilization.

BIG IMPLICATIONS

Stepping away from the trees of my argument, it is now time to survey the wider aspect of the forest. What are the big implications that one can draw from this comparison? I draw out two sets of conclusions. The first concerns research on social movements and the second concerns whether we can see Falun Gong as in some way progressive or proto-democratic.

On Social Movements

For social movements, I have asked why Falun Gong was better able to mobilize as a protest movement than Minyun. The answers I gave relate to religion, global China, and social movement modularity. Falun Gong's character as a religious movement is crucial to understanding the manner in which it mobilized as a social movement. When Falun Gong gained momentum in China during the mid-1990s, some members of its grassroots community mobilized to "defend the Fa" through letter-writing campaigns, and then through sit-ins and vigils between 1996 and 1999. Defending the Fa and spreading the Fa to attract new religious recruits emerged as complementary and self-reinforcing. Eventually, practitioners widely came to construe nonviolent and public affirmations of Falun Gong, which were simultaneously claims that bore upon authorities, as a moral and religious obligation offering transcendent rather than only worldly benefits.

How diaspora Falun Gong activists responded to repression in China, including the conventions of proselytizing and protest created by fellow practitioners in the homeland, was not independent of what happened in China. Falun Gong's tactical repertoire in diaspora, especially its central emphasis on persuading the bystander and mainland Chinese publics, grew out of the *hongfa* and *hufa* activism. Although one might debate whether or not Falun Gong protest in China constituted a social movement campaign, as defined in Chapter 1, there is a clear historical path linking Falun Gong's style of protest in China to its social movement activism in diaspora. Falun Gong's diaspora social movement mobilization was an interactive outcome dependent on the total theater of global China.

Global China mattered for Minyun activists as well, because they also carried with them a pattern of activism from China into diaspora. But without a proselytizing religious subculture, activists largely operated within the bounds of the shared secular culture of post-Mao China. This cultural toolbox and set of dispositions provided little incentive for activists to decentralize mobilization or to orient claim making toward publics rather than directly to authorities. Not only did Minyun fail to sustain mobilization, the form of mobilization it undertook had less formal "social movement-ness" than that of Falun Gong. Minyun voiced claims against authorities on behalf of the public, rather than turning to the public as fellow citizens who are the ultimate source of legitimate authority and whose opinion, participation, and resources could help pressure authorities in China.

Third, the comparison also matters for understanding the modularity of social movements. The within-group culture of Falun Gong as a new religious movement had a kind of elective affinity with the social movement protest model, whereas the within-group culture of Minyun did not. These differences influenced how each attempted to mobilize overseas, and can be seen with particular vividness relative to how each oriented themselves to publics. Modularity of social movements is therefore conditioned by a group's within-group culture. Modularity entails more than simply a collective actor picking up the toolbox of social movement in order to protect its self-evident interests. Different groups are differently able, these two cases suggest, to adopt the social movement model. Furthermore, modular appropriation is dynamic and interactive. Group culture can change as a result of mobilization as a social movement. For Falun Gong, becoming a modern protest movement led to reformulations of ideology, collective identity, and religious mission, with consequences for Falun Gong even after politicization subsided.

The Progressive Potential of Falun Gong?

In the Introduction, I discussed the question, raised by Craig Calhoun, of the relationship between movements speaking in the name of tradition and the actual social change to which they contribute. Traditionalist movements, it was argued, can, in some cases, foment progressive social change even within an ideological framework that celebrates the recovering of lost tradition. I have signaled this theme a few times in the book when I spoke of the "progressive potential" of Falun Gong mobilization, especially in reference to how practitioners acted on their own initiative in a decentralized way and to how they emphasized persuasive outreach to publics. I also spoke of that progressive potential being undermined by the millenarian turn taken within the movement. Now I would like to revisit this theme in a systematic way.

On the face of it, to speak of Falun Gong having a progressive potential rings an odd note. In terms of ideology, Falun Gong is better characterized as reactionary rather than progressive, at least in regards to sexuality, race, gender, science, and liberalism. Yet, there are good reasons to also see within the movement progressive aims and social forms. First, Falun Gong protest mobilization was initially an assertion and defense of freedom of religion, even if emic terminology prevented participants from defining it as such. If Falun Gong any time after 1999 had successfully won back the right to believe in their faith, assemble, associate, publish, and proselytize, which was in sum the substance of their claims against authorities the day they surrounded Zhongnanhai in Beijing, the rights they would have won back were effectively the rights of freedom of religion. These rights, argues Jose Casanova, are "the precondition of all modern freedoms," because the right to privacy of conscience is necessary for "the modern institutionalization of a private sphere free from government intrusion as well as from ecclesiastical control" (Casanova 1992:

17–18). Regardless of the ideological contents of Falun Gong, the battle itself has a progressive character, because the rights at stake are those at the core of liberal democratic modernity.

Second, we can also see the progressive potential of Falun Gong in the form its mobilization took among participants. Here I speak of people learning the skills and subjectivities that go with being citizens of a democracy rather than of an authoritarian regime. These include expectations for public participation, developing the networks and know-how of civil society and for protest mobilization, in particular, and forging shared symbolic frameworks that represent and institutionalize relations between an individual, his/her conscience, official authority, and voluntary association. Could the Falun Gong, or any new religious movement speaking in the name of tradition, be a source of this kind of progressive cultural change? In other contexts, movements speaking in the name of tradition and drawing upon Chinese indigenous cultural sources have played such a role. Robert Weller (1999) and Richard Madsen (2007) have shown that indigenous forms of Chinese religiosity, which, like Falun Gong, did not share cultural and historical foundations with modern liberalism, have strengthened and interacted positively with Taiwan's democratic evolution (also see Cohen 1994). How tradition and progressive social change intersect is not essentially determined but contingent. How does Falun Gong diaspora look from this vantage point? Was it ever, or could it have become, a source of progressive social change?

I suggest that there are primarily three areas in which we can see a progressive potential in Falun Gong activism. Although that progressive potential was ultimately neutralized by external and internal forces, it remains valuable to identify and describe how the movement at times expressed progressive directionality, especially because other movements at other times and places might be able to carry that potential through to fuller realization.

The first area I consider is the practical field of grassroots activism. Falun Gong diaspora activism facilitated widespread political participation within its community. All participants eventually became activists. The majority of those activists were immigrants from mainland China who did not have much or any prior activism experience. Many practitioners, moreover, such as women and unemployed seniors, had relatively subordinate social positions. For them, protest campaigning entailed realizing a degree of new political agency. Moreover, Falun Gong is a heterogeneous community that includes different linguistic groups, levels of education, and economic classes. The egalitarian ethic of Falun

Gong, in which all cultivators are essentially equals before the supremacy of the transcendent Dafa and its sole teacher Li Hongzhi, deeply pervaded how people organized. The duty to act on one's conscience was widely felt. Practitioners respected one another for undertaking activism according to each person's own conscience, as long as it was consistent in general with Falun Gong teachings. On-the-ground conflicts and decisions were often made through the mutual exchange of ideas (*jiaoliu*) in a way that emphasized consensus, listening, and equality. In practical matters, activism led people to learn skills that amplified their voice in public affairs. Practitioners learned how to execute a petition, march through a major city, conduct lawsuits to protect rights, produce a newspaper, lobby elected officials, get motions through the US Congress, hand out leaflets on street corners, use local and national laws to protect rights, register a 501c3 nonprofit organization in the USA, issue press releases, coordinate transnational information and telephone campaigning, and so forth. All of this mobilization, especially because it was so decentralized and emphasized individual initiative, facilitated skill development and politically consequential forms of agency.

Another way that Falun Gong activism might be seen as contributing toward progressive social change is what we might call its spillover effects. That is, some forms of activism may have had, or will have, progressive consequences beyond the intended aims of the activists. For example, media projects associated with Falun Gong have included newspapers, websites, and television and radio networks. Although many programs, editorials, articles, and advertisements focus on Falun Gong-specific topics, much of the news and reporting is unrelated to Falun Gong and operates simply as alternative noncommercial, nongovernmental sources of information and entertainment. The Chinese edition of *The Epoch Times*, which is often free and easily available in many major cities, stands out among overseas Chinese-language newspapers for its commitment to publishing watchdog, critical news from mainland China. For example, it claims to have been the first media source to report the SARS cover-up in China in 2003. Over the years, the incentives of being supported through advertising and increasing readership have pushed the newspaper toward greater professionalization and to increasingly orient itself toward the needs and interests of its widest readership. Simply by increasing the plurality of voices in the diaspora Chinese-language public sphere, *The Epoch Times* is playing a progressive role, even though the community's pariah status limits its impact. It is also conceivable that an organization like *The Epoch Times* could evolve into a more mainstream publication while retaining its critical independence and moral watchdog mission. Similar spillover effects may be occurring through Falun Gong human rights activism, lawsuits, software development, and lobbying of states and international agencies.

Still one more spillover effect of Falun Gong activism may be its demonstration role among the Chinese dissident and diaspora community. I have occasionally encountered evidence in my research that non-Falun Gong actors are taking lessons from Falun Gong activism. For example, I visited a Minyun organization in Las Vegas that included a Chinese art and culture show as part of their annual democracy movement meeting. When I asked an organizer why, he told me that they had seen Falun Gong successfully use art shows to attract public support and so decided to try it as well.[3] Spillover might also be occurring across generations. In Hong Kong, I interviewed a young woman whose parents were core Falun Gong activists in North America. Raised in the USA as an American citizen, she spent her childhood attending marches and other Falun Gong "clarifying truth" activities. When I met her, she was loyal to her family heritage as a practitioner of the Dafa, but young people like her may eventually take other paths in adulthood. And, whatever her path, due to her experiences in childhood and as a young adult, she will already have inscribed in herself many skills and orientations that could be useful toward speaking out and organizing with others on matters of public significance.

A third way that Falun Gong protest demonstrated a potential for progressive social change was that it facilitated for its mainland Chinese participants a radical break in consciousness relative to established Chinese authority. In comparing the tactical repertoires of Falun Gong and Minyun, we saw that Minyun activism, for all of its intellectual acuity and genuine sacrifices, never departed, even in North America, very far from enactments of established Chinese norms of authority. Protest was enacted as a confrontation between counter-elites and authorities, rather than as a triadic project of leveraging public opinion and resources to pressure authorities. By contrast, Falun Gong made a much more radical, even revolutionary, break with tradition. We see this in the grassroots-based, diffuse nonviolent protest campaigning and in how participants

---

[3] The person with whom I spoke did not know of my research on Falun Gong. Email correspondence, 2010.

oriented their activism toward the public as a means of influencing political power holders.

The break with tradition leads to two further implications. The first implication restates, but with new significance, the idea that the modularity of social movements is mediated and contingent upon cultural processes within a challenger group. The adoption of social movement activism by actors from an authoritarian context entailed more than the instrumental picking up of new tools for collective action or even learning new routines of action: adoption of the social movement form also entailed reformulating intersubjective notions of legitimate political authority. The traditional elite-led form of protest enacted, and, thus, reproduced, a patriarchal or paternalistic model of authority, whereas the public-oriented activism of Falun Gong emphasized the agency of the public, thereby enacting a set of relations that was fundamentally more democratic.

The second implication of this break from tradition concerns the role of charismatic authority in making this break occur. Max Weber's classic theory of how cultural structures of legitimate authority can change historically suggests one possible explanation for why Falun Gong was able to make this more radical break than Minyun. Minyun was, as argued in Chapter 7, highly conventional in its models of authority and protest. This was true in spite of its ideological mission of modernist democratization. Minyun's collective action did not facilitate decentralized forms of grassroots activism, as we saw in Falun Gong, nor was it congenial to the triadic relations implicit to social movement activism. In Minyun, we observed more continuity with tradition than rupture. By contrast, Falun Gong was based upon a living charismatic authority, a man who declared all prior religions, science, and political authority as inferior to the message he had come to deliver. Li Hongzhi made a contemporary Chinese version of the archetypal charismatic claim noted by Weber, "It has been written ..., but I say unto you ... " 1978 [1968]: 1115). Falun Gong's break with traditionalistic forms of protest was authorized by a radical break from the past made possible through charismatic leadership. The aim of the movement was to forge a new kind of person – a cultivator, a Dafa disciple – and complete the project of a new age, the age of Fa-rectification (*zhengfa shiqi*). Such a radical cultural break made possible new forms of social organization and new enactments of selfhood.

In this way, one might see Falun Gong bearing resemblance to the Puritan movement, which Max Weber, Michael Walzer, and Philip

Gorski argued in different ways contributed to the evolution of the modern democratic, capitalist citizen. Although there are many differences, Falun Gong was like Calvinism in that it emerged during a period of turbulent social transition and became popular in part due to its "bold effort to shape a new personality against the background of social 'unsettledness'" (Walzer 1965: 312). Calvinism, also like Falun Gong much later, invented an "ethic of self-discipline" and "a variety of techniques for achieving it: regular Bible reading, daily journals, moral log books, and rigid control over time" (Gorski 2003: 20). Falun Gong similarly emphasized self-cultivation based on an ascetic moral credo of "truthfulness, compassion, and forbearance." These three virtues were often juxtaposed against the dishonesty, corruption, and injustices that had frequently been perceived to go unchecked and unpunished in reform-era China. And like Calvinism, cultivating Falun Dafa entailed various daily techniques to realize "a new spiritual nature," to borrow Calvin's phrase (Gorski 2003: 20). Those techniques included regular study of Li Hongzhi's texts, daily self-cultivation exercises, doing the collective "sending forth righteous thoughts" (*fa zhengnian*) prayers, and "clarifying truth" through volunteer campaigns. Through all this public activism, and, again, similar to Calvinism, Falun Gong reinforced worldly, practical lessons that are not contained in its ideology. "Calvinism," according to Walzer, "was not a liberal ideology," but its "congregational life was surely a training for self-government and democratic participation" (1965: 301). Falun Gong, too, does not offer a liberal ideology, but its corporate life has given diaspora participants ample opportunity to learn and master a wide variety of practices that go with social movement activism in modern democracies.[4]

Seeing the Falun Gong case from this perspective also brings together two big ideas that have heretofore, to my knowledge, only been treated separately: the first is the idea, from Weber, that charisma tends to become routinized into institutionalized practices; the second is the idea, primarily from Tilly, that the modern social movement is an historically particular form of collective action. The Falun Gong case brings these two ideas together because the religious movement's protest mobilization is an instance of charisma being routinized into a modern social movement.

---

[4] In drawing the comparison, I do not, of course, mean to suggest that we should grant to Falun Gong a comparably significant historical role for China that Puritanism occupied for Western modernity. I am instead simply identifying a common process or mechanism.

Weber's classic theorization sketched a variety of trajectories by which charisma can be routinized into institutionalized practices:

Thus the pure type of charismatic rulership is in a very specific sense unstable, and all its modifications have basically one and the same cause: The desire to transform charisma and charismatic blessing from a unique, transitory gift of grace of extraordinary times and persons into a permanent possession of everyday life. This is desired usually by the master, always by his disciples, and most of all by his charismatic subjects. The charismatic following of a war leader may be transformed into a state, the charismatic community of a prophet, artist, philosopher, ethical or scientific innovator may become a church, sect, academy or school, and the charismatic group which espouses certain cultural ideals may develop into a party or merely the staff of newspapers and periodicals. (Weber 1978 [1968]: 1121)

Not on his list of outcomes, but worthy of being included, is the routinization of the charismatic blessings into a protest movement, including a protest movement of the sort celebrated and studied in the social movements literature.

But charismatic authority offers, also as Weber theorized, only a faux revolutionary departure from traditionalistic and personal structures of authority. Routinization of charisma leads back to recreating traditional authority. Li Hongzhi's charismatic claims and the movement that grew up around them may have initially authorized the break from tradition that facilitated social organization as a protest movement, but the same charismatic leadership also ushered in the millenarian interpretation of repression and undermined the progressive potential that was implicit in Falun Gong protest. We saw this through the ideological innovation of interpreting contention as a cosmic battle and protesting as saving souls. We also later saw the millenarian framework used to justify concentrating public activism on the Shen Yun art shows because such shows, Li argued, were a superior technology of saving souls than the more explicitly political practice of "clarifying truth." The charismatic leadership that unleashed the progressive potential of Falun Gong also stifled it.

This last point indicates, moreover, some other limits to seeing the Falun Gong tactical repertoire as progressive. In spite of the formal similarities between the ideal typical social movement repertoire and Falun Gong protest campaigning, the meanings that organized activism were always substantively at odds with the progressive, democratic directionality of social movement activism. At the ideational level, the protest movement was never independent of the dynamics of charismatic authority. Falun Gong participants were throughout committed to the charismatic idealization of Li. This charismatic dream conflicted with the progressive potentiality of the social movement, as activists formally carried it out through their tactical repertoire. When Falun Gong activists turned to the public as a means to protest homeland authorities, they enacted the triadic relations of a social movement; but, at the same time, they decreasingly came to view the public as the ultimate source of legitimate authority and increasingly to view the public as the unconverted, the as-yet-unsaved. In Falun Gong, which is a totalizing movement that ultimately denies distinctions between religious and political, the only final source of authority is the person of Li Hongzhi. The turn to the public may initially have been an attempt to tap the legitimate authority of public opinion and public support, but as the millenarian interpretation of protest took hold, the turn to the public became a traditionalistic effort to bring the public into the universe described and authorized by Li Hongzhi alone. Inevitably, this had marginalizing consequences for the movement relative to mainstream societies.

FINAL REMARKS

I conclude by recalling an especially human moment I had during my field research. I was in Tokyo and had been included in a Sunday collective study of *Zhuan Falun*, Li Hongzhi's book. I was sitting on a carpeted floor at a low table, Japanese style, with several Chinese practitioners. Two, in particular, were giving me their attention: a young man in his late twenties, who worked in a food import company and who had a long scar running the length of his arm, and an older woman, who had come to Japan to be with her daughter and son-in-law. Along with many others, these two practitioners had been very helpful to me, answering my questions and enthusiastically sharing their personal experiences. It felt nice to be in their community and to be speaking with them. Then, the older woman startled me with a direct question: how was my research going to represent them, to represent Falun Gong? For a moment, I choked.

Although I had entered the field originally hoping to write a sympathetic portrayal of Falun Gong, I knew my overriding obligation was to be true to the facts and experiences as best as I could understand them. Already, I recognized, I was on a path that would disappoint the hopes of those people who allowed me to treat them as objects of research. My portrayal of the movement, while emphasizing the ways in which activists impressively adopted the social movement form of activism, also would need to reveal, as it has, the many ways that Falun Gong has rallied around fantastical claims about cosmic reality, history, and the super-natural. And while I have felt loyalty to, and sincere respect for, the genuine and legitimate aspirations for the good that motivate many Falun Gong practitioners, I have also observed little in the actions and teachings of the charismatic leader to inspire my trust or respect. Often I have paused to wonder, what kind of leader would condemn to divine punishment those who renounced Falun Gong under torture? What kind of leader would fail to try to mitigate the suffering of his flock in China, as he might have tried to do after July 1999? Similarly, I have worried at times for my research subjects, when they warned me of the dangers of thinking or speaking critically of Falun Gong. Had these earnest people trapped themselves in a coercive hall of ideological mirrors?

Forced to respond in the moment to the fair, but penetrating, question, and to do so in a language in which I master no eloquence at all, I did my best to express that whatever I write, I will endeavor to convey respect for their common aspirations, their shared relationships with one another, and their authentic pursuit of dignity in the face of defamation and persecution. Under the disciplining constraints of social science writing, I fear that I have not even achieved that modest goal. In a last effort to redeem my promise, let me state my feelings this way: The beliefs of Falun Gong practitioners are not my beliefs. But I have not worn their shoes and walked the miles they have walked. Beneath such tenacity of spirit and such commitment to embody their idealization of the good, there are many, many individual biographies – each unique and none free of hard-ships. Were I to know each of these biographies, as each one must be known to the person who has lived it, I am confident that a profoundly sympathetic portrayal of Falun Gong would be simple to write. Then, I would be better able to keep the promise I made on that Sunday in Tokyo.

APPENDIX
Research Design, Methods, and Sources

This book relies on multiple methods of data collection and analysis. I combined document-based research drawn from movement publications with ethnographic investigation in order to explore two different levels of analysis: the macro-historical level by which the broad trajectories of the movements could be considered across historical time and global space, and the micro-sociological level at which the religious culture of Falun Gong activism could be observed *in situ*. These different levels of analysis allowed me to synthesize micro-sociological observations with an analysis of case histories that reveal broad patterns over time and place. My research ultimately fell into three domains: (1) fieldwork investigating contemporary Falun Gong religious and political activity, supplemented with some similar research on contemporary Minyun diaspora activism; (2) close readings and summary analysis of communications on the Minghui website; and (3) protest event trends drawn from comparative historical data published in movement sources for both Minyun and Falun Gong. I now proceed to describe the sources and data collection methods for each of these domains.

ETHNOGRAPHIC FIELDWORK

I conducted ethnographic and observational fieldwork at events by Falun Gong and Minyun, participant observation in a Falun Gong community in one small New England city, and interviews. Formal interviews were semi-structured and deliberately open-ended enough to draw out rich accounts of my preselected concerns, such as "clarifying truth" activities or asking for personal stories of "gaining the Fa." In addition to formal interviews, field observations gave me many opportunities for impromptu interviews, based on interactions that occurred as I observed public events. Even for these impromptu conversations, I identified myself as a researcher and, if the conversation evolved into an in-depth interview, I sought verbal consent to participate in research from interviewees.

For the Falun Gong research, I spent about 160 hours in the field, more than 90 hours of which were conducted in Japan, Taiwan, and Hong Kong, and the remainder in various US cities. In addition, I attended as an audience member six Falun Gong "gala" cultural productions (four Shen Yun and two separately labeled) in New England, New York, and Chicago. I conducted my research between January 2006 and July 2015, with my most active periods in the spring of 2006 in New England; in July 2007 in Japan; in the summer of 2009, which included visits to Washington DC and New York; in 2013 in Japan and Taiwan; and one month in 2015 in Hong Kong.

In the field, I had two typical modes of entry. The first was as a participant observer, including 40 hours of participant observation in one New England community. There, I learned to do the Falun Gong exercise and meditation practices, attended a weekly beginners class offered by a practitioner at a local community center, joined in some publicity events, and, on one occasion, joined an outdoor group cultivation session on a frigid winter Sunday morning. Whenever I intended to participate in an event at which practitioners would be doing the Falun Gong exercises and meditation, I attempted to contact the organizers in advance, using Falun Gong's publicly available contact lists for local practice sites. I would explain my research purposes and ask for consent to do the research. In the exceptional instance when I did not have advance contact, I immediately introduced my research purposes. Participating in the exercises and meditation often helped secure acceptance for me as someone with a serious intention. If I performed the exercises poorly, as happened frequently enough, it sometimes attracted helpful instruction, but other times consternation. Nevertheless, much like Cheris Chan's account of her ethnographic experience (2013), after a while I found little research value to doing the exercises and mediation, so I focused my efforts on observation and interviews.

At no point in my field research did any Falun Gong community consider me as a true insider, although I was frequently encouraged to "study the Fa" as a practitioner and abandon my outsider position. As a consequence of my outsider status, my research is not able to provide insight into the backstage operations of the movement. For example, senior practitioners in diaspora use private and encrypted Internet communication platforms to which I was never given access. To gain access, I would have needed to present myself not as a researcher, but as a true practitioner and secretly embedded myself in the community. Given the politics of repression in which the movement is unhappily involved, I did not see an ethical justification for such subterfuge. My research could have been construed as spying or might in fact have led to the exposure of information that could have been used to further damage the community. Furthermore, since my research focus was on the political mobilization of ordinary practitioners, who also do not have access to the backstage workings of the central leadership, this limitation in my research did not undermine my ability to fulfill my research aims.

In contrast to my participant observation work, I used a different mode of entry into the field when I observed large Falun Gong political demonstrations or cultural performances. Although sometimes I participated in activities that would help me experience the event, such as candlelit vigils, more frequently I remained an observer. As an observer, I frequently spoke with participants in the style of informal, unstructured interviews. Being Caucasian with strong, but not native, spoken Mandarin (Putonghua) and Japanese language skills, I was often successful in generating useful conversations. I was usually first perceived as an interested member of the public who might be open to learning about Dafa. After explaining my research purposes, most practitioners seemed to view me as a benign academic, a potential source of bystander support, and/or a potential new recruit to the community. Occasionally I was rebuffed by practitioners in my attempts to talk with them and was treated as a threat or distraction from the urgent tasks of "clarifying truth" to the public.

I also engaged in about 30 hours of fieldwork and interviews with contemporary Minyun participants. This research took place in Washington DC, New York City, Las Vegas, and Los Angeles. Although my field research on Minyun was helpful for providing context, background information, and interviews, I have not used this relatively sparse research to make strong claims in the book. In a few instances, the two movements "collided" for me in the field, such as the incident in front of the Los Angeles Chinese Consulate. In another instance, Minyun activists tried to rally attention to their cause and support from the local Chinese community by hosting a Chinese cultural art show, which Minyun organizers explicitly told me was inspired by observing the success of similar Falun Gong shows. These interactive settings were not only rich opportunities to view the movements in action, but also served as reminders that the cases are not in fact independent, even though, for research purposes, I mostly treated them as if they were.

MINGHUI WEBSITE

The second domain of research I explored was through the websites and media of Falun Gong. The most influential website, Minghui,[1] is vast, with many thousands of postings that have been archived by the site operators (for detailed descriptions, see Chen, Abbasi, and Chen 2010; Ownby 2008: 200–207; Penny 2012: 30–33). Falun Gong publications and the Minghui website, in particular, have been a common source for research in studies of Falun Gong (Chen, Abbasi, and Chen 2010; Junker 2014a;, 2014b; Lu 2005; Ownby 2008; Palmer, D. A. 2007; Palmer, S. J. 2003; Penny 2012; Thornton 2010). The website is a key site of Falun Gong activity and global interaction, especially between the charismatic leader, the Minghui editors, and the globally dispersed population of practitioners and potential recruits. The site is also frequently used to share practical information. Naturally, the picture of Falun Gong that emerges from the Minghui website does not entirely match the picture that emerged from my ethnographic research. Both views of the movement are legitimate, but the Minghui website might be best understood as a stage by which practitioners and leader can perform idealized versions of themselves, i.e., versions of self that emphasize doctrinal conformity, ideological purity, commitment, and piety. In the field, practitioners may try to live out these images of themselves, but usually the lived experience of Falun Gong looked different, less zealous, and more human(e).

Minghui was founded in May 1999 in Canada; soon after, it became the central Falun Gong website, recognized as the movement's most authoritative source (Ownby 2008: 200–201; Palmer 2007: 252; Penny 2012: 30). Minghui is an internally targeted website, meaning that its audience is primarily Falun Gong practitioners. Most postings were written by the users of the website, although reposting of news and information from other sources is common. During my research, I observed that postings were

---

[1] The web address is www.minghui.org for Chinese, www.clearwisdom.org for English. Also examined were the closely related sites www.minghui.ca, www.falundafa.org, and www.falundafa.ca.

edited and formatted by the website managers and organized into several categories, such as daily updates on the persecution of Falun Gong in China, overseas Falun Gong activism, technology topics, cultivation experiences, and so forth. Because the website was accessible from China through censorship-evading software, such as that produced by Falun Gong practitioners, the website linked the underground mainland Chinese Falun Gong community to overseas practitioners. The website operates in multiple languages (eleven as of 2012). I took the Chinese version to be more comprehensive than the English, in part because the majority of practitioners are Chinese and also because the Chinese site contained much material that was not translated into English.

Minghui served a dual integrative function for the Falun Gong movement: on the one hand, it fostered communication between the overseas Falun Gong community and the mainland practitioners, and, on the other hand, the website fostered the cultural integration of Falun Gong religious life and its political mission. In addition, and especially important for my use of Minghui as a domain of research, the site's managers and contributors have been self-conscious about preserving its content to document Falun Gong's place in history. The archive contained virtually everything posted to it since January 2000, as well as still earlier material.[2] One can search by date, to see the articles posted on any given day, or search by topic, key word, and the like. Due to the archive, Ownby argues that "the site comes close to representing the whole of the 'virtual' Falun Gong experience since 1999 as seen by practitioners and, actually, since the inception of the movement, as many historical documents are available as well" (2008: 206). The Chinese version of the website archive, for example, contained about 150,000 article titles for the years 2000–2008 when I examined it in March 2009. My research has relied on this archive for compiling activism narratives in the protest event study; for analyzing leadership communications to followers during the period of Falun Gong's initial politicization; for examining other facets of the movement, such as a genre of postings called "solemn declarations," and for learning about telephone call activism.

The archive covered all types of postings, but two special categories were available by direct link from the homepage: statements made by the charismatic leader and statements made by the Minghui website editors. After Li's own statements, those of the editors were understood to be the most authoritative source of Falun Gong doctrine and policy. The website

---

[2] Strictly speaking, there were several related websites in 1999 that appear to have been retrospectively ordered and combined into the single Minghui website.

did not identify any editor by name. Nevertheless, it is said that Mr. Ye Hao founded the Minghui site. In contrast to Li, who never attended college, Ye's biography suggests the picture of a capable and sophisticated administrator. He graduated from China's second most prestigious university, Tsinghua, in 1959, and spent a career working in China's Ministry of Public Security, from which he retired in 1996. His final fifteen years of his career were spent as a cadre in the Eleventh Bureau of the Ministry of Public Security, which is in charge of cyber security and policing. Ye had become an associate of Li Hongzhi in the early years of Falun Gong's rise to popularity. He migrated from China to North America about the same time as Li and appears to have remained a major figure in the movement.[3] It is plausible to conjecture that Ye Hao has been involved in the writing of editorial postings, if not all important postings on the website, including even those of Li Hongzhi. My research has not attempted to uncover these backstage processes.

According to statistics reported by the editors of Minghui in April 2009, on the tenth anniversary of Falun Gong's April 25 protest event in Beijing,[4] the Minghui site had a large following in the Chinese diaspora. In 2004, says the report, Minghui received nearly six million visits, or an average of about 16,000 hits per day, from unique IP addresses located outside of China. In 2005 it received 8.2 million visits, and this number increased in 2007 to a peak of 16.7 million visits, or about 46,000 visits per day. Visits declined in 2008 to 12.2 million. These statistics, says the report, only represented visits from overseas computers; visits from mainland Chinese computers, which must first pass through censorship-busting software, were not included. According to the report, if visits from PRC computers were also counted, the total would be much higher still, since much user-generated material posted on the site comes from the mainland. Further, the website "confirmed and posted" 254,000 firsthand reports of persecution incidents since the PRC government banned Falun Gong in July 1999. Although it was not possible for me to independently

---

[3] Information for this profile was taken from a variety of pro-Falun Gong, independent, and anti-Falun Gong websites. These details all appear consistently across the spectrum. Specific sources are: http://boxun.com/forum/200906/qglt/61558.shtml, www.hkhkhk .com/64/messages/11767.html, www.youtube.com/watch?v=D2fFquqkLrM, all retrieved on May 9, 2013, and www.tianjian.org/forum.php?mod=viewthread&tid=11033, retrieved on July 25, 2013.

[4] "Shi zhounian jiang lin zhi ji minghui bianji bu da duzhe wen" (Minghui editors ask readers on the occasion of the tenth anniversary), www.minghui.org/mh/articles/2009/4/ 19/199284p.html, retrieved on April 21, 2009.

confirm these statistics,[5] they suggest the central and robust role that the Minghui website has played in the Falun Gong movement.

As a source for research, Minghui's archive is rich, but requires skepticism because it is the product of a movement engaged in a representational battle with the Chinese state. Website operators, for instance, have removed or altered statements by Li Hongzhi that later became seen as problematic (e.g., Palmer 2007: 268). In the present work, Chapter 8 relies most heavily on interpreting the evolution of the movement's politicization through the Minghui website. When gathering evidence for that analysis, I compared both the Chinese and English versions and also compared statements against an independent Internet archive, when available.[6] Also, I am persuaded by historian David Ownby who, after evaluating the validity of Minghui documents, concluded that, in reference to firsthand experiences of persecution and activism, "little in Falun Gong documentation suggests outright fabrication" and "the accounts found on the Clear Wisdom [Minghui] site are largely credible" (Ownby 2008: 163, 194). While the level of detail, plethora of accounts, and corroborating statements in interviews suggest a meaningful degree of plausibility, I remained skeptical toward aggregate claims, such as statements claiming how many Falun Gong practitioners there are or how many people have "Quit the CCP" in Falun Gong's campaign.

For Chapter 8, I used Minghui to understand the evolution of doctrine by the charismatic leadership. I read all statements (about 150) by Falun Gong leadership, including Li Hongzhi and the Minghui editorial department, posted during the period of transnational politicization between 1999 and 2001. In addition, using titles and electronic searches for key words, I identified and read many relevant statements from the charismatic leader and other leadership from before 1999 and after 2001. Some postings in the two languages are direct translations, but some materials that appear in Chinese never appeared in English, and vice versa. By triangulating the Minghui archive against other sources, I was also able to discover some texts that were missing or deliberately excised from the Minghui archive, such as a public statement made by Li Hongzhi on the day Falun Gong was officially banned in China. In addition, I read

---

[5] Ownby reported that his many efforts to communicate directly with website editors were rebuffed; the internal workings of these sites remain a mystery to outside researchers (2008: 201).

[6] http://archive.org/web/web.php

all of Li Hongzhi's publicly available statements for 1999, as well as his
major publications from earlier in the movement, which have also been
described in the secondary literature (Chang 2004; Ownby 2008; Penny
2012). These materials allowed me to construct an analysis of leadership
discourse during the period when "clarifying truth" emerged. The sources
document the "official" doctrine, but cannot tell us about backstage
processes that influenced their production or how ordinary followers
reacted.

Reading official communications is an imperfect way to infer what
widely held religious ideas, interpretations, and concerns were involved
in Falun Gong's politicization. For instance, if one were to use officially
published CCP discourses to gauge what party members think and care
about, one would draw flawed inferences for certain. But in the case of
the Falun Gong, official discourse is a valuable window into
interpretations and widely shared beliefs within the movement. Several
reasons support my assertion. First, Falun Gong followers, especially
those from mainland China, treat the communications from Li Hongzhi
as sacred texts, called *jingwen*, which is also the standard term for
scripture in Buddhism. Not only are all followers expected to read
jingwen as revelation, but followers also regularly study *jingwen*
together by reading texts aloud in unison and commenting on how
points in the texts are proven through one's own personal experience.
Like *jingwen*, communications from the anonymous editorial board of
Minghui also enjoy the status of having Li Hongzhi's approval. Since
Falun Gong is a voluntary association based largely on shared beliefs,
interpretations, and ideas communicated through "official" channels are
enormously influential. A second justification for relying on official
communications is that a major portion of Li Hongzhi's *jingwen*
include apparently verbatim transcriptions of his talks, in which
questions were asked by followers and answered by Li. These
transcripts offer a window into the interactive dynamics of the
charismatic leader and his followers. Finally, efforts (my own and that
of others) to contrast Li's preaching against the beliefs of active followers
typically reveal a high degree of correspondence between the leader's
preaching and beliefs among the core Chinese membership (Chan 2004;
Palmer 2003) as well as homogeneity of beliefs across diverse national
settings (Chan 2013).[7]

---

[7] Burgdoff (2003) came to opposite conclusions, but that was drawn from a more limited
   sample.

PROTEST EVENT TRENDS

My third domain of data collection focused on protest event information that I used to compare Minyun and Falun Gong activism. I constructed a data set of protest events drawn from published sources in both movements. My methodology was a form of protest event analysis, which is a common research method among scholars studying social movements (Earl et al. 2004; Koopmans 1993, 1998; Kriesi 1995; Rucht, Koopmans, and Neidhardt 1998; Tilly 1995b). My data set differs from the standard approach in two important and related ways. First, I collected and coded data from sources authored by movement participants, rather than independent media newspaper reports. Much of the activity of a social movement occurs in ways that fail to attract newspaper reportage (Taylor and Van Dyke 2004: 268). Accounts of activism authored by activists, by comparison, include a broader range of happenings and thus better document events, especially for a relatively marginal movement like Falun Gong, in which the vast majority of activism that constitutes a participant's experience never surfaces in the mass media. Newspapers report what seems newsworthy to a general public, whereas activist-generated narratives, what I call "activism narratives," are accounts "from the trenches" and are written primarily for other activists in order to share information and sustain mobilization. Activism narratives are relatively rich sources of information about the practices that activists do, even if those practices are inconsequential relative to the wider world of events reported on by independent news media.

A second way in which my data collection differed from the typical study of protest events is that I used the software called Program for Computer-Assisted Coding of Events (PC-ACE), which was created by Roberto Franzosi of Emory University in order to carry out the method of quantitative narrative analysis (QNA). Data presented in Chapter 5 was collected and validated using this software as part of research funded by the National Science Foundation. PC-ACE allowed for an open-ended coding approach such that all forms of collective action mentioned in an activism narrative could be recorded for each event, which was defined by date and place.

Comparing Minyun and Falun Gong protest events also entailed making decisions about time periods. Although the Minyun diaspora began in 1982 and is still active, the most valid period by which to compare the tactical repertoire of Minyun to Falun Gong is during Minyun's one episode of widespread participation and "upward scaling" (Tilly and Tarrow 2007). Therefore, I collected data on Minyun protest events for a two-year period, spanning from February 1989 to January 1991. This period encompasses the emergence and dissipation of the diaspora movement's only robust era.

One cannot identify a similar period of peak political activism for Falun Gong, since the protest movement has sustained itself with considerable vigor since 1999. Nevertheless, because the collective action repertoire of more recent years has been influenced by what preceded it, an early period of Falun Gong diaspora mobilization logically offered the better comparison to Minyun. As the Minghui archive was only available starting from January 1, 2000, I could not collect protest event data for the initial months of repression, which might have otherwise been ideal.

My time period selection was also influenced by another concern, which was finding a two-year period in which the overall pattern of contentious dynamics for Falun Gong was in some meaningful way analogous to that of Minyun. This led me to select a two-year period of Falun Gong protest events between October 2000 and February 2002. During this time, the arc of contention in China between Falun Gong and the Chinese state followed a trajectory similar to that found in the Minyun history. Two events in the Falun Gong experience of this time stand out. Falun Gong activists mounted a major disruptive demonstration on National Day, October 1, 2000, after which the state severely increased repression against the movement. Second, in January 2001, due to the "self-immolation incident" (see Chapter 3), the Chinese state successfully and decisively turned public opinion against Falun Gong. By late winter 2001, Falun Gong activism in China had gone underground and only diaspora activists could continue public contestation of the repression.

This home country dynamic roughly parallels what occurred for Minyun: home country contention started in February 1989 with the publication of an open letter calling for the release of Wei Jingsheng, student demonstrations began in April, and the June 4 repression marked a major turning point for domestic mobilization and the end of overt public resistance. During the period after June 4, which constitutes the majority of the time period for which data were collected, Minyun activism was severely repressed in China, but efforts were made to keep it alive in diaspora. These roughly analogous event dynamics across the two movements provide the two sets of protest event data with a stronger contextual framework for comparison. In summary, I collected data on the early phase of Falun Gong in diaspora, from late 2000 to early 2002, and on the two most robust years of Minyun mobilization, from 1989 to 1991. For those readers interested in further details, the remaining portion of the appendix addresses the technical complexities of this comparison using PC-ACE software and the particular features of the sources from which data were collected for the protest event analysis.

Falun Gong Data

The two-year Falun Gong data set was drawn from postings to the "Diaspora News" category of the Minghui website, published between October 1, 2000 and September 30, 2002. Within these two years, the Minghui website archived a total of 8,796 postings classified as diaspora news (roughly twelve per day). From these, SPSS was used to generate a random sample of 535 articles, or about 6 percent. These articles were all read and coded for information on protest events undertaken in diaspora. Not all articles contained information on protest events and some articles contained information on more than one event. The total data set from the sample included 367 articles and 506 events, defined by unique start time and place.

The Minyun Data

Because the 1989 democracy protests in China occurred before the Internet, Minyun diaspora communication about protests followed other channels. In consideration of these constraints, Minyun data were compiled from two different sources, each of which parallels the Falun Gong data in different ways.

The Minyun Electronic ("Online Minyun") Data

Online Minyun transcripts from 1989 online communication during the Tiananmen protests share significant structural similarities with the Falun Gong data. Nevertheless, the Online Minyun source also has important limits. First, unlike the Internet today, access to internationally networked computers was limited in 1989 and therefore selected for certain types of users. Minyun participants who used the "Social Culture China" online community had access to it through a university-owned networked computer. Another constraint of the era was that Chinese fonts for electronic communication had not yet been invented. All communication was in English. Therefore, in order to contribute to what became the Online Minyun data, a person needed to be comfortable communicating in English and have access to a networked computer. In spite of this limitation, it appears that many overseas Chinese students and scholars met these conditions. Also, information passed through electronic channels was secondarily shared through social networks and contributing writers frequently wrote and posted messages on behalf of friends who did not have direct access.

Still two more shortcomings from the electronic mail transcriptions need to be noted: the data source only covers six months of time and the publishing editors at Stockholm University abridged the contents such that selection bias may distort the picture of collective action that emerges from the materials (Ståhle and Uimonen 1989a: vol. 1, xxxiii–xxxvi). The published transcripts are in two volumes. Volume one, which covers February to June 4, contains many more protest event narratives than volume two, which covers June 5 to July 4. If editorial selection rules were applied inconsistently, favoring commentarial texts over protest event narratives in the second volume, distortion in the data would occur. However, there is no reason to believe that selection practices were systematically related to the types of action narrated by the original authors. Furthermore, the overall portrait of Minyun's repertoires derived from Online Minyun looks plausible when compared to In-print Minyun.

In collecting event data from Online Minyun, all of the transcripts were read and all articles narrating any kind of collective action outside of mainland China were coded. Unlike in the Falun Gong data, Online Minyun was coded in the style of a census rather than a sample: the total population of events were included. Online Minyun included a total of 435 protest events, defined by unique start time and place.

The Minyun Journal ("In-print Minyun") Data

Given the limitations of the Minyun electronic data, I also compiled data from two diaspora Chinese democracy journals: *China Spring*, which was published out of New York in Chinese on a monthly basis throughout the period of data collection; and *Minzhu Zhongguo*, which translates either to "Democracy China" or "People Rule China." The latter was the flagship journal of the Federation for a Democratic China (*Minzhu zhongguo zhenxian*) (1990–1991), which was founded in the fall of 1990 in Paris by leaders of the Tiananmen Square protests who had fled abroad. The journal's first issue was published in September 1990; it came out bi-monthly for the remainder of the data collection period. Given that both journals were only distributed in print, contents were edited and subject to cost considerations. Although dissimilar from the Minghui data in that regard, the democracy journals data have the benefit of being in Chinese and covering a much broader span of time.

The data from the democracy journals cover two years, from February 1989 through to January 1991. As in the Online Minyun data, all articles mentioning diaspora collective actions were coded. The In-print Minyun data included a total of 464 protest events, defined by unique start time and place.

Coding Procedures

Falun Gong and In-print Minyun data were coded by a single bilingual coder. Online Minyun was coded by two coders who cannot read Chinese. Their work was secondarily verified by the bilingual coder. Inter-coder reliability was assured by following common coding procedures, randomized input–output verification, and semantic coherence verification for all data (Franzosi 2009: 89–90).

Event dates are the initial date of action mentioned in the event narrative. Some events lasted for more than a day or were regularly occurring. Regularly occurring forms of action, like daily vigils conducted by Falun Gong activists outside of embassies and consulates, only appear occasionally in the source, so are significantly undercounted. Such undercounts are probably more common for Falun Gong than Minyun.

References

Aberle, David Friend. 1982 [1966]. "A Classification of Social Movements" pp. 315–33 in *The Peyote Religion among the Navaho*. Chicago: University of Chicago Press.

Ackerman, Susan E. 2005. "Falun Dafa and the New Age Movement in Malaysia: Signs of Health, Symbols of Salvation." *Social Compass* 52(4):495–511.

Agence France-Presse. 2001. "Falun gong demonstrators defy Beijing; Blood flows again in Tiananmen Square; as police arrest, beat protesting dissidents." The Globe and Mail (Canada), January 2, p. A8.

Al Saud, Hussa Salman Abdulaziz. 2012. "The Weiquan Lawyers' Movement in China: Does It Have a Future?" *Asia-Pacific Journal on Human Rights & the Law* 13(2):44–73.

Alexander, Jeffrey C. 2006. *The Civil Sphere*. Oxford; New York: Oxford University Press.

2017. "Seizing the Stage: Social Performances from Mao Zedong to Martin Luther King Jr., and Black Lives Matter Today." *The Drama Review* 61 (1):14–42.

Aminzade, Ronald and Elizabeth J. Perry. 2001. "The Sacred, Religious, and Secular in Contentious Politics: Blurring Boundaries" pp. 155–78 in *Silence and Voice in the Study of Contentious Politics*, edited by Ronald Aminzade. Cambridge; New York: Cambridge University Press.

Amnesty International. 2015. "*China: Submission to the United Nations Committee against Torture, List of Issues, 54th Session, 20 April-15 May 2015.*" London: Amnesty International Publications.

Ashiwa, Yoshiko and David L. Wank. 2009. *Making Religion, Making the State: the Politics of Religion in Modern China*. Stanford, CA: Stanford University Press.

Associated Press. 2002. "Falun Gong Followers Detained: China Rounds up 2,000 Members." Calgary Herald, April 26, p. A19.

Bell, Mark R. and Taylor C. Boas. 2003. "Falun Gong and the Internet: Evangelism, Community, and Struggle for Survival." *Nova Religio: The Journal of Alternative and Emergent Religions* 6(2):277–93.

Benford, Robert D and David A Snow. 2000. "Framing Processes and Social Movements: An Overview and Assessment." *Annual Review of Sociology* 26(1):611–39.

Biao, Teng. 2014. "A Chinese Activist: Out of Prison but Not Free." *The Washington Post*, September 7.

Black, George and Robin Munro. 1993. *Black Hands of Beijing: Lives of Defiance in China's Democracy Movement*. New York: John Wiley.

Brook, Timothy. 1998. *Quelling the People: the Military Suppression of the Beijing Democracy Movement*. Stanford, CA: Stanford University Press.

Brown, Nathan. 2013. "Buddhist group sues town; Deerpark's planning decisions challenged." Times Herald-Record, September 6.

Burgdoff, Craig A. 2003. "How Falun Gong Practice Undermines Li Hongzhi's Totalistic Rhetoric." *Nova Religio: The Journal of Alternative and Emergent Religions* 6(2):332–47.

Calhoun, Craig J. 1995. *Neither Gods nor Emperors: Students and the Struggle for Democracy in China*. Berkeley, CA: University of California Press.

2012. *The Roots of Radicalism: Tradition, the Public Sphere, and Early Nineteenth-Century Social Movements*. Chicago, IL: University of Chicago Press.

Casanova, Jose. 1992. "Private and Public Religions." *Social Research* 59 (1):17–57.

Chan, Anita and Jonathan Unger. 1990. "China after Tiananmen: It's a Whole New Class Struggle" pp. 79–81 in *The Nation*. New York: The Nation Company, L.P.

Chan, Cheris Shun-ching. 2004. "The Falun Gong in China: A Sociological Perspective." *The China Quarterly* 179:665–83.

2013. "Doing Ideology Amid a Crisis: Collective Actions and Discourses of the Chinese Falun Gong Movement." *Social Psychology Quarterly* 76(1):1–24.

Chang, Maria Hsia. 2004. *Falun Gong: the End of Days*. New Haven, CT: Yale University Press.

Chao, S. Y. 2001. "Power of the Wheel: The Falun Gong Revolution." *Pacific Affairs* 74(4):591–92.

Chen, Chiung Hwang. 2005. "Framing Falun Gong: Xinhua News Agency's Coverage of the New Religious Movement in China." *Asian Journal of Communication* 15(1):16–36.

Chen, Jie. 2014. "The Overseas Chinese Democracy Movement after Thirty Years: New Trends at Low Tide." *Asian Survey* 54(3):445–70.

Chen, Li and Wei Lu. 1993a. "权利先于是非 – 中国民联简史 (第五部分)." 北京之春 (Beijing Spring), issue 1.

1993b. "民主的乐章 – 中国民主团结联盟"十年简史 (连载)." 中国之春 (*China Spring*), issue 119, pp. 97–103.

1993c. "永远的伤痛 – 中国民联简史(第十部分)." 北京之春 (Beijing Spring), issue 6.

1993d. "搞民主要优雅一点 – 中国民联简史(第七部分)." 北京之春 (Beijing Spring), issue 3.

1993e. "民联"、"民阵"之间 – 中国民联简史(第九部分)." 北京之春 (Beijing Spring), issue 5.

1993f. "曲折的道路 – 中国民联简史(第六部分)." 北京之春 (Beijing Spring), issue 2.

1993-1994. "'中国民主团结联盟' 简史（连载)." 中国之春 (China Spring) and 北京之春 (Beijing Spring).

1994. "挫折与反思 – 中国民联简史(第十五部分)." 北京之春 (Beijing Spring), issue 13.

Chen, Nancy N. 1995. "Urban Spaces and Experiences of *Qigong*" pp. 347–61 in *Urban Spaces in Contemporary China: the Potential for Autonomy and Community in post-Mao China*, edited by Deborah Davis. Washington, DC: Woodrow Wilson Center Press and Cambridge University Press.

2003. *Breathing Spaces: Qigong, Psychiatry, and Healing in China*. New York, NY: Columbia University Press.

Chen, Xi. 2008. "Collective Petitioning and Institutional Conversion" pp. 54–70 in *Popular Protest in China*, edited by Kevin J. O'Brien. Cambridge, MA: Harvard University Press.

2012. *Social Protest and Contentious Authoritarianism in China*. New York, NY: Cambridge University Press.

Chen, Yi-Da, Ahmed Abbasi, and Hsinchun Chen. 2010. "Framing Social Movement Identity with Cyber-Artifacts: A Case Study of the International Falun Gong Movement." *Security Informatics* 9:1–23.

China Spring. 1982. "告海内外同胞书 (Introductory Letter for our Chinese compatriots overseas and in China)." 中国之春 (China Spring), pp. 5–7.

1989-1991. 中国之春 (China Spring).

Chinese Human Rights Defenders. 2015. *Civil Society Information Submission to the Committee against Torture for the Review of the Fifth Periodic Report of China (CAT/C/CHN/5)*. Washington, DC: Chinese Human Rights Defenders.

Chiou, Chui Liang. 1995. *Democratizing Oriental Despotism: China from 4 May 1919 to 4 June 1989 and Taiwan from 28 February 1947 to 28 June 1990*. New York, NY: Macmillan; St. Martin's Press.

Cohen, Myron L. 1994. "Being Chinese: The Peripheralization of Traditional Chinese Identity" pp. 88–108 in *The Living Tree: the Changing Meaning of Being Chinese Today*, edited by Tu Weiming. Stanford, CA: Stanford University Press.

Cook, Sarah and Leeshai Lemish. 2011. "The 610 Office: Policing the Chinese Spirit." *China Brief* 11(17):6–9.

Davenport, Christian, Sarah A. Soule, and David A. Armstrong. 2011. "Protesting While Black?" *American Sociological Review* 76(1):152–78.

Della Porta, Donatella and Sidney G. Tarrow. 2005. *Transnational Protest and Global Activism*. Lanham, MD; Oxford: Rowman & Littlefield.

Ding, Chu. 2008. 大梦谁先觉：《中国之春》与我的民主历程. Hong Kong: Haifeng Publishing.

Duara, Prasenjit. 2003. *Sovereignty and Authenticity: Manchukuo and the East Asian Modern*. Lanham, MD; Oxford: Rowman & Littlefield Publishers.

Earl, Jennifer, Andrew Martin, John D. McCarthy, and Sarah A. Soule. 2004. "The Use of Newspaper Data in the Study of Collective Action." *Annual Review of Sociology* 30(1):65–80.

Eckholm, Erik and Elisabeth Rosenthal. 2001. "China's Leadership Pushes for Unity." *New York Times*, March 9, pp. A1.

Economist. 2002. "A jail by another name." *The Economist*, December 19.

Edelman, Bryan and James T. Richardson. 2003. "Falun Gong and the Law: Development of Legal Social Control in China." *Nova Religio: The Journal of Alternative and Emergent Religions* 6(2):312–31.

Esherick, Joseph W. and Jeffrey N. Wasserstrom. 1990. "Acting Out Democracy: Political Theater in Modern China." *The Journal of Asian Studies* 49(4): 835–65.

Federation for a Democratic China. 1990–1991. *Min Zhu Zhongguo (Democracy China)*. Paris: Min Zhu Zhongguo Magazine.

Festinger, Leon, Henry W. Riecken, and Stanley Schachter. 2010 [1956]. *When Prophecy Fails*. London: Pinter & Martin Ltd.

Fisher, Gareth. 2003. "Resistance and Salvation in Falun Gong: The Promise and Peril of Forbearance." *Nova Religio* 6(2):294–312.

Franzosi, Roberto. 2004. *From Words to Numbers: Narrative, Data, and Social Science*. Cambridge; New York, NY: Cambridge University Press.

2009. *Quantitative Narrative Analysis*. Thousand Oaks, CA: Sage.

2012. "On Quantitative Narrative Analysis" pp. 75–98 in *Varieties of Narrative Analysis*, edited by James A. Holstein and Jaber F. Gubrium. Los Angeles, CA; London; New Delhi; Singapore; Washington, DC: Sage Publications, Inc.

Gao, Zhisheng. 2007. *A China More Just: My Fight as a Rights Lawyer in the World's Largest Communist State*. San Diego, CA: Broad Press USA.

Goldman, Merle. 1994. *Sowing the Seeds of Democracy in China: Political Reform in the Deng Xiaoping Era*. Cambridge, MA: Harvard University Press.

Goossaert, Vincent and David A. Palmer. 2011. *The Religious Question in Modern China*. Chicago, IL: University of Chicago Press.

Gorski, Philip S. 2003. *The Disciplinary Revolution: Calvinism and the Rise of the State in Early Modern Europe*. Chicago, IL; London: University of Chicago Press.

Guo, Xuezhi. 2012. *China's Security State: Philosophy, Evolution, and Politics*. New York, NY: Cambridge University Press.

Gutmann, Ethan. 2014. *The Slaughter: Mass Killings, Organ Harvesting, and China's Secret Solution to its Dissident Problem*. Amherst, NY: Prometheus Books.

Han, Minzhu and Huasheng Zhang. 1990. *Cries for Democracy: Writings and Speeches from the 1989 Chinese Democracy Movement*. Princeton, NJ: Princeton University Press.

Harrell, Stevan and Elizabeth J. Perry. 1982. "Syncretic Sects in Chinese Society: An Introduction." *Modern China* 8(3):283–303.

He, Rowena Xiaoqing. 2014. *Tiananmen Exiles: Voices of the Struggle for Democracy in China*. New York, NY: Palgrave Macmillan.

Hochschild, Adam. 2004. "Against All Odds: the First Great Human-rights Campaign" pp. 66+ in Mother Jones: Foundation for National Progress.

Hon, May Sin-mi. 2002. "Subversive' group will not be targeted, pledges justice chief." South China Morning Post, June 28, p. 1.

Hooper, Kate and Jeanne Batalova. 2015. "Chinese Immigrants in the United States" in *Migration Information Source*. Washington, DC: Migration Policy Institute.

Hu, Ping. 2005. 法轮功现象 *(The Falun Gong Phenomenon)*. Hong Kong: Xinlidong yinshuadingzhuang gongsi.

Human Rights Watch. 2002. *Dangerous Meditation: China's Campaign against the Falun Gong*. New York, NY: Human Rights Watch.

2015. *Tiger Chairs and Cell Bosses: Police Torture of Criminal Suspects in China*. New York, NY: Human Rights Watch.

Hurst, William, Mingxing Liu, Yongdong Liu, and Ran Tao. 2014. "Reassessing Collective Petitioning in Rural China: Civic Engagement, Extra-State Violence, and Regional Variation." *Comparative Politics* 46(4):459–82.

Jasper, James M. 1997. *The Art of Moral Protest: Culture, Biography, and Creativity in Social Movements*. Chicago, IL: University of Chicago Press.

Johnson, Ian. 2004. *Wild Grass: Three Stories of Change in Modern China*. New York, NY: Pantheon Books.

2017. *The Souls of China: the Return of Religion after Mao*. New York, NY: Pantheon Books.

Junker, Andrew. 2014a. "Follower Agency and Charismatic Mobilization in Falun Gong." *Sociology of Religion* 75(3):418–41.

2014b. "The Transnational Flow of Tactical Dispositions: The Chinese Democracy Movement and Falun Gong." *Mobilization: An International Quarterly* 19(3):329–50.

2018. "Live Organ Harvesting in China: Falun Gong and Unsettled Rumor." *American Journal of Cultural Sociology* 6(1):96–124.

Keck, Margaret E. and Kathryn Sikkink. 1998. *Activists beyond Borders: Advocacy Networks in International Politics*. Ithaca, NY: Cornell University Press.

Kilgour, David, Ethan Gutmann, and David Matas. 2016. *Bloody Harvest/The Slaughter: An Update*. International Coalition to End Organ Pillaging in China, pp. 680. Retrieved on June 25, 2016, from https://endtransplantabuse.org/an-update/.

Kniss, Fred and Gene Burns. 2004. "Religious Movements" pp. 694–715 in *The Blackwell Companion to Social Movements*, edited by David A. Snow, Sarah Anne Soule, and Hanspeter Kriesi. Malden, MA: Blackwell Pub.

Koopmans, Ruud. 1993. "The Dynamics of Protest Waves: West Germany, 1965 to 1989." *American Sociological Review* 58(5):637–58.

1998. "The Use of Protest Event Data in Comparative Research: Cross-National Comparability, Sampling Methods and Robustness" pp. 90–110 in *Acts of Dissent: New Developments in the Study of Protest*, edited by

Dieter Rucht, Ruud Koopmans, and Friedhelm Neidhardt. Berlin: Edition Sigma.

Kriesi, Hanspeter. 1995. *New Social Movements in Western Europe: a Comparative Analysis.* Minneapolis, MN: University of Minnesota Press.

Kristof, Nicholas D. 2009. "Tear down this cyberwall!" *New York Times,* June 18.

Kuhn, Philip A. 2008. *Chinese among Others: Emigration in Modern Times.* Lanham, MD: Rowman & Littlefield Publishers.

Kurien, Prema. 2004. "Multiculturalism, Immigrant Religion, and Diasporic Nationalism: The Development of an American Hinduism." *Social Problems* 51(3):362–85.

2007. *A Place at the Multicultural Table: the Development of an American Hinduism.* New Brunswick, NJ: Rutgers University Press.

Lalich, Janja. 2004. *Bounded Choice: True Believers and Charismatic Cults.* Berkeley, CA; London: University of California Press.

Leijonhufvud, Göran. 1990. *Going against the Tide: on Dissent and Big-character Posters in China.* London: Curzon.

Li, Angela. 2002. "Local delegates to call for tighter rein on sect." *South China Morning Post,* March 3, p. 3.

Li, Hongzhi. 2001. *Essentials for Further Advancement (English Version).* Minghui. Retrieved on July 23, 2013, from http://falundafa.org/eng/eng/jjyz.htm.

2003. *Zhuan Falun: Turning the Law Wheel.* Taiwan: Yih Chyun Bok Corp., Ltd.

2005. *Essentials for Further Advancement II.* Minghui. Retrieved on July 23, 2013, from http://falundafa.org/eng/eng/jjyz2.htm.

Lian, Xi. 2010. *Redeemed by Fire: the Rise of Popular Christianity in Modern China.* New Haven, CT: Yale University Press.

Lim, Louisa. 2014. *The People's Republic of Amnesia: Tiananmen Revisited.* New York, NY: Oxford University Press.

Lofland, John. 1985. *Protest: Studies of Collective Behavior and Social Movements.* New Brunswick NJ: Transaction Books.

Loh, Christine. 2010. *Underground Front: the Chinese Communist Party in Hong Kong.* Aberdeen; Hong Kong: Hong Kong University Press.

Lowe, Scott. 2003. "Chinese and International Contexts for the Rise of Falun Gong." *Nova Religio: The Journal of Alternative and Emergent Religions* 6 (2):263–76.

Lu, Yunfeng. 2005. "Entrepreneurial Logics and the Evolution of Falun Gong." *Journal for the Scientific Study of Religion* 44(2):173–85.

2008. *The Transformation of Yiguan Dao in Taiwan: Adapting to a Changing Religious Economy.* Lanham, MD: Lexington Books.

Lum, Thomas G. 2003. *China and "Falun Gong."* Washington, DC: Congressional Research Service, Library of Congress.

Madsen, Richard. 2000. "Understanding Falun Gong." *Current History* 99(638): 243–47.

2007. *Democracy's Dharma: Religious Renaissance and Political Development in Taiwan.* Berkeley, CA: University of California Press.

Masuzawa, Tomoko. 2005. *The Invention of World Religions, or, How European Universalism was Preserved in the Language of Pluralism.* Chicago, IL: University of Chicago Press.

Matas, David and David Kilgour. 2009. *Bloody Harvest: Organ Harvesting of Falun Gong Practitioners in China.* Woodstock: Seraphim Editions.

Matas, David and Torsten Trey. 2012. *State Organs: Transplant Abuse in China.* Woodstock: Seraphim Editions.

McAdam, Doug. 1982. *Political Process and the Development of Black Insurgency, 1930–1970.* Chicago, IL: University of Chicago Press.

McAdam, Doug, Sidney G. Tarrow, and Charles Tilly. 2001. *Dynamics of Contention.* New York, NY: Cambridge University Press.

McCarthy, John D. and Mayer N. Zald. 1977. "Resource Mobilization and Social Movements: A Partial Theory." *The American Journal of Sociology* 82(6): 1212–41.

McDonald, Kevin. 2006. *Global Movements: Action and Culture.* Malden, MA; Oxford: Blackwell.

Melton, J. Gordon. 1985. "Spiritualization and Reaffirmation: What Really Happens When Prophecy Fails." *American Studies* 26(2):17–29.

Michels, Robert. 1966. *Political Parties: a Sociological Study of the Oligarchical Tendencies of Modern Democracy.* New York, NY: Free Press.

Morris, Aldon D. 1984. *The Origins of the Civil Rights movement: Black Communities Organizing for Change.* New York, NY: Free Press.

Nathan, Andrew J. 1985. *Chinese Democracy.* New York, NY: Knopf.

Nathan, Andrew J. and E. Perry Link. 2001. *The Tiananmen Papers.* New York, NY: Public Affairs.

Noakes, Stephen and Caylan Ford. 2015. "Managing Political Opposition Groups in China: Explaining the Continuing Anti-Falun Gong Campaign." *The China Quarterly* 223:658–79.

O'Brien, Kevin J. 2008. *Popular Protest in China.* Cambridge, MA: Harvard University Press.

O'Brien, Kevin J. and Lianjiang Li. 2006. *Rightful Resistance in Rural China.* Cambridge; New York, NY: Cambridge University Press.

Olson, Mancur. 1971. *The Logic of Collective Action: Public Goods and the Theory of Groups.* Cambridge, MA: Harvard University Press.

Overmyer, Daniel L. 1981. "Alternatives: Popular Religious Sects in Chinese Society." *Modern China* 7(2):153–90.

2003. "Religion in China Today: Introduction." *The China Quarterly* 174: 307–16.

Ownby, David. 1999. "Chinese Millenarian Traditions: The Formative Age." *The American Historical Review* 104(5):1513–30.

2003a. "A History for Falun Gong: Popular Religion and the Chinese State since the Ming Dynasty." *Nova Religio* 6(2):223–43.

2003b. "The Falun Gong in the New World." *European Journal of East Asian Studies* 2(2):303–20.

2008. *Falun Gong and the Future of China.* New York, NY: Oxford University Press.

Palmer, David A. 2007. *Qigong Fever: Body, Science, and Utopia in China.* New York, NY: Columbia University Press.

———. 2008. "Heretical Doctrines, Reactionary Secret Societies, Evil Cults: Labeling Heterodoxy in Twentieth-Century China" pp. 113–34 in *Chinese Religiosities: Afflictions of Modernity and State Formation,* edited by Mayfair Mei-hui Yang. Berkeley, CA: University of California Press.

———. 2009a. "Religiosity and Social Movements in China: Divisions and Multiplications" pp. 257–82 in *Social Movements in China and Hong Kong,* edited by Gilles Guiheux and Khun Eng Kuah Kuah-Pearce. Amsterdam: ICAS/Amsterdam University Press.

———. 2009b. "China's Religious *Danwei.*" *China Perspectives* 4:17–30.

Palmer, Susan J. 2003. "From Healing to Protest: Conversion Patterns Among the Practitioners of Falun Gong." *Nova Religio: The Journal of Alternative and Emergent Religions* 6(2):348–64.

Pan, Philip. 2001. "Human fire ignites Chinese mystery." *The Washington Post,* February 4.

———. 2002. "Falun Gong members receive stiff sentences." *The Washington Post,* September 21, pp. A13.

Penny, Benjamin. 2002. "Falun Gong, Prophecy and Apocalypse." *East Asian History* 23:149–68.

———. 2003. "The Life and Times of Li Hongzhi: Falun Gong and Religious Biography." *China Quarterly* 175:643–61.

———. 2008. "Animal Spirits, Karmic Retribution, Falungong, and the State" pp. 135–54 in *Chinese Religiosities: Afflictions of Modernity and State Formation,* edited by Mayfair Mei-hui Yang. Berkeley, CA: University of California Press.

———. 2012. *The Religion of Falun Gong.* Chicago, IL: University of Chicago Press.

Pepper, Suzanne. 2008. *Keeping Democracy at Bay: Hong Kong and the Challenge of Chinese Political Reform.* Lanham, MD: Rowman & Littlefield Publishers.

Perry, Elizabeth J. 2001. "Challenging the Mandate of Heaven: Popular Protest in Modern China." *Critical Asian Studies* 33(2):163–80.

———. 2002. *Challenging the Mandate of Heaven: Social Protest and State Power in China.* Armonk, NY: M.E. Sharpe.

Pils, Eva. 2006. "Asking the Tiger for His Skin: Rights Activism in China." *Fordham International Law Journal* 30:1209.

———. 2009. "Rights Activism in China: the Case of Gao Zhisheng" pp. 243–60 in *Building Constitutionalism in China,* edited by Stephanie Balme and Michael W. Dowdle. New York, NY: Palgrave Macmillan.

———. 2015. *China's Human Rights Lawyers Advocacy and Resistance.* Abingdon, New York: Routledge.

Piven, Frances Fox and Richard A. Cloward. 1977. *Poor People's Movements: Why They Succeed, How They Fail.* New York, NY: Pantheon Books.

Pomfret, John. 2002. "Fight over banned Chinese sect moves to U.S.; Falun Gong activists irk Beijing by filing human rights lawsuits in American Courts." *The Washington Post,* March 12, pp. A15.

Porter, Noah. 2003. Falun Gong in the United States: an Ethnographic Study. MA thesis. Tampa, FL: University of South Florida.

Poston, Dudley L., Jr. and Hua Luo. 2007. "Chinese Student and Labor Migration to the United States: Trends and Policies Since the 1980s." *Asian and Pacific Migration Journal* 16(3):323–55.

Pringle, James. 2001. "Beijing police take batons to Falun Gong." The Times (London), January 2.

Pye, Lucian W. 1990. "The Escalation of Confrontation" pp. 162–79 in *The Broken Mirror: China after Tiananmen*, edited by George L Hicks and Asai Motofumi. Harlow; Chicago, IL.: Longman Current Affairs; St. James Press.

Robbins, Thomas and Dick Anthony. 1995. "Sects and Violence: Factors Enhancing the Volatility in Marginal Religious Movements" pp. xxvi, 394 in *Armageddon in Waco: Critical Perspectives on the Branch Davidian Conflict*, edited by Stuart A. Wright. Chicago, IL: University of Chicago Press.

Robbins, Thomas and Susan J. Palmer. 1997a. *Millennium, Messiahs, and Mayhem: Contemporary Apocalyptic Movements*. New York, NY: Routledge.

———. 1997b. "Patterns of Contemporary Apocalypticism" pp. 1–27 in *Millennium, Messiahs, and Mayhem: Contemporary Apocalyptic Movements*, edited by Thomas Robbins and Susan J. Palmer. New York, NY: Routledge.

Roy, Denny. 2003. *Taiwan: a Political History*. Ithaca, NY: Cornell University Press.

Rucht, Dieter, Ruud Koopmans, and Friedhelm Neidhardt. 1998. *Acts of Dissent: New Developments in the Study of Protest*. Berlin: Edition Sigma.

Rudolph, Susanne Hoeber. 1997. "Introduction: Religion, States, and Transnational Civil Society" pp. 1–24 in *Transnational Religion and Fading States*, edited by Susanne Hoeber Rudolph, and James P. Piscatori. Boulder, CO: Westview Press.

Sacco, Stephen. 2008. "Questions remain in Deerpark death: No investigation scheduled; religion rules out autopsy." Times Herald-Record, May 6.

Saich, Tony. 1990. *The Chinese People's Movement: Perspectives on Spring 1989*. Armonk, NY: M.E. Sharpe.

Schwarcz, Vera. 1986. *The Chinese Enlightenment: Intellectuals and the Legacy of the May Fourth Movement of 1919*. Berkeley, CA: University of California Press.

SCMP. 2002. "No keeping politics out of court; the trial of 16 people over a Falun Gong protest took on a significance way beyond that of the minor offences involved." South China Morning Post, August 16.

Sheffer, Gabriel. 1986. "A New Field of Study: Modern Diasporas in International Politics" pp. 1–15 in *Modern Diasporas in International Politics*, edited by Gabriel Sheffer. London: Croom Helm.

Slater, Dan. 2010. *Ordering Power: Contentious Politics and Authoritarian Leviathans in Southeast Asia*. Cambridge; New York, NY: Cambridge University Press.

Smith, Christian. 1991. *The Emergence of Liberation Theology: Radical Religion and Social Movement Theory*. Chicago, IL: University of Chicago Press.

1996a. *Disruptive Religion: the Force of Faith in Social Movement Activism.* New York; London: Routledge.

1996b. *Resisting Reagan: the U.S. Central America Peace Movement.* Chicago, IL: University of Chicago Press.

Smith, Jackie. 2008. *Social Movements for Global Democracy.* Baltimore, MD: Johns Hopkins University Press.

Smith, Jackie G. and Hank Johnston. 2002. *Globalization and Resistance: Transnational Dimensions of Social Movements.* Lanham, MD.: Rowman & Littlefield.

Spence, Jonathan D. 1999 [1990]. *The Search for Modern China.* New York, NY: W.W. Norton.

Spires, Anthony J. 2011. "Contingent Symbiosis and Civil Society in an Authoritarian State: Understanding the Survival of China's Grassroots NGOs." *American Journal of Sociology* 117(1):1–45.

2012. "Lessons from Abroad: Foreign Influences on China's Emerging Civil Society." *The China Journal* 68:125–46.

Spires, Anthony J., Lin Tao, and Kin-man Chan. 2014. "Societal Support for China's Grass-roots NGOs: Evidence from Yunnan, Guangdong and Beijing." *The China Journal* 71:65–90.

Ståhle, Esbjörn and Terho Uimonen. 1989a. *Electronic Mail on China.* Stockholm: Föreningen för orientaliska studier.

1989b. *Electronic Mail on China*, volume 1. Stockholm: Föreningen för orientaliska studier.

1989c. *Electronic Mail on China*, volume 2. Stockholm: Föreningen för orientaliska studier.

Stamatov, Peter. 2010. "Activist Religion, Empire, and the Emergence of Modern Long-Distance Advocacy Networks." American Sociological Review 75(4): 607–628.

Stark, Rodney and Eric Liu. 2011. "The Religious Awakening in China." *Review of Religious Research* 52(3):282–289.

Sun, Yanfei and Dingxin Zhao. 2008. "Environmental Campaigns" pp. 179–204 in *Popular Protest in China*, edited by Kevin J. O'Brien. Cambridge, MA: Harvard University Press.

Tarrow, Sidney G. 1995. "Cycles of Collective Action: Between Moments of Madness and the Repertoire of Contention" pp. 89–115 in *Repertoires and cycles of collective action*, edited by Mark Traugott. Durham, NC: Duke University Press.

1998. *Power in Movement: Social Movements and Contentious Politics.* Cambridge: Cambridge University Press.

2005. *The New Transnational Activism.* New York, NY: Cambridge University Press.

2011. *Power in Movement: Social Movements and Contentious Politics*, Revised and Updated 3rd Edition. Cambridge: Cambridge University Press.

2012. *Strangers at the Gates: Movements and States in Contentious Politics.* Cambridge; New York, NY: Cambridge University Press.

Taylor, Verta and Nella Van Dyke. 2004. "'Get up, Stand up': Tactical Repertoires of Social Movements" pp. 262–93 in *The Blackwell*

Companion to Social Movements, edited by David A. Snow, Sarah Anne Soule, and Hanspeter Kriesi. Malden, MA: Blackwell.

Thornton, Patricia M. 2002. "Framing Dissent in Contemporary China: Irony, Ambiguity and Metonymy." *The China Quarterly* 171:661–81.

2008. "Manufacturing Dissent in Transnational China" pp. 179–204 in *Popular Protest in China*, edited by Kevin J. O'Brien. Cambridge, MA: Harvard University Press.

2010. "The New Cybersects: Popular Religion, Repression and Resistance" pp. 215–38 in *Asia's Transformations*, edited by Elizabeth Jv Perry and Mark Selden. London; New York, NY: Routledge.

Tilly, Charles. 1995a. "Contentious Repertoires in Great Britain" pp. 15–42 in *Repertoires and Cycles of Collective Action*, edited by Mark Traugott. Durham, NC: Duke University Press.

1995b. *Popular Contention in Great Britain, 1758–1834*. Cambridge, MA: Harvard University Press.

2007. *Democracy*. Cambridge; New York: Cambridge University Press.

2008a. "Invention of the Social Movement" pp. 116–45 in *Contentious Performances*. Cambridge; New York, NY: Cambridge University Press.

2008b. *Contentious Performances*. Cambridge; New York, NY: Cambridge University Press.

Tilly, Charles and Sidney G. Tarrow. 2007. *Contentious Politics*. Boulder, CO: Paradigm Publishers.

Tilly, Charles and Lesley J. Wood. 2013. *Social Movements, 1768–2012*. Boulder, CO; London: Paradigm Publishers.

Tong, James W. 2002a. "Anatomy of Regime Repression in China: Timing, Enforcement Institutions, and Target Selection in Banning the Falungong, July 1999." *Asian Survey* 42(6):795–820.

2002b. "An Organizational Analysis of the Falun Gong: Structure, Communications, and Financing." *China Quarterly* 171(636–660).

2009. *Revenge of the Forbidden City: the Suppression of the Falungong in China, 1999–2005*. Oxford; New York, NY: Oxford University Press.

2012. "Banding after the Ban: The Underground Falungong in China, 1999–2011." *Journal of Contemporary China* 21(78):1045–62.

UN Commission on Human Rights. 2006. *Report of the Special Rapporteur on torture and other cruel, inhuman or degrading treatment or punishment, Manfred Nowak*. New York, NY: Economic and Social Council.

United States Congress. 2013. Chen Guangcheng and Gao Zhisheng: Human Rights in China: Hearing before the Subcommittee on Africa, Global Health, Global Human Rights, and International Organizations of the Committee on Foreign Affairs, House of Representatives, One Hundred Thirteenth Congress, first session, April 9, 2013. Washington, DC: House Committee on Foreign Affairs. Subcommittee on Africa United States Congress, Global Health Global Human Rights. Washington: U.S. Government Printing Office.

US Department of State. 2007. *Human Rights Report: China*. Washington, DC: Bureau of Democracy, Human Rights, and Labor.

2008. International Religious Freedom Report 2008. Retrieved on October 2, 2018, from www.state.gov/j/drl/rls/irf/2008/108404.htm.

Wallis, Roy and Steve Bruce. 1986. "Sex, Violence and Religion" pp. xi, 359 in *Sociological Theory, Religion and Collective Action*, edited by Roy Wallis and Steve Bruce. Belfast: Queen's University.

Walzer, Michael. 1965. *The Revolution of the Saints: a Study in the Origins of Radical Politics*. Cambridge, MA: Harvard University Press.

Wang, Gungwu. 1991. *China and the Chinese Overseas*. Singapore: Times Academic Press.

——— 2000. *The Chinese Overseas: from Earthbound China to the Quest for Autonomy*. Cambridge, MA: Harvard University Press.

Wang, Yuhua and Carl Minzner. 2015. "The Rise of the Chinese Security State." *The China Quarterly* 222:339–59.

Wasserstrom, Jeffrey N. 1990. "Student Protests and the Chinese Tradition 1919–1989" pp. 3–24 in *The Chinese People's Movement: Perspectives on Spring 1989*, edited by Tony Saich. Armonk, NY: M.E. Sharpe.

Wasserstrom, Jeffrey N. and Elizabeth J. Perry. 1994. *Popular Protest and Political Culture in Modern China*. Boulder, CO: Westview Press.

Weber, Max. 1958 [1946]. *From Max Weber: Essays in Sociology*. New York, NY: Oxford University Press.

——— 1978 [1968]. *Economy and Society: an Outline of Interpretive Sociology*. Berkeley, CA: University of California Press.

——— 2001 [1930]. *The Protestant Ethic and the Spirit of Capitalism*. New York, NY: Routledge.

Weller, Robert P. 1999. *Alternate Civilities: Democracy and Culture in China and Taiwan*. Boulder, CO: Westview Press.

Wessinger, Catherine. 2003. "Falun Gong Symposium Introduction and Glossary." *Nova Religio: The Journal of Alternative and Emergent Religions* 6(2):215–22.

WOIPFG. 1999. *Master Li Hongzhi Met with Chinese Media in Sydney*. Hyde Park, MA: World Organization to Investigate the Persecution of Falun Gong.

Wong, Yiu-chung. 2006. ""Super Paradox" or "Leninist Integration": The Politics of Legislating Article 23 of Hong Kong's Basic Law." *Asian Perspective* 30(2):65–95.

Wood, Elisabeth Jean. 2001. "The Emotional Benefits of Insurgency in El Salvador" pp. 267–81 in *Passionate Politics: Emotions and Social Movements*, edited by Jeff Goodwin, James M. Jasper, and Francesca Polletta. Chicago, IL: University of Chicago Press.

Wood, Richard L. 1999. "Religious Culture and Political Action." *Sociological Theory* 17(3):307–32.

——— 2002. *Faith in Action: Religion, Race, and Democratic Organizing in America*. Chicago, IL: University of Chicago Press.

Xie, Y. U. E. 2012. "The Political Logic of Weiwen in Contemporary China." *Issues & Studies* 48(3):1–41.

Xu, Jian. 1999. "Body, Discourse, and the Cultural Politics of Contemporary Chinese Qigong." *The Journal of Asian Studies* 58(4):961–91.

Yang, Fenggang. 2006. "The Red, Black, and Gray Markets of Religion in China." *The Sociological Quarterly* 47:93–122.

Yang, Guobin. 2003. "The Internet and the Rise of a Transnational Chinese Cultural Sphere." *Media, Culture & Society* 25:469–90.

    2005. "Environmental NGOs and International Dynamics in China." *The China Quarterly* 181:46–66.

    2009. *The Power of the Internet in China*. New York, NY: Columbia University Press.

Yeung, Chris. 2002. "Beijing pushing for territory to introduce subversion law." South China Morning Post, February 28.

Young, Michael P. 2006. *Bearing Witness against Sin: the Evangelical Birth of the American Social Movement*. Chicago, IL: University of Chicago Press.

Zhang, Boli. 2002. *Escape from China: the Long Journey from Tiananmen to Freedom*. New York: Washington Square Press.

Zhao, Dingxin. 2000. "State-Society Relations and the Discourses and Activities of the 1989 Beijing Student Movement." *American Journal of Sociology* 105 (6):1592–632.

    2001. *The Power of Tiananmen: State-Society Relations and the 1989 Beijing Student Movement*. Chicago, IL: University of Chicago Press.

    2010. "Theorizing the Role of Culture in Social Movements: Illustrated by Protests and Contentions in Modern China." *Social Movement Studies* 9 (1):33–50.

Zhu, Huiguang. 1994. "演播室里转 "法轮" (Turning the 'Law Wheel' in the Broadcast)." 现在养生, May, pp. 2–7.

Zhu, X. and B. Penny. 1994. "The *Qigong* Boom." *Chinese Sociology and Anthropology* 27(1).

Zong, Hairen. 2002. 朱镕基在1999. Hong Kong: Ming jing chu ban she.

Index

CPSIA information can be obtained
at www.ICGtesting.com
Printed in the USA
BVHW031743050422
633465BV00002B/8